How To Be
A Better Parent

How To Be
A Better Parent

Cassandra Jardine

Vermilion
LONDON

For my children, without whom I would not have found
out all this.

3 5 7 9 10 8 6 4 2

Copyright © 2003 Cassandra Jardine

First published in 2003 by Vermilion,
an imprint of Ebury Press, Random House
20 Vauxhall Bridge Road, London SW1V 2SA
www.randomhouse.co.uk

Random House Australia (Pty) Limited
20 Alfred Street, Milsons Point, Sydney,
New South Wales 2061, Australia

Random House New Zealand Limited
18 Poland Road, Glenfield,
Auckland 10, New Zealand

Random House (Pty) Limited
Endulini, 5A Jubilee Road,
Parktown 2193, South Africa

The Random House UK Limited Reg. No. 954009

Papers used by Vermilion are natural, recyclable products
made from wood grown in sustainable forests.

Typeset by Palimpsest Book Production Limited,
Polmont, Stirlingshire
Printed and bound in Great Britain by
Mackays of Chatham plc, Chatham, Kent

A CIP catalogue record for this book is available from the British Library

ISBN 0–09–188972–3

ACKNOWLEDGEMENTS

I should like to thank: Noël Janis-Norton and Luke Scott, for their patient tuition; the staff at the New Learning Centre, especially Gillian Edwards and Miriam Chachamu, who let me come to their classes and watch them in action; the other parents I met in parenting classes, who allowed me to hear about their problems and solutions; all those friends who have been fellow travellers; my sister Theresa; niece-in-law Georgina, who helped with computing; and, of course, my husband William and our children, who have co-operated with my attempts to be a better parent.

CONTENTS

PREFACE

Children, like dogs, are judged by their behaviour. As parents, we love them, but we cannot expect others to like them if they are rude, demanding, uncommunicative and either loll around all day saying, 'I'm bored' or pick fights.

Since the first of my five children was born, I have read many books about how to make children behave well. Many of them have been inspiring, enlightening and sometimes funny too, but often, when I put these books down, I feel frustrated. I want to achieve the nirvana they outline, but I am left stuck in the same old ways, making the same old mistakes and getting into the same old rows with my children.

This book, I hope, will be different. It will tell you not so much what to achieve – that is for you to decide – but how you might do it. In effect, it is the child-training manual that many people say they wish they had been given when they first became parents.

It is aimed at parents, like myself, with children who are past the baby stage – where masses of advice is available – and not yet into the teenage years. The decade in between – three to thirteen – is the time when parents are left to cope on their own. 'Middle-aged' children may not present problems as dramatic as those induced by a new arrival or hormonal upheavals, but this is the time when children learn the habits that form what is perceived as their personality, the habits that will carry them through socially, academically and emotionally to later life.

The wisdom this book contains is not my own, acquired simply by virtue of having children: it is a distillation of the advice given to me by two experts in parenting, Noël Janis-Norton and Luke Scott.

Theirs is a practical approach, and one, I found, that I could apply to the flashpoints of daily life. Every child, they say, is capable of far better behaviour than their parents believe. If we expect it of them and train them in the skills they need, we will not only enjoy their company more, we will be 'hard-wiring' children for success. As adults, we spend fortunes on courses to help us eliminate our bad habits and replace them with more productive ones; it is much kinder – and easier – to train children in good habits from an early age.

INTRODUCTION

Two events, which occurred in the space of a few months, led me to embark on the explorations that resulted in this book. Together they made me realise that what my unruly children needed from me was not so much love, which they could take for granted, but training. The first of the prompts, which could be called the human element, came during one particular week when I made what I imagined would be routine telephone calls.

Before I describe those calls, I shall explain my situation. With five children of my own, aged at the time of writing between thirteen and three – a boy, three girls and then another boy – I have always been eager to learn what lies around the next developmental corner. For this I rely on tales from the coalface, recounted by friends with older children.

It was in the course of one of these casual chats that I found myself shocked. That particular sunny morning I had rung the mother of two teenagers to hear her news. She appeared slightly distracted and I discovered why when I asked after her children. At first, there was an embarrassed silence, then, after much evasion, she came clean. I had caught her, she admitted, bucket in hand, about to discreetly flush away the pool of vomit that her seventeen-year-old son had left outside her house. 'Only, just as I reached the kerb,' she said, 'a car came up and parked on top of it.'

Her son was in the habit, she explained, of going out with friends and returning at all hours, drunk. He was barely attending school and not getting the grades he deserved. And he wouldn't listen to a word she said – if he could hear her, that is, above the deafening noise of rock music.

'Par for the course, with teenagers,' I soothed, but this mother was no longer looking for reassurance. She had already exhausted all the usual excuses: blaming the school, his friends, the temptations of London life. This time she had come to a new conclusion. She had started going to parenting classes and she was finding, to her chagrin, that for years she had been acting in ways that had, she now saw, landed her in this bucket-in-hand mess. 'I've been too indulgent,' she said.

Although that mother was still facing the pool of vomit outside the house, she and her husband felt they were, at last, getting back in control. 'I'm trying some new techniques,' she said, 'and they seem to be working. At least my son and I are talking.'

At the time I had scarcely heard of parenting classes. Or rather, I had read about them but dismissed them as a nannyish prescription for parents whose delinquent offspring were setting fire to piles of tyres on street corners when they should have been at school. Despite the evidence that they work at that end of the spectrum, it had never occurred to me that well-educated, reasonably well-balanced people such as my friends – or, indeed, myself – would ever need them. Even the idea of turning the word parent into a verb irritated me; it made it sound as if parenting was a skill, like fishing, that could be learnt.

I had always preferred the notion that being a good parent would come as naturally as the love I felt for my newborn babies. I never assumed it would be easy or relaxing, but I did presume that all I had to do was listen to the dictates of my heart. And now here was someone telling me that her similarly liberal and kindly approach had landed her in a situation that made her wonder where and why she had gone wrong.

Although that first mother's tale rocked me, I was still feeling smugly that my children would be bound to turn out delightful, when, later that same week, I made another phone call and heard a similar horror story of the teen troubles that might be to come from another articulate, happily married mother of my acquaintance. This doctor, who had largely given up work to care for her sons, was also – or, at least, had been – in despair.

Her two sons, both in their teens, were, she said, intolerably rude and uncooperative. They didn't tidy their rooms, left the kitchen a tip, swore at her and stayed out whenever and wherever they chose.

This woman, like the one I had spoken to a week before, has always struck me as sensitive, affectionate and no more neurotic than most of us. Her boys had also always appeared in public to be perfect specimens – successful, pleasant, helpful – but now she was admitting that they had made her and her husband acutely unhappy. What was more, she felt, it was all her fault.

As she saw it, her own mother had been a disciplinarian and so, when she had her turn at being a parent, she had wanted to do things differently. 'I never laid down the law and now I'm reaping the consequences,' she said. 'The boys feel they can do anything, and life has become horrendous.

'I wanted to be a friend to my children, but I found I had turned into just the kind of mother I didn't want to be. I had stopped listening and being sympathetic because I was so angry with them. When they demanded something I would lose my temper and shout, "No, you can't have any more money." Then I would feel that I'd let everyone down.'

She too had taken herself off to parenting classes and was finding them so helpful that, as soon as one course ended, she was signing up for another. In part, she admitted, she enjoyed the solace of hearing how others were dealing with similar situations. 'It makes you feel less alone,' she said. 'Often their problems are far worse than your own.'

But the classes she described weren't just a form of group therapy: they involved learning skills with arcane names that meant nothing to me, such as 'descriptive praise' and 'reflective listening'. What's more, they seemed to be making a difference. After six months' regular attendance, she was confident that the atmosphere in her home had changed for the better. Her attitude to being a parent had also altered. 'I no longer think it is just a matter of following instinct. Now I see bringing up children without guidance as a bit like trying to drive a car without either lessons or an instruction manual.'

This conversation was an eerie rerun of the earlier one. The great regret both these women expressed was that they had not studied parenting years before. Had they done so, they felt, bringing up children could have been so much more enjoyable. They could have got their children into better habits, established more balanced relationships and avoided some of the pitched battles of the teenage years.

It was too powerful a message to ignore. Examining my own home life, I could not honestly say that the atmosphere was beyond improvement. My children have no special problems, and most of the time they are a delight, but a week does not pass without me being reduced to fury or tears by their fights, rudeness or apparent inability to behave as I want them to. In more honest moments I could admit to feeling as if I were tackling a stream of problems without the expertise to handle them adeptly.

At times I would think ahead gloomily to the teenage years and quake, but, until I had spoken to those two friends, I had assumed there was nothing I could do other than brace myself and continue to muddle on, making it up as I went along, responding to quarrels and tantrums according to my mood. Firefighting, in other words, which sometimes took the form of pouring myself another glass of wine and tuning out the noise of warring, whining children, and at others of rising to the bait and exploding.

My comfort was the optimistic conviction that children from relatively happy circumstances usually turn out fine in the end. This was just an assumption – an unquestioned belief; it wasn't as if I didn't know that it was not always the case. Many is the time when the children of delightful parents have left me speechless with irritation as they behave boorishly around our house. They make a mess without clearing up, help themselves to food from the fridge without asking and rarely admit to either gratitude or shame.

Maybe these are minor problems, but I know families so unruly that their relations would rather cancel Christmas than have them to stay. These pariah children interrupt, demand attention and presents, squabble, crash about, bellow and seem quite unaware of the adults who can barely restrain themselves from slapping them.

I was also aware that this might not just be a fascinating phenomenon that I could observe in others, but one on view in my own home. Way back, when my first child was a toddler, I had tea with a retired nursery school teacher, who observed me alternately smile forgivingly and chide weakly as he rampaged around her house. Bravely, she took me aside and said, 'You are storing up problems for the future.' My reaction at the time was an arrogant, 'What does she know?' But it did sow a seed of self-doubt.

When the children's behaviour got me down, I would reassure myself that I was not treating my children very differently from many other parents whom I knew. It was only when, in the course of my work as an interviewer for the *Daily Telegraph*, I met Joan Collins that I began to wonder whether a collective madness might lie at the heart of the problem.

Collins, a glamorous actress and writer, had just remarried at the age of sixty-eight and was rumoured to be eager to adopt a child with her much younger husband. I asked her if this was indeed the case. She turned her perfectly made-up face to me and stared in disbelief. 'Children these days are a nightmare,' she said. 'They take up all your time and money and they behave appallingly. Their parents seem to be afraid of chastising them for fear of losing their love.'

Inwardly I blushed, being well aware that neither my children's behaviour nor the balance of power at home was as it should be. No expertise in body language was required to read the recoil in those who came across my family at one of those moments when the older children were swearing about some appalling injustice or the younger ones screeching to get their own way.

At such times I wondered whether I should follow the more authoritarian tack taken by those of my friends whose children appeared rather better behaved. These paragons went to bed on time, did their homework, behaved impeccably at meals and were never (at least in front of me) rude to their parents. But often I found their parents' ways too harsh and old-fashioned – they would send children to bed hungry, or 'gate' them for what seemed to be minor misdemeanours. Imbued with the current child-centred approach to being a parent, I feared those parents ran the risk that their children might decide, as soon they left home, to distance themselves from their oppressors.

I wanted to remain what I considered a 'nice person', yet I had no idea what else to do to regain control. So I had carried on veering between soppy liberality and outbreaks of angst, knowing that I was not doing as well by my children as I – and, indeed, my husband – might have wished.

These thoughts were swilling around in my head when I received a call from Battersea Dogs' Home. Like many women who have had their last child and crave something additional to cuddle and care for, I had applied to have a puppy – for the children's sake, of course. And now, six months after I had registered, the woman at the end of the line was saying that ours was waiting for us.

Molly, a mongrel politely known as a Labrador cross, came with a leaflet on puppy behaviour and training, the message of which was the second prompt that led to this book. The introduction contained a section entitled 'Why do things go wrong?' to which the answer was 'Because we fail to guard against disaster'.

'Most dogs,' it said, 'are perfectly well behaved despite the approach and attitude that owners adopt, but not necessarily because of it. In other words, you can do all the wrong things and get away with it, but this is not very responsible and, unfortunately, if things do go wrong, it is the dog that unjustifiably gets the blame. So we must look upon doing the "right" things as a form of insurance against problems developing instead of reacting when they occur.'

Having no idea about rearing a dog, I immediately enrolled myself in a dog obedience class, just as I had automatically signed up for ante-natal classes before my first child was born. Whereas the latter's guidance ceased with the final push – leaving new mothers to work out by trial and error how to proceed – the former dealt with raising the dog.

The classes had their comic side, as thirty pets woofed and tied their owners up in knots, but they were led by a man whose two dogs obeyed his commands instantly and to the letter. If we wanted our dogs to acquire good habits, he told us, we should make sure that we teach and reward them properly. So, instead of bellowing 'Sit' over and over again to a bewildered animal, we were made to help them into that sitting position. Once they had done as we asked, we were instructed to give them a pat and a treat. If they stayed quiet, we were not to take advantage of the peace and start talking among ourselves: we were regularly to praise the dogs for doing as we wanted.

From that first lesson I learnt a ragbag of tips, among them that the key to happiness with a dog is to establish who is boss right from the start. When walking along the road, even entering the house – and definitely at mealtimes – the owner has to take precedence. Of course, the trainer said, when the dog is an adorable puppy we might let it get away with sitting on the sofa or jumping up, but we had to be aware that it would soon be fully grown, and then this kind of behaviour would drive us mad.

So true, I thought, considering the behaviour of my children. A toddler who hogs the best seat and throws tantrums is sweet, but a teenager who sprawls all over the sofa and won't get up for an aged aunt is maddening.

Other insights followed. We were told to have consistent words for every action we wanted. When I asked the trainer whether it was better to tell my puppy to 'Lie' or 'Stay', his reply was sharp: 'You can say "Bacon" – it really doesn't matter so long as you stick to it.' It was my first lesson in rule-setting.

Another piece of advice was that it was sensible to teach a dog to lie down on command. 'Why might that be?' the trainer asked. No one knew. He sighed. 'If a dog starts barking, he won't stop on command,' he explained, 'but you can tell him to lie down and then he will be unable to bark.' This was the first time that it dawned on me that the best way to cure an undesirable behaviour was not to ban it but to overprint it with a desired one. As a dog's adoptive parents, we were learning how to make it easy for the dog to please us.

Throughout this training session my children had been watching patiently from the sidelines. As I got up to go, I summoned them with a wave: it was the dog trainer who turned to them with a smile. 'Thank you for being so good,' he said. They beamed and I realised to my embarrassment that, while I was absorbing the trainer's message that dogs need to be constantly encouraged and rewarded if they are to acquire good habits, I was assuming my children would just pick up desirable behaviour.

Soon after, I bought some books on dog training and booked a one-to-one dog-training session with the behaviourist. As I did so, it struck me as odd that I could be bothered to learn how to make the dog behave well yet leave the training of my children, so infinitely more precious, to chance and amateurish instincts.

The hunt for guidance

Fired with a determination to teach my children to sit, come to heel and stop barking before their lack of discipline got them into trouble, I asked the women who had alerted me to the idea of parenting classes to put me in touch with those who could help me train my children. Following their leads, I soon discovered a kaleidoscope of individuals and organisations eager to help parents make a better fist of bringing up their children.

There are men-only groups for out-of-touch fathers, and groups that specialise in dealing with acute family crises. There are the parties, similar to those thrown to sell risqué underwear or jewellery, at which women sit drinking coffee in someone's living room discussing the week's child-rearing nightmares. There are many groups, too, that help adults examine the legacy with which child-hood has left them burdened when bringing up their own families.

None of those options appealed. What I wanted was manage-ment skills and practical tips for handling the day-to-day situa-tions that bedevilled my attempts to be a calm parent. Just as I had had no idea how to stop my puppy pulling on the lead, since saying 'No' repeatedly had zero effect, I hadn't a clue how to get my chil-dren to behave in a civilised manner at mealtimes, since telling them to sit still, eat up and stop teasing each other didn't seem to do the trick.

Again and again those who spoke to me in wonderment about the miraculous transformation in their households – some deeply troubled, other coping with what I would call an ordinary level of chaos – mentioned two names: Noël Janis-Norton and Luke Scott.

When I spoke to Noël and Luke I found their optimism and insights, combined with the sheer detail of their advice, made me heave a great sigh of relief. I began by talking to them casually but soon found myself attending classes, discussing every situation that arose in my own life and listening intently to other class members' problems. Their emphasis was invariably on finding solutions, not on wallowing in the drama and emotion of the upsets.

I invited each of them to meet my family and observe the chil-dren's behaviour and my handling of it. 'You may not like what I am going to say,' Noël warned me before she delivered her first dose of feedback, and often I didn't. The comments from Noël and Luke made me realise how impulsive, inconsistent and irritating I could be, so – naturally – my words and actions were not having the desired effect on the children. Their advice, however, proved so easy to follow and so effective that I started to write a series of articles for the *Daily Telegraph* about their parenting guidance. If they can help me, I thought, their wisdom might be useful to others too, and so it proved. Many readers wrote to say they were sticking the articles on their fridges and passing them on to their friends.

As I became more deeply involved with Noël and Luke – and my home life improved – I found I was fascinated not just by their prescriptions for coping with homework hassles or bedtime bolshiness, but by the systematic thought that lay behind their advice. For my own sake, as well as others', I wanted to set out their wisdom in such a way that it was easy to turn to in a moment of crisis.

When cooking, I refer to a recipe; when training the dog, I look up a step-by-step technique. Why shouldn't it be possible to do the same for children? This book, I hope, will be the equivalent for humans of the instruction leaflet that I was given by the dogs' home, only more detailed, because children and the environment that they have to learn to cope with are infinitely more complex.

But, before I convey what they said in answer to my endless and varied enquiries about every aspect of child-rearing, I would like to introduce you to my two experts.

Noël Janis-Norton is a softly spoken American who is so skilled at taming even the most unruly children that she is considered the 'horse whisperer' of the child world. Many years ago, when teaching in a primary school, she noticed that difficult children, even those with autism or attention deficit (hyperactivity) disorder (AD[H]D), behaved well in her classes. As soon as those pupils left her care, however, she noticed that their behaviour deteriorated. The change began at the school gates where, she observed, parents would make a simple, affectionate gesture, such as offering to take the child's schoolbag. 'Parents mean well,' she says, 'but their good intentions can give children the message that everything will be done for them.'

To change children's behaviour, she felt she had first to tackle the parents, so she set up the first of her parenting classes in the USA. Seventeen years ago she left that country for Britain, where she had spent much of her teens. In part, this was because she had become exasperated by the child-rearing culture that, even in the nineteenth century, led Oscar Wilde to remark: 'It's amazing how well American parents obey their offspring.'

Although British children used to be much better behaved than their counterparts in the USA, Noël finds 'the gap is closing' and British parents have not yet caught the American enthusiasm for taking parenting seriously as a set of skills. 'Parents in Britain no longer feel they are in charge,' she finds and the trouble this causes for both parents and children is evident to her daily at the New Learning Centre (NLC), the north London base from which she disseminates her ideas on creating cooperative and successful children through proactive parenting practices.

There she runs classes teaching her 'Calmer, Easier, Happier Parenting' programme, gives individual advice and leads a team of specialist teachers who help children, including those who have been excluded from school, to learn the social and academic skills that will allow them to prosper. Watching her in action, it is remarkable how a child who first arrived kicking and screaming is, a few weeks later, asking permission to leave the room and producing meticulously accurate written work.

Noël's personal experience has some bearing on her work. Her liberal intellectual parents divorced when she was very young and gave her and her younger sister the feeling that they were more interested in them as achievers than as individuals, thereby exacerbating sibling rivalry.

She attended numerous schools on both sides of the Atlantic, including Summerhill, the British flagship of the movement to set children free from the negative constraints of the adult world. 'Some children seized their opportunities,' she observed, 'but many, when left to decide whether they wanted to attend lessons, left without an education.'

That experience left her with the belief that it was naive to imagine that children could grow up free of adult influence – and also undesirable. 'It is parents' right and responsibility to have an impact on their children,' she says.

While still at college – where she studied English, psychology and education – she married and began her own family. In her twenties, by which time she had a son and a daughter, she divorced, yet remained geographically close to her ex-husband so that they could share the care of their children. Currently she has a foster child and five grandchildren.

Rearing children added the insights of personal experience to her academic work on psychology and education, and at times she wished she knew more about how to be a good parent. She did not, for example, know instinctively how to help her children discuss their feelings, and was 'puzzled and stymied' when they weren't as confiding as she would have liked. It baffled her too when the children weren't doing things that they knew how to do. 'Then one day I reflected on my own experience and realised that there were hundreds of things that I knew how to do – such as taking exercise – but didn't do regularly. I simply wasn't in the habit of doing them.'

Her determination to be positive and look for the good in a situation or in a child's behaviour may have been enhanced by her life-long tendency to bouts of depression. But, although Noël is candid about her personal experiences and gladly draws upon them, it would be a mistake to view her teachings in their light alone. Many years of thought, study and work with families at solving a wide range of problems lie behind the advice that she gives.

Luke Scott trained with Noël Janis-Norton at the New Learning Centre, but he has a distinctly different take on many of the problems with which I presented him at our regular weekly sessions.

A single man with, as yet, no children of his own, he remains close in spirit to some of the uncertain, worried young people whose lives he helps to transform either by working with them directly, or through educating their parents. He has a particular rapport with boys of around the age that he was himself (nine) when his father left home and his world was cast into confusion.

Where Noël is systematic, Luke tends to approach behavioural problems by looking at the emotional mainsprings of a situation. He is not so much an educator as a wise friend to those families and individuals whom he helps. His emphasis lies not so much on what to do as why change is desirable. The details of how to bring that change about he sees as a secondary consideration.

He was brought up in the best 1960s' liberal tradition by a father who was in rebellion against his authoritarian upbringing. Dyslexic and slow at exams, he failed the eleven-plus and was considered by his teachers thereafter as a source of profound frustration, a bright boy who had no self-discipline. 'My parents never told me to do my homework, so I didn't do it,' he says. 'Instead, I expressed myself all day long and ended up not going to university, which I now regret.'

After his parents' divorce, Luke and his younger brother were brought up by their mother. Although he remained in contact with his father, he felt, as a teenager, that he lacked a strong male role model and was left to work out for himself how he might grow up to be a man.

This experience led him (once he had spent several years going wild and nowhere) into working with Youth at Risk, where he helped young offenders to rebuild their lives. There he met Noël, became interested in her methods and trained with her at the New Learning Centre, working with her until he set up on his own as a specialist family adviser. Since then he has helped individuals and groups to train their children in good habits of motivation and communication and shown them how to take a constructive approach to the conflicts that bedevil family life.

He has also worked in a special school where children and adults with autism are taught and trained in every life skill from literacy to how to flirt and order food in a restaurant. He now divides his time between London and his home in Norfolk; in the summer he runs workshops for fathers and sons.

Through his work with anxious parents, many of them successful and well-to-do, he has come to see that their needs are every bit as pressing as those of less privileged families. It amazes him how often parents who are effective in other aspects of their lives are unable to assert themselves with their children. 'The children of such parents are often more out of control,' he says, 'because they have had everything bought for them and everything done for them all their lives. They have no concept of having to earn their privileges: they get the new trainers however badly they behave. Their parents seem so wary of their children that they put up with, and even reward, intolerable behaviour. They clear up after their children, drive them everywhere, give them money and let them invite their friends over, even if their children shout abuse and make a mess. I have couples who tell me that their child won't go to bed, and it turns out that they are talking about a six-year-old. By the time that child is a teenager, the parents will be screaming at him.'

Their ideas

On every specific question that I presented to them, I found that Noël and Luke had interestingly complementary and, on occasion, divergent views, but they are as one on the fundamental principles of child-rearing and training. They consider themselves, as Luke puts it, 'old-fashioned behaviourists', and use an approach, not dissimilar to dog training, that went out of fashion when therapy came in, and with it the vogue for examining the past in order to illuminate the present.

'It's not that history is unimportant,' says Noël, 'but we have to deal with the situation as it is today. The past affects us all, but we have to move on. Unfortunately, therapy often encourages us to dwell on the bad things about the past. That makes us depressed; taking action makes us feel more positive. No situation is so bad that it can't be changed for the better.'

Similarly, although there is a host of reasons why being a parent is uniquely difficult today – dual careers, single-parent families, lack of support from the extended family – Noël and Luke don't see any circumstances as so hideous that children cannot be guided into calm and cooperative ways. Many times they have seen families transformed more quickly and dramatically than anyone would consider possible.

Their starting point is the conviction that all behaviour is caused – so if a child is in the habit of throwing a tantrum, it will be because he has discovered that it is the best way to get what he wants, which is likely to be parental attention. 'Change the environment and the child cannot but change,' says Noël. 'It is never too late: I've seen remarkable improvements, even with parents whose children are in their twenties.'

They also share a belief that children, however wild and rude, are keen to behave well. 'Children want nothing more than to please their parents,' says Noël. 'If they seem to have lost track of how to do so, it will probably be because they are so used to criticism that they have given up trying. Of course, it is hard not to screech when a child is deliberately winding you up. It may even be what the child is hoping for. But screeching, "Stop that immediately," is not going to solve the problem.

'You are never going to get children to behave better by reacting emotionally. That approach doesn't work in the office, where no one would stand for being bawled at if they had done something wrong, and it works even less well at home because children are yet more ruled by their emotions than adults, and less able to see reason.'

Noël and Luke agree, too, on many of the fundamentals of good parenting: the need to be 'positive, firm and consistent' – Noël's mantra – and how hard it can be to achieve that when faced with a real-life situation. Nor does either of them underestimate the intelligence or the excellent intentions of the parents who ring them up in despair. As Luke says, 'We all know what is common sense – that children shouldn't hit each other or eat lots of junk food – but most parents are bewildered when, even after they've asked their children nicely again and again not to behave in a certain way, they carry on doing it. Parents don't know what else to try.'

The thrust of their teaching is to encourage parents to stand back, put their emotions on hold and use their brains. 'Just having a go is OK a lot of the time,' says Luke. 'Sometimes it will work, and sometimes it won't. It's like going out on a tennis court and hitting the balls around. Sometimes you are bound to hit them, but you will only become a better tennis player if you put some energy and intelligence into learning the game.

'Parenting is just like any other aspect of our lives: we make more progress if we analyse what went wrong and why. If a child won't do her homework, for example, and still refuses, however many times you say, "Do it, do it, do it," you have to find a different way. As Albert Einstein said, "A definition of madness is doing the same thing again and again and expecting a different result."'

The key to change, they both say, is to accept the need for training. 'Children are immature,' says Luke, 'they do things slowly, they are impulsive and disorganised. They want to have everything their own way, but that doesn't mean they feel comfortable with it. Instead of shouting at them for something outside their own control, parents should teach them how to be more mature. You are not responsible for their happiness but you are responsible for their ability to cope with life.'

Noël's long experience has led her to believe that the core problem in many homes is that parents are focused on getting things done, and done quickly. 'If you think your job is to get things done, children are bound to irritate you because children's needs inevitably slow you down and interfere with efficiency,' she says. 'But if you see it as your job, while the children are awake, to train them into good habits and values, your day becomes less stressful. Parents are fearful that everything will take longer, but in the long run you will get more done.'

As Abraham Lincoln said, 'When you look for the bad in mankind, expecting to find it, you surely will.' The reverse is equally true, and Noël and Luke have seen thousands of families transformed once parents have dared to believe that their home lives can be calmer, easier and happier.

Many an ex-convict has learnt to be a useful member of society.

It is much easier for children to change their behaviour. After all, they want to please their parents; they just may not know how.

How to use this book

In each section of this book I shall pass on my experts' advice about handling the specific situations that cause trouble in family life. As illustration, I shall draw upon my own experiences, since they provided the subject matter of my weekly sessions with Noël and Luke. I shall also mention the difficulties and the suggested solutions that I learnt from other parents at classes. Some situations lend themselves to a series of tips, others do not.

You might find it most useful to read the whole book first to get the general idea before homing in on a trouble spot. The key is not just to read the words and agree or disagree, but – as they both had to keep reminding me – to put the advice into practice. 'The problem with the bullet-point mentality,' says Noël, 'is that it makes people think they can just do it but it's not easy to change our habits. Grasping something intellectually is not the same as putting it into practice day after day, even when you're tired and irritable. Only doing is doing.'

At the end of each section there will be a reminder of the key action points for a given situation. This is the equivalent of the homework that they ask those who attend their classes to do in between weekly sessions. Individuals set their own targets for something they intend to do differently. Knowing they have to report back the next week on what happened is a good way to focus on action.

The very thought of homework may induce in parents the same instant rebellion that many children feel when work eats into their free time, but this homework is different. While children have to get out their books, sharpen their pencils and find a quiet place to sit, parenting homework is all set up and waiting for you as you open the front door. If you are going to look after children, you might as well experiment with some tried and tested methods for getting the best results.

Before beginning, Noël and Luke advise sitting down with your partner or a friend and listing the situations that cause the most problems in your home life. Some parents choose to tackle these problems one by one. Many parents, however, find that it is actually easier to apply the skills that Noël and Luke teach to all the problem areas simultaneously. This way works well because parents are getting lots of practice, improving rapidly and soon become more confident. The result is that the children's behaviour improves more quickly, and in many areas at the same time, which is cheering in itself, and raises everyone's confidence.

The changes in the level of cooperation and calm should be noticeable week by week. With a particularly stubborn situation, it may take three months to effect a total turnaround, but they promise encouraging improvements will be visible within two to four weeks, often even sooner.

Energy, concentration and determination will be required. 'Change is hard not just because it involves finding new ways of doing things,' says Noël. 'It is easier to change our entrenched habits when we remember that we always have a choice about how we react to situations. On different days the same person could react differently to the same situation. But inconsistency, which is typical of many parents' reactions, is counter-productive.

'We can improve our children's habits but we, the adults, have to change our habits first.'

1

PARENTING SKILLS

Where do I begin? Do I need to know
anything before I start?

Before launching into the specific situations that concern parents, I shall outline the sixteen skills that Noël applies to any given parenting situation. The skills will keep cropping up throughout the book, but it is as well to run through them first. Some will be familiar and scarcely need explanation; others, notably 'descriptive praise' and 'reflective listening', were new concepts to me and may well be to you, so I have described them in more detail. No one skill is a magic wand, but taken together they can solve most problems.

Luke broadly agrees with the skills Noël has identified, but his approach to parenting problems is more free-form. As he says, 'The skills are useful when you know what you are trying to do, who you are and, from that, what you want to give your children. If we're not sure what our job is, it is hard to use the skills since they are the way of bringing our aims, values and expectations into existence.'

Summarising the preparation he would like parents to do before tackling problems at home, he says, 'We should treat children not as they are but as we would like them to become.'

Perhaps the best way to learn to use the skills would be to read through them quickly now and refer back to them when, having thought through what you aim to achieve in a specific instance, you will be able to make better use of them.

1. Prepare for success

Most situations go awry because we haven't thought them through in advance. A parent who takes a tired, hungry child to the supermarket and expects peace is asking for trouble. Prepare for the worst and you won't end up in a rage.

But planning takes mental effort. It requires you to anticipate what is likely to happen and what you will realistically be able to do about it when it does. Whenever I have complained to Noël or Luke about not having the time to plan, they are firm. 'Planning takes three minutes,' they say. 'Dealing with an upset child takes far longer.'

2. Have clear expectations

Knowing what behaviour you expect of a child is vital; then you have to communicate it. The key is to create clear rules and discuss them.

Obviously, parents have to be realistic. When we expect the earth, children are bound to fail. The result is a frustrated parent and a confused child. 'It is fine,' says Noël, as an example, 'to expect homework to be done, but quite unreasonable to expect children to enjoy doing it.'

Perfection is not an option; Noël and Luke advise parents to expect 90 to 95 per cent cooperation once they are using the sixteen skills. 'Don't even aim for 100 per cent,' says Luke. 'You or society may not be right in your expectations and, while you want cooperation, you probably don't want total obedience as that doesn't always make for future happiness.'

Luke suggests that one way to find out whether your expectations are reasonable is to carry out a reality check with other parents. But, Noël warns, 'Don't pander to popular opinion. You know your child best, and he may need more sleep than his best friend. Particularly when you get to the teenage years, what's typical may have nothing to do with what's right.'

3. Present a united front

Research shows that 90 per cent of arguments between parents are about disciplining the children. Opposites attract, and living together and bringing up children polarises differences. What seems to one parent harmless cheekiness may strike the other as downright rudeness.

Children are swift to spot those inconsistencies and play their parents off against each another to get a later bedtime or an additional sweet, or just for the fun of seeing their parents rowing. 'You and your partner may not agree on everything,' says Noël, 'but you probably agree that you both want family life to be calmer, easier and happier. We find that parents are usually willing to make the effort to agree once they see that we are not judging them, blaming them, or saying that they have been doing it all wrong while their partner has been doing it all right. Becoming a united front always requires both parents to do things differently.'

When I told Luke that I tend to put a child's grumpiness down to low blood sugar while my husband looks for a psychological cause, he told us to establish more common ground by spending fifteen minutes each day not sighing over what has gone wrong, but working out joint solutions.

4. Use descriptive praise

Everyone needs praise. It's the great motivator. We all know that. I say 'Well done,' 'Clever you' and 'That's brilliant' to my children constantly. Noël and Luke are not impressed. 'You were probably given that kind of praise when you were a child: did it make you feel wonderful?' asks Noël. 'If anything, it probably made you feel less confident. The problem with that kind of "super, marvellous" praise is that we can always think of someone who is cleverer or more brilliant, so we don't believe it. In fact, it can even make us feel worse.'

Luke has often observed the harmful effects of this 'evaluative' praise: 'In households where there are expectations of high achievement, children almost always read into that kind of praise the idea that they could have done better.'

The answer, they say, is not to let the praise dry up – evaluative praise is better than no praise at all – but to try a better form of appreciation, which is known as 'descriptive praise'. This kind of praise carries no negative connotations, is not exaggerated, and is the key to motivating children to cooperate. It is delivered in a casual voice, not an excited exclamation, and, like a cuddle, it lowers the emotional turmoil and changes the mood.

'It's about noticing and describing all the good things a child has done right,' Noël explains, 'and about noticing effort rather than just results. Even in a difficult situation, there is always something that a child is not doing wrong that you can praise.'

Examples of descriptive praise
'Ah, you've got one sock on.'
'You didn't spill your orange juice.'
'Two brothers sitting next to each other and nobody screaming.'
'You're doing your homework.'
'You've made a sensible choice. You didn't hit your sister back.'
'You are on your bed even though I know you don't want to go to sleep.'

The rationale behind this kind of praise is that what you notice you get more of – not just from the child in question, but from siblings who also want praise. It changes the mood because it makes a parent more aware of the child's efforts to do what's required (attempts often masked by irritating behaviour), and thus makes the parent more positive and optimistic.

Luke finds that the easiest way to get into this new habit is to make an effort to praise descriptively in a situation that gives you constant headaches, such as getting the children to bed. 'You've found your pyjamas. Now what do you have to do next? Yes, brush your teeth. That's right. I really like the way you haven't tried to go downstairs even though you want to, etc.'

Noël prefers to give parents the exercise of starting the praise from the very beginning of the day and asks them to keep it up all day long. That doesn't mean the occasional remark but a constant flow. 'Before the children leave the house in the morning,' she says, 'you should have descriptively praised each of them at least ten times. Why? Because each child will have done many not-wrong things already that morning, and they deserve to be acknowledged. If we praise only the rare wonderful moments, we miss many chances to appreciate the myriad OK moments.'

As you become more practised, they say, and as children get older, you can move from praising actions to praising more abstract achievements, such as being organised or patient or brave.

But there are caveats. Never use descriptive praise when you are angry as it sounds like sarcasm. Never praise a child for a habit he acquired long ago: it sounds patronising. Also, expect that sometimes the praise will remind a child of the misbehaviour he could be getting up to. Praising a child for not whining on a long walk, for example, can start the child moaning. 'Ride it out,' says Noël. 'It's temporary and will soon disappear.'

Some people are coy about using descriptive praise, feeling it to be false, but Noël's and Luke's response to that is: 'Like medicine, you don't have to like the taste for it to work.' When you see how effective it can be, they imagine that you will expand the use of its magic powers into other – and eventually all – aspects of life.

Another common fear is that it creates praise junkies, reliant on constant fixes of admiration: 'It is the child who doesn't feel good about himself who craves praise,' says Noël. 'Children who receive a lot of descriptive praise start to internalise these new statements. Their confidence, maturity, self-reliance and cooperation all increase significantly.'

5. Do reflective listening

Just as we all think we praise our children, so we all think we listen to them. Again we may not, according to Noël and Luke, be giving the most useful form of attention. Often, they find, parents interrogate and ask for facts. Certainly, whenever I ask a distressed child what is upsetting her, I invariably receive the answer, 'Nothing,' which leaves all parties no wiser, and usually rather crosser.

Luke and Noël advocate an alternative kind of listening, one that bypasses the level of facts – you don't really need to know who said what to whom about disputed gel pens – and goes straight to the often uncomfortable and difficult-to-express emotions that lie behind the behaviour. 'A child,' says Noël, 'can't listen to a parent's words of wisdom when in the grip of an emotion, so you have to make that child feel understood. He will then automatically start to calm down.'

Not only does reflective listening make a child feel you understand – or want to – it also, says Noël, makes the child feel you are on her side. 'And, over time, it teaches the child a vocabulary for expressing feelings so that she doesn't have to bottle them up or act them out inappropriately. It also shows a child that feelings are important and that expressing them is beneficial.'

This kind of listening calls for putting yourself in the child's shoes. 'Maybe you are feeling sad because you wanted your friend to come to tea with you but she has invited someone else round,' Noël suggests, might be a way of encouraging the child who says nothing is wrong to open up. 'If you are wrong, the child will probably put you right. Even if you are spot on, the child may deny it and stomp off but she will have the feeling that you understand.'

Useful ways to show a child that you care about her feelings
'I can see you are upset.'
'You look pretty cross.'
'It seems as if you are trying to show me you are angry.'
'You seem to be feeling confused by this.'
'You want to let me know how disappointed you are right now.'

Reflective listening, they point out, is not just for the inarticulate child. Many children are precociously good talkers but they may not be any better at identifying and expressing their feelings than a more monosyllabic child. 'Boys,' Luke warns, 'are often harder to get talking. If you do something together, they are more likely to open up, but don't expect quick results.'

Reflective listening is not a way to get to the bottom of an immediate problem, although it does achieve that. Nor is it a prelude to fixing something, or an end in itself. It is a way of dealing with the emotion dominating a child as a prelude to moving on and taking action. It is about helping a child to manage his own feelings, about building confidence and maturity and about developing a vocabulary that reflects the fine distinctions between feelings. As such, it is a long process involving patience. Often a child offers an opening just when you are at your busiest. In that case, they suggest, make a brief comment to show you are interested and a promise to return to the subject later.

Some parents worry that if they listen to a child's feelings, they will find it more difficult to assert their authority. Luke scotches that misconception: 'You don't have to condone an action just because you have listened to the feelings that caused it.'

Noël adds, 'Respecting a child's feelings does not mean having to take their opinions equally seriously. Their feelings are valid but their opinions, by definition, are often immature.'

She recommends attempting to listen reflectively to a child at least ten to fifteen times a day, whenever he or she is annoyed, out of sorts, or signals through body language that some uncomfortable feeling is preoccupying her. 'Doing it often will get you into the habit,' says Luke. 'Really you should be aiming to do it as often as necessary.'

> *I had given Eugenie all the words in the world, but what she needed was the proof that her mummy loved her.*
>
> Sarah, Duchess of York,
> after staying with her daughter in hospital

6. Practise the dos and don'ts of communication

On average, Noël and Luke observe, a child receives nine negative remarks for every positive one. I fear that if I had to listen to myself when I'm tired or ratty I would hear criticism, reminders, groans, rhetorical questions ('Why on earth . . . ?') and all the other grumpy habits of speech that make children feel they can't do anything right.

Anyone would find it hard to bake a cake with only negative instructions: don't put the butter in when it is too cold, don't leave it in the oven for too long. Better results come from putting a more positive spin on your conversation, just as you would with an adult.

Another 'don't' is to guard against labelling and name-calling. We don't call adults lazy, stupid or disorganised – at least not to their faces – yet parents often do not realise how demoralised children can become from hearing such words. This fondness for telling others about themselves is a major cause of escalating friction. It is also unproductive: 'You are a lazy brute' rarely gets the required response.

One particular personal criticism seems to sear into every brain. Years after the accusation, adults can remember how hurtful it was being told they were 'selfish', and one of the New Learning Centre teachers traces her tendency to be too obliging to her children to having been called selfish as a child.

'Instead of thinking she is selfish or lazy,' says Noël, 'remember that the child is only doing whatever it is you are not happy about because she is not yet in a better habit. Finding a positive way to put a criticism won't instantly or automatically make a child do as you wish, but it will defuse the situation. If you want to change your child's habits, you must praise all the little steps in the right direction.'

But sometimes we do get upset. Then, instead of blaming the child, stick to saying how you feel, as in: 'I get upset when you use that tone of voice.' By speaking about your feelings rather than about the child's actions, you are not being insulting or allowing misinterpretation. As long as you can do it in a calm, friendly way it will help the child to see the world from someone else's point of view.

Communication is not just about speech; it is also about body language, eye contact and whether you bellow up the stairs or make a request face to face. It easier to convey firmness and calm determination rather than annoyance or impatience after you have thought about what this means in terms of body language, eye contact, tone of voice, timing, pace, choice of words, waiting for a response, praise and use of questions.

THE DOS AND DON'TS OF COMMUNICATION
- Don't nag, argue, generalise, defend yourself, threaten, lecture, ask why, judge, sympathise, reassure or instruct.
- Talk less and do more.
- Don't answer children's questions: let them answer them themselves.
- Be friendly – smile.
- Keep and use your sense of humour.
- Use silence as a tool.
- Find new ways to say things – don't repeat yourself.
- Say what you mean and mean what you say.

---

7. Follow through

There is no point making a rule if a child only has to nag and whine long enough for you to say, 'Oh, all right then . . .' Without consistent boundaries a child can feel unsafe, which can lead both to anxiety and resentment.

Inconsistency encourages children to be manipulative, to keep pushing at the boundaries to find out where they lie today. If some days you can't be bothered to limit computer time, why should children stop obediently on the rare occasions when you do take a stand?

8. Don't do for children what they can do for themselves

Luke is impassioned about this one, having seen so many teenagers go adrift as soon as they leave home. Parents often think they are being loving by picking up their children's clothes and cooking for them when they could perfectly well do those things for themselves – often from a surprisingly young age. The effect is to keep children dependent by rendering them helpless. 'Never do anything for a child that he can – or could with some teaching or training – do for himself,' is his maxim. 'And that includes thinking.'

9. Practise and provide a sensible lifestyle

Even adults behave badly if they don't take enough exercise or if they eat a diet that creates blood sugar highs and lows. Children are far more sensitive organisms than adults, so you can't expect them to behave well if they follow your poor example. 'And let's not forget TV, videos, computers, Playstations and Game Boys,' adds Noël. 'Many parents complain about the quantity and quality of their children's "screen time", but feel unable to establish more wholesome routines. As parents, we have more experience, maturity and wisdom than our children do, so *we* need to be in charge of our children's lifestyle.'

In my own home a major steps towards a more cooperative atmosphere came with the installation of a trampoline one Christmas. An exercised child is far easier to deal with.

> *If having a child doesn't kick you out of your immaturity, I don't know what will.*
>
> Uma Thurman, actress

10. Teach and train versus nag and hope

Luke and Noël are clear about the distinction between teaching and training. Teaching results in a child knowing a fact (such as that you should look people in the eye when responding to questions), or in knowing how to do something (such as how to make a bed). Training results in doing it automatically and regularly without needing to be reminded: in other words, training results in habits.

Children can learn new routines surprisingly fast, they say, if properly taught in manageable steps, but the skills will only become habits if children are trained to use them.

When I looked rebellious at the thought of how much work was involved, Noël was bracing: 'Training a child may seem laborious at first,' she said, 'because parents assume, often incorrectly, that bad habits are hard to drop and new ones slow to be established. Even when that is true, training will save time in the long run. The alternative – hoping and nagging – results in countless wasted hours of correction and recrimination.'

11. Be in charge

In this democratic age it may seem wrong to lay down the law but, Noël says, 'Parents who are in charge relieve children of the burden of being the most important people in the house. Adults have the maturity to take decisions; children don't. Since you are training children rather than telling them what to do, you are influencing them rather than bossing them about.'

When my children complain about a decision, she has advised me to toss the question back to them. 'Ask, "Why do you think I'm insisting on this?" Usually they know perfectly well and will find it a relief that someone is taking charge. Just because children like the idea of doing exactly as they please doesn't mean they are comfortable with it.'

Nevertheless, when I first learnt of Noël's methods I was concerned that they were a way to control children by hemming them in with rules. 'Many parents think that initially,' she says, 'but they change their minds when I tell them that I don't care what their rules are, or even if there are no rules at all, so long as they are consistent. Call them guidelines or policies, if you prefer. Being in charge is not the same as controlling: controlling means that you want something to happen in a certain way, right now, like this, and when it doesn't happen you get cross. Being in charge means you know what you want to achieve, you know how to achieve it and you carry out your plan without giving up.'

She rarely meets over-controlling parents of the kind who make their children cowed. 'The parents I see vacillate between bossiness and permissiveness because they haven't thought through what they are trying to achieve. They are scared of their children and tiptoe around them. I often hear them use expressions such as "My child refuses . . ."'

Being just such a parent, I once asked Noël if it wasn't reasonable to be concerned that, if I was too much in charge at home, my children might rebel later. 'That's a myth,' she said. 'Particularly rebellious teenagers have usually been rebellious throughout their childhood. Innate temperament plays a more important part than we realise in whether children adapt to rules and routines easily and quickly or with struggle and protest.'

> *When I was a child and I was upset about something, my mother was not capable of containing that emotion, of letting me be upset but reassuring me, of just being with me in a calming way. She always got in a flap, so I not only had my own baby panics, fears and terrors to deal with, but I had to cope with hers too . . . In a way, she had managed to put me in charge of her.*
>
> John Cleese, actor and writer

12. Pay attention to detail

Noël's way of helping a child to develop good habits involves describing in detail what is required, praising every tiny step in the right direction and picking up on every tiny misbehaviour by asking for an action replay. In an action replay the parent has the child repeat the scenario, but this time substituting the behaviour you want.

Action replays, she says, are a *very* effective consequence for the numerous minor misbehaviours that parents would otherwise be tempted to ignore or to scold – neither of which responses helps children into good habits.

'Thirty action replays a day is quite normal to begin with, but it soon drops off when the children see you are paying attention to detail.'

13. Lead by example

We expect children to copy our good traits rather than our bad ones, but why should they stop shouting if we regularly bellow at them?

Luke and Noël suggest creating whole-family rules and making sure everyone – parents included – sticks to them. 'You don't have to be perfect,' says Luke, 'but you should at least show your children that you are actively working to overcome your own bad habits and problems.'

14. Take care of yourself

No one can be positive, firm and consistent if they are feeling imprisoned by their children. It takes energy to change, so parents need to recharge their batteries and prevent themselves dwindling into joyless 'child-rearing units'. Noël's formula for parental time off is one night each week, one weekend each month and one week each year.

I can't afford all that childcare, I protested to her. Noël did not back down. Instead she told me to explore creative solutions, such as swapping with other parents.

Many parents say they are too busy to train their children, to which Luke responds that they should review their lives and make more time for 'being' rather than 'striving'.

15. Time alone together

When a child has frequent, predictable time alone with a parent, Noël finds that this invariably strengthens the bond between them. The more time a parent and child spend together, the more the child wants to be like that parent and take on his or her values. 'Children become much less demanding because an important need is being met. Also, siblings get on much better when they each have frequent, predictable time alone with each parent.'

When parents protest, as I did, that they are too busy to spend much time alone with each child, she is brisk. 'Presumably,' she said, 'you had children in the first place in order to be able to enjoy their company.'

16. Make the time and take the time

Training, says Noël, takes time in two senses. Not only must it happen over a period of time – training can't be achieved in a day – it also takes time when you are doing it as it is a slow and careful process.

As the mother of nine children once told me, the single thing she had learnt from all her experience was this: 'Never rush a child.'

RECIPES FOR DISASTER
- Ignoring bad behaviour in the hope that your child will learn that bad behaviour doesn't win attention.
- Repeatedly saying 'Stop', etc.
- Reasoning, asking a child why he did something.
- Threatening consequences but not following through.
- Offering a treat or bribe for good behaviour.
- Ignoring behaviour until someone else seems bothered by it.
- Making a child feel guilty.
- Saying things you don't mean.
- Doing nothing because the misbehaviour is not that bad or important.

2

DAILY ROUTINES

How do I get the children up in the morning?
How do I get the children to go to bed and stay there?
What do I do about nightmares?

When I first turned to Noël and Luke to improve my family life, the issues of routine dominated my mind. It was rare to get the children off to school without a crisis, and equally unusual for bedtime to pass without drama. In that, I soon learnt, I was typical of those who come to them yearning for a calmer, easier, more cooperative family life.

I suspected the roots of our problems lay in infancy. When my first child was born I had read the books about child-centred behaviour and allowed him to eat and sleep pretty much when he wanted. Since I had to go back to work soon after, it suited me that he had nothing resembling a schedule because it meant I saw more of him. This policy, if it can be called one, remained unchanged as the other children came along. My husband and I weren't thrilled with the results, but we were too tired to do things differently.

This undisciplined approach would, I feared, get me into trouble with my parenting experts. I had underestimated their kindliness. They did not tell me that I had made a rod for my own back by failing to set routines; they didn't need to. They only asked whether I was happy that the children came downstairs for snacks when they should have been asleep, and migrated into our bed in the middle of the night. If not, they could help me install different routines.

Luke doesn't work much with babies, but he understands how hard it is to know what to do for the best in those early months when there is so much conflicting advice. 'Some things are clear: that breast-feeding, for example, is good both for the child's health and for bonding. But habits such as feeding on demand and sleeping in the parents' bed are very much an individual matter. The early years are so stressful that the last thing parents need is to be told that they are not doing it right.'

Nevertheless, having been brought up in a laissez-faire way himself, which left him having to create his own good habits, he does think that it is kinder to children to establish a routine. 'The routines you want your children to stick to are common sense. If you establish them when they are young, they will have internalised them. If you wait until the children are teenagers before, for instance, establishing a daily bath, you will meet with rebellion.'

One of my excuses for not having fixed routines was that, because of work, my husband and I were not always there to see them through; sometimes a babysitter was left in charge. 'That,' says Noël, 'is no excuse. It's far easier for others to look after your children if the routine is established and, preferably, written down.'

But they did not want me to spend too much time on justifications or regrets; they wanted to help me set the routines. This was my first encounter with their cheering belief that it doesn't matter how you got into a mess, the point is to get out of it. Questions of routine are all about setting rules and sticking to them, so the first thing they wanted me to do, with my husband, was to decide on the rules.

What are rules and why are they a good thing?

'Rules are a parent's way of transmitting their values to their children,' says Noël. 'They are not about revelling in red tape, but about thinking through what we want our children to be like in a few years' time, and the skills they need to acquire. A rule regularly enforced becomes a routine, so the rules have to be thought through at a calm time, not made up on the spur of the moment. When made on the hoof they are often hard to follow, inconsistent and don't carry much authority.'

Rules, she explains, make children feel secure. They are something children can depend upon and get right in a bewildering world. They remove the personal and the arbitrary from a situation and prevent unnecessary clashes. As Luke says, having been brought up without many rules, 'Knowing exactly what you are meant to be doing leaves you more energy to put into all the other, more creative aspects of life.'

The classrooms in which Noël teaches children excluded from school are festooned with rules. Like most parents, my jaw dropped when I first saw them: 'I know it appears alarming,' she says, 'but the rules are simple and are there to remind children of all the things they usually do right, such as flushing the loo after they have used it.'

Of course, it can be difficult to be equally explicit in your own home as you may not know what the rules are yourself – I didn't – so setting them becomes an exercise in working out what you mind about and what you don't. Noël and Luke asked me to talk through, with my husband, what needed to be done at the beginning and end of the day – in great detail. Should the children put out their clothes the night before? Who would get how much story time when? At what juncture should the children brush their teeth? Were we going to stagger bedtimes so that the older ones had special privileges? Were the children to get dressed before they came downstairs for breakfast, or eat first and dress afterwards?

The point was to create a sensible and fixed order of events so that the children knew exactly what was expected. They recommend that rules should be written down, and that children should take part in the rule-setting, not by dictating the rules, which would mean bedtime set at midnight, but by reflecting back the rules that they believe are already in place. Often they come up with far more rules than you knew existed.

Children then need to be trained in those routines – and possibly even taught the skills involved – until they are able to operate on automatic pilot. Merely telling children the rules is not sufficient, they warn, because children are creatures of impulse, are easily distracted and find it hard to follow sequences of operations. Training takes energy, but they are adamant that children equate firm guidance with love.

Even so, I worried that the children would think I had gone mad when I asked them what they thought the rules were about bedtime. In fact, I discovered that their natural instincts were those of camp commandants and that they were setting far earlier bedtimes than those they actually stuck too, which were also far earlier than I was about to set myself.

This should not, perhaps, have been a surprise. Whenever the children – particularly the girls, I notice – set up a game, they invariably establish EU quantities of regulations governing the behaviour of each participant. 'You have to stand there, wear this and say that,' says the self-appointed leader. Their doors bear copious instructions about who may enter and how. They wallow in rules; it is only adults who are shy of asserting themselves.

TIPS FOR SETTING RULES

- Rules are needed only to cover potential or actual problems. Let a child make as many small decisions for himself as possible.
- A new rule, especially one that won't be popular, should be announced well in advance. 'From next week people who are rude have to go to bed earlier,' or 'From next week I'm going to confiscate everything I find on the floor.' The announcement should be made by both parents face to face with the children, making eye contact, with smiles and cuddles as appropriate.
- Frequent references should follow so that when next week comes the children know what is expected – and so do you. If the child is unhappy about the new rule, you can listen reflectively to their feelings without being swayed into changing the rule.
- To help a child succeed in the new routine, talk or even walk them through it *before* they have to do it for themselves. The parent should do this by asking questions and allowing the child to come up with the answers. 'Tell me how you are going to make sure your clothes are ready for tomorrow . . . Right, so you put them on the chair, and where will you find a clean pair of socks?'
- Allow plenty of time for every process. Adults may be able to jump out of bed, throw on some clothes and eat breakfast in the car, but children can't. By expecting them to do things fast we are setting them up to fail; rushing invariably leads to confrontation.

- If instructions need to be given, try to weave them into a conversation, don't bark them out like a sergeant major. Not, 'Brush your teeth now,' but 'Let's go and find your toothbrush and see if we can squeeze a little blob of toothpaste on to it very carefully.'
- For complicated activities, write out a chart so they don't forget the sequence of events and ask, say, for the bedtime story before the clothes have been put out.
- Keep them on track if they falter, not by telling, but by asking: 'What do you think you have to do next?'
- Be prepared to wait for a child to do something. Treat a child's silence as thinking time, not resistance.
- Notice and praise every step in the right direction.
- Don't despair of disappearing under a forest of routines that seem to take forever: soon they will become automatic and infinitely speedier.
- Once one skill is mastered, move on. There's always the next skill to teach and train.
- Rather than making or suggesting a rule and then finding yourself in negotiation with your child about it, anticipate any valid objections *before* you speak. That way you won't be thought to be backing down.

Note: Rules don't have to be inflexible. There can be exceptions but, Luke says, 'You should be the one to decide when and what, and you should always give a good reason so that it is clear (to you and to the child) that you are not giving in to whining or intimidation.'

Morning mayhem

Having learnt the basics about setting routines, we discussed the ways in which I might improve the atmosphere in the mornings. Breakfast in my household was an indigestible mixture of cereal, boiled eggs and hysteria. Low early morning blood sugar seemed at war not only with the *Today* programme but with all civilised behaviour, and day after day we would have fights over control of the cereal packets, panics over lost items of uniform and last-minute crises over packed lunches.

One of our daughters would routinely get into a terrible state over anything from finding the right pair of tights to her spelling test. The scene usually ended with her being inserted into the car, wailing and kicking, with her lunchbox and book bag thrown in after her. My husband would then announce gloomily, 'It can't go on like this,' but it did.

Following Luke and Noël's advice we improved our routines, so the children were getting up earlier, going to bed earlier and (sometimes) putting clothes out the night before, but we still had chaos, and I was tempted to follow the example of a colleague who buys chocolate for her son on the way to school if he gets into the car on time. 'That will be fine until he hits eighteen stone aged twelve,' jokes Luke. Rather than bribe children with chocolate bars, he and Noël suggest harnessing their natural desire to get things right and to please their parents.

They advised me to start by making a list of all the operations that have to be done in the morning – brush teeth, make bed, etc. – and to go over it with the children so that they are in no doubt as to what needs to be done and in what order. 'Organisation' is Noël's watchword; 'self-reliance' is Luke's; and helping the children become more aware of what needs to be done meets both priorities.

Both of them often say that parents are either part of the problem or part of the solution, so I had to learn to be more realistic about how long each operation takes. As Luke pointed out, 'Children are too immature to know that it is no fun being in a rush and feeling flustered, so you have to take charge.' If dressing takes fifteen minutes, there's no point setting aside five minutes for it.

Leaving plenty of time for each operation, with some to spare, will probably mean getting up earlier at first, but they assured me that the process would soon speed up. One reason for this is that once children see a parent means business, they will cooperate more readily, dawdle less and put their own clothes out the night before.

When I groaned at the time it might take to reach that happy state, Noël reminded me of the point of training. 'All parents say they want children to do as they are told. What parents want even more than cooperation is self-reliance: children doing the right thing *without* having to be told each time. When we train children to follow routines, they learn to solve their own problems. Very soon there is less friction because children don't like being told what to do and how to do it any more than adults do.'

What do you do about children who won't get out of bed?

The reason we are usually in a rush is that the children don't get up when woken; some need two or three shakes at ten-minute intervals. This, Luke says, is a habit I should break immediately. Ideally, I should put them in charge of their own alarm clocks but, if a parent is to do the waking, an announcement should be made that, from now on, there will be only one call and no further reminders.

'Otherwise, as they get older,' he says, 'they will ignore the first three wake-up calls and get up only on the fourth when you shout the house down and they know you really mean it. Even if you are only doing it for their sakes, they will resent you for it and you will feel angry and hurt.'

What can be done about early morning grumps?

Noël is hot on the dietary causes of early morning grumpiness. Her first move would be to cut out all caffeine during the day – that includes chocolate – as it interrupts the sleep cycle. She would outlaw sugar and other refined carbohydrates for the same reason.

When I ascribed my children's early morning humour problems to low blood sugar she suggested that I wake each child with a mood-improving glass of orange juice, but she warned me that it mightn't work.

Often she finds that sensitive children can't cope with the mornings because in many households this time of day is hectic and tension-inducing. A child would rather hide under the duvet than face a mother saying, 'Hurry up, let's go . . . We're going to be late . . . Why are you always . . . ? Can't you ever . . . ?'

There may also be something happening at school that the child can't face. Time for reflective listening . . .

Although many such problems can be solved, Noël advised me to accept that some people – children included – are just foul in the morning. If so, I should prevent the screaming matches by setting aside a place to eat for those who wish to be solitary.

As it is, the grumpy ones, when forced to socialise, create walls of cereal packets. This is only the junior equivalent of disappearing behind a newspaper. If the packets themselves become the cause of fights, Luke advises keeping them in the cupboard for three days running until everyone agrees not to fight.

What do I do about a child who won't get ready on time?

With young children, Luke suggests making getting ready into an enjoyable game, with a reward at the end. Little ones are happy with a cuddle, a story and, of course, plenty of descriptive praise. Older ones might need further incentives – star charts, perhaps, which could be linked to their pocket money.

'Motivation is a function of habit,' he believes, 'but until the habit is established, you have to help children by letting them feel the rewards and consequences of their behaviour.' So, rather than endure a daily white-knuckle ride in order to leave the house tidy and get to school before the register is taken, he suggests announcing that from next week (always give warning of a change) you will not be leaving until the mess on the floor has been cleared up – even if that means missing registration.

The pain of being looked at by the rest of the class may be sufficient to start the reform process. 'You could even explain to the teacher,' he says, 'that your daughter may be late for the next few days because you are trying to train her. Ask the teacher not to be too indulgent. The child needs to be given a late card.'

'But what if a child has left his lunch behind?' I wailed. Noël told me not to fuss or drive back to school with the missing item. 'Let him have school dinner this once. Nor will it do any harm if an eight-year-old has to sit out swimming for a lesson.'

TIPS FOR CALMER MORNINGS
- Make a calculation of how long everything should take and work backwards from departure time to set the wake-up time.
- Talk the schedule through with the children and get them to prepare as far as possible the night before. PE kits, swimming stuff and book bags can be left by the front door; most of a packed lunch can be done in advance, too.

- If the child is in a panic, you could say that for a week you will help him think through putting his clothes out. Each day of that week, require a bit more self-reliance. After that, he can manage on his own.
- Get yourself dressed before going downstairs. Power-dressing is as important at home as in the office. Pyjamas or nightie do not give authority, and it is easier to insist on a child getting dressed before breakfast if you have already done so yourself.
- Parents who are grumpy in the morning should have something to eat before the children get up and get on their nerves.
- Wake children only once and decisively. Better still, give them the means to wake themselves.
- Teach them how to make their own breakfast. And don't, Noël begs, give children refined carbohydrate. 'Many cereals are metabolised like sugar. Would you give your child a bowl of sugar?'
- If they are still not ready in time, get them up even earlier – most children would do anything for longer in bed.
- If something causes problems – in our household it is hairdressing – create a rota.
- If the child won't go to school, use force if necessary, but only the minimum and not in anger. If the child is hysterical, say that you will discuss her feelings only when she is calm.
- If all else fails, Luke suggests a useful exercise that is particularly effective for those who are adept at dodging responsibility for their own lateness. Ask if the child would be at school on time if there were a £1 million reward. The answer is always, 'Yes.' Then find out what they would do to guarantee the reward – and do it.

Note: Don't forget to descriptively praise all improvements.

Bedtimes blues

Here Luke and Noël imparted a great universal truth: all children think they need less sleep than they really do. Left to themselves, they will party until they drop; then you not only have to carry them to bed, you also have to deal with overtired grumps the following day.

To make sure children get enough of this elixir of good temper, parents must assert themselves at bedtime. This requires planning, determination and the understanding that to get children into bed in a frame of mind that makes them stay there means starting rather earlier than you might like. 'The key is to be calm, develop a routine and talk the children through it,' says Luke. 'They should know the sequence of events and what is and is not allowed. To begin with, at least, parents have to stick to the rules precisely – no deciding to skip stories tonight because you are going out.'

Of course there will be times when, despite following the routine to the letter, children are over-excited and won't settle. Then, he suggests, you should set logical consequences to their actions. 'If they stay up late, you can tell them, they will not be allowed their extra half hour before bedtime at the weekend. Setting that kind of rule and letting the child know exactly what consequence will follow takes the emotion out of a situation. It will mean that you no longer have to scream, "You are driving me mad." You only have to say, "You know what will be the result." It is useful training in cause and effect.'

'And never give children the impression of having a choice when they don't,' warns Noël. 'If you ask, "Would you like to go to bed now?" you know what the answer will be. Then, when you insist on bedtime, the child will have every reason to feel angry. It is very important that children go to bed in a calm and happy frame of mind.'

What should I do about bedtimes when I get home late from work?
Parents who are at home all day tend to be rather good at getting children to bed because they have had enough of them. Agony aunt Claire Rayner admitted that on one occasion, when she needed to go out, she got hers into bed at 4.30 by bringing all the events of the day forward.

Those, like me, who work outside the home are less good at

bedtimes because we come home with our minds full of happy dreams about snuggling up on the sofa, reading stories and hearing the children trill out their accounts of the day. The reality is, of course, different: the children either carry on with what they were doing, or start moaning and demanding until the parent cracks and announces, in none-too-calm tones, that it is 'BEDTIME' and orders them upstairs.

Particularly in the summer, when it is light, this leads to a chorus of protests, snack attacks and suddenly recalled homework projects, and the scene usually ends with slammed doors and tears.

However much children need attention, Noël advised me to find ways of giving it to them earlier in the day – early morning chats, calls home from the office, starting and ending work sooner, anything to prevent me keeping them up late.

She feels it is essential not only that the children get sufficient rest but that the parents have some time to themselves. To assuage any guilt, she would have parents say to themselves that they need that time for their children's sake. 'You owe it to the children to be in a positive frame of mind. Unless you replenish yourself by having at least two hours' free time after the children are in bed, you will resent the children and that will effect how you treat them.'

With older children, Luke adds, it is not so much a matter of sending them to bed as of making sure they respect your need for private time.

Can you make children more aware of time?

At one of my classes, a woman with children aged five and three, who had been suffering from interminable bedtime battles, jumped up, having had a brilliant idea. 'I know what I must do! I must put clocks everywhere so that I can make the children realise that when it is seven o'clock they must go upstairs.'

An awareness of time would certainly help the children take charge of their own routine, said the person taking the class, but she wondered whether the parent was being realistic. At such a young age the children would not be able to tell the time; a better idea might be to get a timer. She could then make the children aware of bedtime looming by setting it to ring in ten minutes and announcing that now was the time to clear up because when it went off it would be time to go upstairs.

What happens when there's a babysitter?

If there is a babysitter, Noël says, he or she should be given a written list of the sequence of events and timings so she can do exactly as you would do. 'That's hard on the babysitter,' I protest. 'No, it's easy for the babysitter,' she replies. 'All she needs to do is ask the children what happens next. "Where do you put your dirty socks? When do you have your story?" It is a mistake to think that when you delegate you should let others do it their way. They will be grateful to know exactly what is expected and then get some peace and quiet.

'Of course, both you and the babysitter should be generous in your descriptive praise when the child does as you want – especially without prompting. And don't forget to praise the babysitter too.'

What if children beg for a later bedtime?

'Children often don't appear to know why they can't stay up until midnight,' says Luke. 'Rather than reasoning with them about why an earlier bedtime makes sense, why don't you reflectively listen to the child's feelings? You could guess at what those feelings are by saying something like, "You probably think it would be much more fun to be downstairs."

'Just because you take time to listen to their feelings doesn't mean you have to do anything differently. You can still be firm and say that they have to go to bed, but they may not feel so angry and upset.'

If there is a concerted campaign to be allowed a later bedtime, Luke suggests putting the onus on the child to prove that she deserves the extra time by demonstrating mature behaviour. He also suggests checking out with other parents what bedtime seems to make sense for a child of a particular age.

'Don't start negotiating too soon. You have the right to say no and not to feel coerced into an agreement. By the time your children are teenagers they may sometimes stay up later than you: at that stage you have to remind them of the house rules, which might be that there is no music after a certain hour and that the kitchen has to be left tidy.'

What do you do with a child who screams for more stories?

One reason why children want to stay up is to get more parental attention – particularly if the attention is hard to come by. At one class I listened to a couple with a three-year-old describe their difficulties. The child so enjoyed his father reading stories to him in bed that he would trap him in his room reading book after book; if he didn't comply, the child would scream the place down, waking up the baby.

'That's blackmail and should be stopped immediately,' says Luke. 'The child should be told how many stories Daddy will read and that should be that. If he screams, the parents should go in after a time and praise him for whatever he is doing right – like staying in bed – but not give in. If necessary, put the baby to bed in a more distant room for a while. With a child of three it should not take too long, or require too much effort, to change a habit.

'But,' he adds, 'the parents should also look behind the behaviour to the message. That child may not be seeing enough of his father. If he can't be home earlier, the father should make a point at weekends of spending one-to-one time with him.'

What about children who won't stay in their own beds?
Luke and Noël find that parents who complain that their children will not settle often did not allow them to develop self-comforting methods as babies because they cuddled them to sleep. But that's history. If children won't settle when they are older, it is usually because parents haven't been consistent in sticking to the routine.

They are adamantly opposed to any lure that might keep children in their rooms – such as television or computer games. They are also anti story tapes, which could get children so used to going to sleep with a burble going on in their heads that they become unable to relax without it.

Noël's plan for children who won't stay in their rooms – often they say they are frightened – is to keep popping in to check on them at regular but lengthening intervals. If the child gets out of bed, silently put him back. Smile, kiss and say goodnight again; no over-exciting ticking off.

'If he shouts but stays in bed, leave it a few minutes. Then go in, comfort, leave. Wait a little longer than previously before returning. Of course, there should be copious praise for the child who has not got up.'

What do I do about nightmares?

My children frequently appear in the middle of the night pleading bad dreams. Often, I suspect, this is an excuse to cuddle up. Luke would take the child back to her own room but give the benefit of the doubt. 'Listen to the fears,' he advises, 'and don't try to sort them out by saying, "Don't be silly, of course a giant isn't coming to eat you." The child must be allowed to feel her fears are taken seriously.

'And don't cross-question children too much on the exact nature of nightmares. They usually can't remember and it makes them feel that their feelings need justifying. A better way to dispel fears is to find a time the following day to talk it through again when the child may have a better sense of proportion.'

TIPS FOR CALMER BEDTIMES

- Don't use bed as a threat or a punishment.
- Play with a child for half an hour earlier in the evening so that he does not crave attention.
- Don't allow snacks after supper.
- No TV or noisy games before bedtime. The hour beforehand should be calm. No child should have a television or computer in the bedroom. If a favourite programme is on too late, record it.
- Don't leave discussion of the worries of the day until last thing.
- Make sure your partner/babysitter does the bedtime routine several times a week, otherwise the child will never go to bed unless you are there.
- Stick to the routine. This might be: tidy up, bath, pyjamas and brush teeth, story/songs, hug.
- Keep lights dim.
- Keep radio or story tapes off. You don't want a child dependent on chatter to get to sleep.
- Don't answer the telephone.
- No bottle in bed. Special blankets or dummies stay in the bed.
- Leave the child to go to sleep alone, otherwise you'll be chained to the bedroom.

Note: Don't forget to give descriptive praise: it ends the day on the right note. And never admit defeat.

3

FEEDING FRENZIES

Why won't the children sit at the table and eat nicely? How do I stop them fighting during meals? How can I get them to eat healthy food? What do I do about a fat child or a faddy one?

A desire to make Sunday lunches more peaceful was uppermost in my mind when I consulted my parenting advisers about my children's eating habits. I soon found myself asking for advice on a host of other issues surrounding food: not just how they eat but what and when.

I know parents who speak of their children's wild enthusiasm for cabbage. I have also read that children, left to their own devices, eat a perfectly balanced diet. But mine turn down vegetables on sight and sneak biscuits from the larder when I'm not looking; some of them would rather die of thirst than drink 'plain' water.

Then there is the agonising problem of body shape. My children are not fat – as yet – but I often wonder how long it will be before they join the ever-growing numbers of children who are obese and heading for a future of heart disease and diabetes. I worry too that their faddiness could develop into the spectre of anorexia in the teenage years.

'Everything surrounding food is very emotive, both for parents and children,' soothed Luke when I asked him and Noël for their advice on how to get the children into better habits. 'So you have to be extra careful to remain calm.'

Table manners

When Mia Farrow (a mother of many) found herself seated next to the late Queen Mother at dinner, she asked her what she felt was the most important thing parents should teach their children. 'Manners,' came the reply. No doubt, she was not thinking only of mealtimes, but for me the trauma of the shared weekend meal is a painful reminder that my children are not as well-behaved (Noël and Luke would say well-trained) as they should be.

A single meal per week eaten as a family should not, one would think, be more than human nature – even young, untrained human nature – can bear. Yet every Sunday lunch we go through the same performance. It goes like this:

1.00   Call everyone to the table.

1.15   Half the family have yet to be rounded up or are still milling around trying to get crisps or chocolate out of the larder while I snarl, 'Wait.'

1.18   The food is served. Cries of 'Yuk!' unless it is roast chicken, when there is a fight over the wishbone.

1.20   Shouts of 'Will you sit down?' start up as the more restless elements fetch drinks, go to the loo, steal food from someone else's plate, start fighting or wander off, saying, 'Call me when it's pudding.'

1.22   My husband and I sit at an empty table, running through a ritual lament about why none of the children have any table manners.

Noël and Luke are quick to provide the answer to that one: you haven't required them to have any. 'But I have,' I protest. 'I tell them to eat what is in front of them, with a knife and fork, to ask to get down, to speak nicely and not to fight. If grown-ups can behave properly, why can't the children simply copy us?'

Dream on, is Luke's reaction: training doesn't come through osmosis, it involves work. Any parent who wants children to have better table manners has to be prepared to be patient and determined. 'You have to accept that while children are being trained, you are not going to have idyllic mealtimes. And you have to lower your expectations: it is not reasonable to hope for intelligent round-table conversations with young children.'

Noël is, as ever, more bullish: 'Parents have too low expectations of their children. You can get them to eat everything if you train them to do so, and you can have sensible discussions at mealtimes if you get rid of the squabbling, the complaints and the parental fussing.'

As always, they believe the starting point is for the parents to sit down together and decide on the rules. Luke would then set up a system of rewards and consequences – it could be a star chart that wins the family a trip to the pizzeria for behaving well for four Sundays in a row. 'Children,' he says, 'will only stay at the table if they want to. Once they have done so a few times, they will have learnt that they can not only do it, but also survive. They might even discover that a civilised meal can be enjoyable.'

Setting rules, Noël points out, may sound laborious but it is less exhausting than trying to ignore or correct bad behaviour. 'It is impossible,' she says, 'for non-saints to keep ignoring annoying behaviour, but if the rules, rewards and consequences are clear, there will be less to be annoyed by. Action replays, descriptive praise and reflective listening are the most effective training tools. And why are you hoping for only one civilised meal a week? Apply your rules to every meal.'

SAMPLE RULES FOR MEALTIMES

- To prevent jack-in-the-box behaviour, Luke suggests a rule that all children should go to the lavatory, wash their hands and equip themselves with a drink before they sit down.
- To discourage fights and fidgets, no one should bring a toy to the table.
- To minimise faddiness, children should be hungry so that they are more likely to try the food. That means making sure there are no snacks around for them to pick at before the meal.
- If you allow juice, it should be drunk after the main course so the children aren't full before they start.
- To encourage an older child to take a leadership role (other than in the creation of mayhem), he advised me to give our twelve-year-old a responsible task, such as carving or opening the wine: 'At that age boys want to be treated like men.'

- And there should definitely be a rule that no one is allowed to say 'Yuk' or anything negative about any of the food – though they can, of course, tell you if they particularly enjoyed something.

How do I deal with a child who says a rule is stupid?

Rarely is the announcement of new rules greeted with delight, and when I started being more prescriptive about mealtime behaviour, there were arguments. 'Why should I eat with a knife and fork?' said one child. 'I like using my fingers.' Arguing and reasoning with him got me nowhere.

I should have prepared the way better, Noël said, by talking through the new routine with the children. Having missed that opportunity, she thought my best tactic was descriptive praise. 'You've stopped arguing and complaining,' she would say during a momentary lull. Then she would do some reflective listening. 'I bet you wish we didn't have a rule about using a knife and fork,' she might say.

At another, calmer moment she would ask, 'Why do you think Daddy and I have a rule about this?' (It is very important, she points out, to make it plain that both parents agree on rules so that one isn't cast as the bad guy.) 'After a while,' she says, 'the child will probably come up with an answer. If it is a facetious answer, descriptively praise their sense of humour and ask for a sensible guess. If the child's guess is sincere but incorrect, find something in the answer that you can descriptively praise, including the courage to take a guess.'

How do I get children to eat what's provided?

Noël has a way of turning children into omnivores which, she promises, 'never fails' if parents are willing to be positive, firm and consistent. The trick is to institute a 'first course' at each meal, consisting of a plate with almost microscopic amounts of a few different foods that you want the children eventually to get used to eating without a fuss. You require the children to finish their first course before moving on to the second course, which is something healthy that you know they enjoy.

'Food preferences,' she explains, 'are purely a matter of habit. Once the children have got used to the tastes of the foods in the first course, they will come to accept them and maybe even, over time, to like them. Ease them into this new regime initially by making the first courses consist of tiny amounts of food that the children already accept. After that you can move on to foods that they don't particularly like. Gradually they will become more adventurous.'

I anticipated battle royal. 'Not if you prepare for success,' said Noël, 'and make sure they understand the rules.' Then, at the actual meal, she advised me to make sure it did not turn into a battleground. So, no urging the children to try the first courses and no remarks such as, 'You never know what you like until you try it' or 'It won't kill you.' The incentive to eat the first courses should be, quite simply, that they don't move on to the second course until the first course is finished.

'I've known rebellious children,' she says, 'who have lasted a whole day – three meals – without eating, but never longer. Of course, you descriptively praise the children for everything they try, or even toy with.'

'It's painful when children say they won't eat anything,' says Luke, 'but most kids won't starve themselves. If the only thing to eat is shepherd's pie, they'll eat it.' However, he adds that parents should be careful to make the food sufficiently attractive to the children to give them an incentive to behave as you wish. 'If you have made skate wings in blackened butter sauce,' he says, 'make sure there is something like pasta on offer too.'

When I say to him that I feel bad about allowing the children only water rather than juice with the meal if the grown-ups are allowed a glass of wine, he is adamant. 'So what?' he replies. 'Be tough.'

How do I deal with disruptive behaviour during mealtimes?

Parents are often told that they should make heroic efforts to react only to good behaviour. 'How easy is that when the children are rioting and squabbling?' I ask. Not at all easy, Noël agrees for non-saints, and not even what she recommends.

She divides disruptive behaviour into two kinds – the impulsive and the deliberate. With the impulsive she would wait a few seconds for it to stop and then descriptively praise the child for stopping the undesirable behaviour. 'If the disruptive behaviour is deliberate,' she says, 'it is not likely to stop. In that case, you remove the child's plate but require him to stay at the table. Don't discuss the annoying behaviour and don't keep saying, "Are you ready to eat properly now?"'

This procedure is, she promises, more effective than any habitual cry of 'Don't do that,' which, she points out, is a totally unproductive instruction. 'Since the child has already done it, what she understands by it is "Don't do it again," which gives the message that it was acceptable the first time. Instead, the very first time you observe the deliberate disruptive behaviour, you should deliver the expected consequence, i.e. remove the plate.'

If children tease each other at the table, she would not be side-tracked. 'Keep descriptively praising the good behaviour. "Even though your sister is teasing you, you have not reacted," you say to the child being teased, and "You are not teasing any more," you say to the child who was doing the teasing, even if she has been calm for only two seconds.'

To a child who starts wailing, she would say something neutral and palliative, such as 'I can see you are upset' without allocating blame. 'The point,' she explains, 'is to remove the moral dimension from misbehaviour and simply make children aware of what works to get them what they want and what doesn't. We want children to notice that it is *easy* to get positive attention.'

A child who is completely out of order will have to leave the room for time out. 'But mine keep bursting back in when I send them out,' I tell Luke. 'So you have to stand by the door to make sure they don't,' he responds. 'I never said this was going to be relaxing.'

After a few weeks of this purgatory, they promise, children will behave better without constant intervention. I was dubious, but at a parenting class I spoke to a mother with two sons aged six and eight, who assured me that the technique worked. She had not only sat down and worked out the rules with her sons, she had also written them out and stuck them on the inside of a cupboard so they could be referred to in case of a dispute.

'It made a huge difference,' she said. 'The children have accepted the rules as a way of life. All I have to say now when they misbehave is: "Are you allowed to kick?" Before, when I mentioned rules only in anger, they seemed to the boys like a ticking off and a punishment.'

How do I tackle bad table manners?

The rules might cover matters such as eating with a knife and fork, using a spoon rather than fingers to serve yourself, and eating with your mouth closed. 'But the rules,' I protested, 'may not always be observed. What happens then?' I asked Noël.

'Action replays,' she replied. 'Don't tell the child off for grabbing a piece of ham with his fingers. Refer to the rules and say, "We'll do that again. Tell me how you are going to pick up the piece of ham this time." When the child tells you, descriptively praise him. When he completes the action replay, descriptively praise him again. He needs to practise doing it right, otherwise the next time he will most probably forget (i.e. tune out your nagging) yet again.'

To an overfilled mouth she would say quietly: 'I know that the next time I look at you your mouth will be closed and you will have only a normal amount of food in it.' The trick then is to watch out of the corner of one eye until the child is doing it right – this may require split-second timing – then give praise.

When should a child get down from the table?

This rule is not as simple as it first appears. Should a child be allowed to get down when he or she has finished? When all the children have finished? When a parent says say so? After pudding?

Noël advises against all of these rules. 'If you allow them to get down when they have finished, the meal becomes a race. If you allow them to get down when the last child has finished, one child can wind up the rest by deliberately eating slowly. If they must ask to get down, they will do so every ten seconds. If you make them wait until after pudding, they will race through the main course.'

Instead, she suggests setting a minimum time for attendance at the table, perhaps twenty minutes. It shouldn't be so long that they are bound to revolt, but long enough for them to have to curb their fidgets. As with all rules, it doesn't really matter what is agreed so long as it is announced to the children in advance (at least the day before) and they know what to expect.

How do I make a child aware of healthy eating?

We know that the choice of fuel affects behaviour. The starkest example is cola: a glass of that and many children, who are more sensitive to caffeine than adults, go wild. Research with adults provides ample evidence that diet affects concentration and self-control, and prisoners have behaved less aggressively when given a balanced diet.

Even so, I still can't get my children to choose healthy options. I tend then to accuse them of being silly and remind them of friends' more sensible children. 'Why don't you try and arrange a swap,' my eldest daughter then says, 'since we are so obviously horrible.'

Lecturing never works, says Luke: 'Everyone knows about healthy eating. Children are taught about it from their first days at school. If a child is eating badly, it will not be out of ignorance but from habit. Also, many convenience foods are packed with salt, sugar and other addictive substances, so of course children want to carry on eating them – if they are available. Look at what food is lying around the house, as well as what is served at meals.'

It is simple, Noël agrees: don't buy rubbish. Let sweets and sweetened drinks be treats that the children have outside the house occasionally, but not their daily fare. If you are training children not to snack, that means (even if you are in a hurry) providing three balanced meals a day and sitting at the table with the children as they eat.'

As for puddings, which are often so tempting that the main course ends up in the bin or the dog while the children rush off to get ice cream, she simply wouldn't offer them. 'If you provide pudding that is as healthy as the main course, you won't mind if they decide to fill up on it.'

When I confessed to Luke that I didn't think I could meet Noël's healthy targets, he was soothing. 'Have the children eat the healthiest diet you can. Aim for the best, but don't feel bad if you don't quite achieve it.'

How do I get children to drink water?

I deeply regret not having insisted on water at mealtimes when the children were tiny so that they had some brand loyalty. However, having landed myself with a brood that thinks unsweetened drinks are 'horrible', I continue to buy tooth-rotting substances because I enjoy the ego boost of their little faces lighting up as they unpack them from the shopping bag.

Noël sighs. 'Parents are unlikely to lose children's affection by insisting on water. You could make it look more appetising by putting a jug of it on the table and adding ice and a slice of lemon. But don't expect children to choose water over squash or cola. You will need to eliminate the unhealthy, "addictive" options if you are serious about your children's nutrition.'

Agonised by the thought of how to introduce the water-only regime, I suggested to her that maybe it would work if I got bottled water. 'You are still tiptoeing around the children,' she noted. 'Make a decision and stick to it. They'll soon get used to the taste of filtered tap water if that is what is on offer. Remember, taste preferences are entirely a matter of habit. And if a child complains and says there is nothing to drink in the house, throw the question back at him and ask what he can think of to drink that is healthy.'

What do I do about a faddy child?

Luke once knew a boy who decided that he would eat only sausages three times a day. 'Of course, he looked pale and unhealthy. Once his parents said, "This is not OK. You are not having only sausages. Eat what's provided," his habits changed.'

The amazing part of that story is that the parents let him eat just sausages for so long. I can understand why: often my children seem so hysterical from low blood sugar that I will give them the food they are most likely to eat rather than food that is good for them but less appealing. That does not impress Noël. 'Adults get hungry too,' she says, 'but that doesn't mean we are allowed to behave badly. We should not allow hunger, fatigue or illness to become an excuse. One of our most important tasks as parents is to teach and train our children to be cooperative and considerate even when it's not so easy to be.

'Parents accept their children's unhealthy eating fads because it feels hard to stand up to a crying or complaining child, and many parents would rather not have the battle. Nagging, lecturing and criticising result in pitched battles, with no one a winner. Stick with the "first course" and within a few months your faddy eater will become much more tolerant of previously "disgusting" foods.

'What is more important to you: a child growing up with unhealthy habits or your feeling of temporary discomfort as you teach and train? Often we go with what feels easy rather than what we know is right.'

What do I do about a child who refuses breakfast?

One of our children went through a phase of refusing to eat before school. I listened to her worries and heard that she hated school because she didn't like her supply teacher. But every morning we had the same scene. I asked Luke what I should do. 'Do you have a way of making her eat? No? Well then, simply telling her to is not working. The phase may wear itself out, so let it ride for a few days, then take action.'

Noël agrees. 'Nip it in the bud. You must intervene because breakfast sets you up for the whole day. Also, you don't want a child to learn to use food to manipulate the world. I would start by not letting children have any food after supper – that includes drinks before bed. Children who refuse breakfast are often not hungry because they ate too late the night before. Remember, food is fuel for action, so there is no need to eat later in the evening. Yes, cocoa, juice or milk before bed can be a cosy, relaxing ritual, but it's not healthy, so replace it with a non-food ritual.

'Another explanation could be that breakfast time is so fraught that the child can't face the hassles of the household in the morning. In that case, improve the morning routine. More time, more calm, more smiles, no telling the children to hurry up.'

But my child says she feels sick in the morning. 'Then she's off school because she is sick and you do the whole ill thing. She must spend the whole day in bed, with no screen, of course, and she will not be able to see friends at the weekend.

'If she decides she's not ill, then she goes to school. There's no halfway line. And if you are going to school, you have to eat breakfast. Start with a tiny amount and build up.

'If she insists that she is ill, you could tell her that you will take her out of school on a particular day to go to the doctor. By all means mention that this means taking a half day off work and is inconvenient, but don't lay it on thick. The prospect will make her feel that you are taking her problem seriously and that you are determined to sort it out.'

What about growing pains?

One of our children, who is very thin, often cries in the night from growing pains. The only way I have found to soothe her is to fetch her a bowl of cereal with milk and spoon it into her in the early hours. 'You are way too sympathetic,' says Noël. 'As far as I know, calcium doesn't help with growing pains. Most so-called growing pains turn out to be muscle spasms, nothing to do with bone growth. Massage and stretching can help with these muscle cramps. When you feed her what is probably helping her to relax is your undivided attention. She may well need more of that than she is getting, but not in the middle of the night. Also, she should not get the attention by crying, or by confusing physical pain with an emotional need.

'She's entitled to be upset by the pain she's experiencing, but you must not make a big thing of it. Don't add to her problems by behaving as if you agree with her that the pain is terrible. Instead, show her how to manage and reduce the pain herself. Self-reliance boosts self-confidence.'

What do I do about a child who wants to make her own food instead of eating the family meal?

On a visit to my home Noël encountered one of my children refusing to eat the meal I was preparing for the others and insisting on making her own food. I growled, but let her get in my way with her own cooking project. Noël took a different approach. 'It must be hard for you eating other people's food when you are such a good cook yourself,' she said to my daughter, reflectively listening to her possible feelings.

Afterwards Noël took me aside and told me to get her out of the habit immediately. 'If you let it ride, soon she will always want something different from what everyone else is eating, particularly if it becomes an attention-getting device.'

Rather than let her cook a separate meal for herself, Noël would establish a rule that anyone who doesn't want the meal provided is allowed to take food from the fruit bowl or the fridge so long as it doesn't require any preparation. The child must still sit at the table and eat with the family, and still wait the prescribed twenty minutes (or however long you have decided) before she can leave the table.

'When children see that they still have to follow the usual routines, they soon decide to eat what the rest are eating.'

What should parents do about a fat child?

Fatness in the early years is a marker for later obesity, and Luke sees many parents who fear they may have ruined their children's health by letting them become overweight. He calms them down by saying that many children go through a podgy phase and, in most, it passes. 'We should do what we can,' he says, 'but we should not get over-excited or else children learn that food is a good way to get parents wound up.

'Before reacting, talk to other parents and take a cool, rational look at the problem. If a child is over-eating because he or she doesn't feel happy or popular, then adding your criticism will only give the problem a further layer. Action and suggestions work better than lectures and conversations.

'The younger a child, the more direct your approach can be. Children don't have willpower – even as adults we have pretty little – so it's up to you to stop buying unhealthy foods. On the exercise side, if you have a non-sporty or uncompetitive child, it's a good idea to make the exercise about something. For example, if he likes natural history, look for fossils on a beach rather than going to a museum.

'Even those who don't like competitive activities often enjoy solitary sports, such as martial arts or rock climbing or dance. When making the arrangement, don't say, "This is because you are fat and it will make you fitter." Say that martial arts will make you better at protecting yourself.

'With a teenager you have to be more oblique, but not indulgent. Pointing to the beauty of a Rubens is no consolation for a girl who is being teased at school and coming home to comfort eat. It is not easy for an overweight child in today's body-conscious society. You could perhaps mention that you are going to try out a new gym down the road. My mum was very good at suggestions like that. She would make them and then not keep referring to them.'

What do I do if a child refuses to take any exercise?

Many children become fat, Noël believes, because tired parents responded to their infant cries by feeding them, even when the cry was not for food. 'A child who is often fed before it is hungry,' she says, 'never learns about recognising a need and having it fulfilled.

'But often we find that children are overweight not because they eat more than others but because they aren't burning it up by taking exercise. It becomes a vicious cycle. The fat child is excluded from playground games and takes even less exercise. And the less fit the child becomes, the less appealing any form of movement becomes.'

A parental show of unity is important to get the child moving, she says. 'You might want to give a child three possible activities to choose from, but do not give him the choice of whether or not to take any exercise.'

If the child is reluctant to join in a class, she would take the child to the class and stay. 'Don't urge the child to join in but praise every step in the right direction.'

And if a child complains about not having the energy to join in, she would look at the child's lifestyle: 'Refined carbohydrates deliver calories but do not provide enough energy for a sustained activity. Also, children who don't get enough sleep may not feel like being very active. We must not expect our children to motivate or organise themselves. That is *our* job.'

What if a parent suspects anorexia or bulimia?

Food, Noël and Luke point out, is not the real issue at the bottom of an eating disorder. Body image is certainly important but it is only part of the story. 'Invariably there is something else going on,' says Luke. 'Food can become a vehicle for a child who doesn't want to grow up to face adult responsibilities, or wishes to control this aspect of her life because other problems are outside her control.'

Those teenagers I know who have an eating disorder are unhappy at home or at school. One sufferer has not seen her father for several years and is terrified of having to leave the security of home and her mother for university. Another is under so much pressure at school that she wants to bottle out of the exam race.

'Seek professional help,' says Luke. 'One of the good aspects of being a parent today is that there is expert knowledge on these issues – books, therapists and counsellors. Don't delay, and if the first expert doesn't help, find another.'

TIPS ON FOOD

- Be clear about the rules and do frequent talk-throughs, with the parent asking the questions and the child describing, in detail, what he should and should not do, and why.
- If they can't find it, they can't eat it. Don't keep a supply of crisps or biscuits, but do keep the fruit bowl full.
- If a child asks for a biscuit, don't say no and provoke a row. Say, with a sweet smile, 'Yes, of course, after you've had your tea.'
- Don't put too much effort into cooking something elaborate that the children may not like because then you will feel angry and resentful when they reject it.
- Stick to regular mealtimes. If lunch on a school day is at twelve o'clock, children will revolt if made to wait until two o'clock on Sunday, unless you provide elevenses.
- Allowing an element of choice does not mean letting children order à la carte. Mealtimes are an opportunity to learn about sharing and tolerance.
- Start each meal with a clean slate. Don't prompt bad behaviour by reminding children of what happened last time. Instead, do a talk-through.
- Allow children to be independent as soon as they can manage a spoon. Feeding a child who can manage for himself leads to tension and manipulation.

- Don't ask children to try unfamiliar food. Instead, use Noël's 'first course' plan. When they do try, praise descriptively.
- Don't discuss their dislikes. Accept that they either eat it or they don't. Show that you are enjoying your meal and are not bothered whether they eat or not.
- Action replays give a child the chance to get it right – that way the meal ends on a happy note.
- My breakthrough with my eldest son came when he started watching Jamie Oliver's cookery programmes. 'There is nothing like a role model,' says Luke, 'but you may not be it.'
- Packed lunches don't have to be unhealthy. Noël suggests taking the children around the supermarket to choose a balanced meal of their own devising.
- Keep water on the table. Introduce it early. Put some effort into presentation.
- Make the last meal of the day no later than 6.30 p.m.

4

DIFFICULT CHILDREN

Are some children impossible? Isn't it true that boys are
more difficult to control than girls? And don't girls
present special problems too?

By this stage I was beginning to get the hang of child training. It
involved planning, optimism, a concerted effort between me and my
husband, the investment of time, and paying attention to every tiny
instance of good behaviour.

Yet the atmosphere at home wasn't changing as fast as Noël and
Luke had led me to believe it could, and I was trying to understand
why. In some ways I knew I was at fault. I would set rules but not
apply them consistently, so the children were operating under
instructions that could sometimes be ignored without the certainty
that I would notice.

Naturally, I didn't like to think that the fault was all mine, so I
spoke to Noël and Luke about the aspects of my situation that made
it hard for me to be in control. Five children close together in age
were surely more difficult to control than one or two? Some of the
children are also quite highly strung – maybe I was facing well-nigh
insuperable obstacles?

They sighed. They were not going to let me off the hook so
easily. These were excuses, not reasons, why I should accept defeat.
Both of them had helped parents with far more difficult children
than mine – children with severe behavioural or learning disorders
– and they had learnt to behave well. 'We can't change the fundamentals of family size, birth order or inborn temperament,' said
Noël, 'but we can alter the way we deal with them. Parents can get
back in charge in two to four weeks, even when a child had been
difficult for a long time.'

The difficult child

'It is very unfair,' says Noël. 'Some people can do the most hideous things and still have children who behave well. Others, who aren't making any really terrible mistakes, have children who make their lives a misery. Even within a family, two children can react perfectly well to a haphazard approach. Then along comes a third child who is more sensitive or more demanding and there is chaos.'

At the New Learning Centre, she teaches some children who are so wild that on their first few visits they have to be restrained to prevent them damaging themselves and others. With the right training, she has invariably found that those children can behave far, far better than their parents had ever imagined possible. These children might have a neurological problem, such as attention deficit (hyperactivity) disorder (AD[H]D), or the more newly recognised oppositional defiant disorder (refusal to do as they are told), but she can still turn them into cooperative human beings.

Most of what we think of as personality, she holds, is a matter of temperament and habit – behaviour learnt from experience. By temperament she means the inborn characteristics that can be discerned in the first three months of a child's life, and sometimes even while they are still in the womb. There are ten of these characteristics, which cover aspects of behaviour such as eagerness to try new things or impulsiveness.

'You can't change a child's temperament,' she says, 'but you can change his behaviour and perceptions. 'All children can change. The "naughty" child can learn self-control, the timid can learn to shine, the aggressive can learn to control their tempers. It's harder for a hyperactive child to develop patience, but not impossible when taught and trained in a positive, firm and consistent way.

'When training a child it helps to separate the temperamental problems from the habits of behaviour. For example, some sensitive children assume that parents or teachers are angry with them because an annoyed or impatient voice sounds to them like shouting. These children often become very argumentative, as they feel they have to defend themselves all the time. So there are two problems to deal with: the unusual sensitivity to even a slightly raised voice, and the behaviour that results from feeling constantly shouted at.

'The first problem, one of temperament, will not go away, but it can be modified by, in this case, gradually getting the child used to louder and louder noises. The second, behavioural, problem can definitely be changed. When, for example, a tendency to act on impulse leads a child to make rude remarks, the child can be taught to think before he speaks.'

Temperament problems usually coincide with learning difficulties, and sometimes it seems as if a new disorder is being identified each week. Naming a syndrome is helpful (if the diagnosis is correct) because it encourages parents to accept a situation and agree on a course of action. The disadvantage of diagnosis is that a label can become an excuse. Diagnoses can also arouse feelings of unwarranted despair in parents.

Many children with AD(H)D, for example, are allowed to get away with disruptive behaviour even when they are on Ritalin, a drug that enables them better to control their impulsiveness and restlessness. 'No syndrome need be a life sentence,' says Noël. 'Just because a problem has been diagnosed does not mean it has to determine a child's future.'

Luke, in the course of his work with autistic people, knows many who have far exceeded others' expectations of them. 'Early on in my work,' he says, 'I met the international director of the Sonrise programme for autistic people who, at the age of three, was diagnosed as severely autistic. His parents were told that he might just be able to feed himself, but certainly not read or write or live independently, but they refused to pigeon-hole him and took him home and educated him. Now he is an impressive, dynamic director of a major organisation.'

Parents, however, often make a sensitive child's problems worse by being by turns over-protective and excessively critical. They tend to see the child's failures as their own and try every means – commonly bribery and punishment – to make him behave better. A difficult child also tends to divide the parents. Men find it particularly hard to accept that their child could have a problem, and deny its existence for as long as possible. Women tend to be overly sympathetic and not firm enough.

Noël and Luke's advice is to help a child with temperament or learning problems by giving him exactly the same treatment as other children, in an even more rigorous form. Nervous, sensitive, impulsive children need the reassurance of knowing exactly what is expected of them. 'They tend to over-react, take everything person-ally and find everything annoying,' says Noël, 'so they need calm, predictable routines that allow them to feel in control.

'They have often become used to being criticised by their parents and teachers; they have received little praise, insufficient supervision and inconsistent consequences for their actions; often, too, they have been over-indulged, so bad behaviour has become a habit; sometimes they even go into revenge mode.

'Although we can never be the completely calm, positive, firm, consistent parents we would like to be we can work on those quali-ties and not add to a sensitive child's problems. We can help that child be calmer and more mature, not more upset. This is hard if you are sensitive yourself and the child grates upon you, but it can be done.'

While there is usually only one problem child in a family, the responsibility (not blame) is everyone's. That child will need everyone's help to learn new, more acceptable forms of behaviour. Home is the place, Luke and Noël believe, to start the changes that affect a child's whole life, since behaviour developed at home is often played out in the larger arena of school.

> If there was suddenly this magical cure for autism, would we take it? It would be like wanting to change him from what he is. So much of his self and charm are connected with his condi-tion, so how can I say I'd want him altered?
>
> Nick Hornby, author, on his autistic son, Danny

Is difficult behaviour always caused by a disorder?

Temperament problems and learning difficulties may or may not require specialist help, but behavioural problems do not usually need professional intervention. They usually stem from a factor common to all children – immaturity. Delightful though some of its symptoms can be when children are younger, immaturity that lasts longer than we would wish means that children act on impulse, are easily distracted and can't always make sense of things, all past the age when we expect to be dealing with those characteristics. Children with a sensitive temperament are often more immature. This leads them to want to be centre stage, to develop a habit of helplessness because it gets them attention, and often to act up because they would rather be thought bad than stupid.

In addition to the temperamental reasons for their immature behaviour, many of the children whom Noël or Luke help have also been 'taught' bad habits by parents who give them too much too easily, do too much for them and make too many excuses for their shortcomings. Those parents, they say, think they are behaving in a loving manner, but they are not doing their best for the child. And it isn't just parents who do it: Luke notices that half- or step-siblings can often make too much fuss of a younger child whom they see only at weekends.

The answer, as always, is to do what is best for the child, not what makes you feel good about yourself as a super-kind parent. That means, among other things, creating rules and sticking to them so that the child experiences and gradually learns to accept and cope constructively with the difficulties and frustrations that he will encounter at school and when he leaves home.

Observing me quake and make excuses when one of my children was being rude and uncooperative, Noël told me to be more assertive. 'You tend to make the assumption,' she observed, 'that circumstances are causing your children to be upset and rude rather than that it has become their habitual way of responding to circumstances they don't like. A child can have supply teachers or whatever is getting her down at the moment without using the upset as an excuse for rudeness or lack of cooperation. One of my basic tenets is that we are bigger than our circumstances.'

While it is important to listen reflectively to a child's worries, she continued, it is over-indulgent to agree with the child that her problems are terrible. 'It is a form of spoiling, and not as harmless as you think. People often joke or even boast about a child being spoilt, but the word means just what it says: you can ruin a child for later life by giving in or by making excuses for bad behaviour.'

How do you make a difficult child behave better?

Noël, when faced with a difficult child, starts right back at the very beginning and builds up the child's confidence. One summer she was asked for help by the mother of a bright ten-year-old dyslexic who was on the point of being excluded from school for his appalling behaviour. His mother, a single parent, was in such despair that she was about to send him to live with her parents because she couldn't cope.

In the boy's first session with Noël the mother was amazed that she began by teaching him how to brush his teeth, breaking this simple activity into steps, starting with putting water on the brush. By learning to master basic routines, and being praised for getting them right, he was transformed during the course of the summer holidays. 'I had no idea that he could be so easy,' says the mother, whose son is now thriving in a mainstream school.

'Consistent routines,' explains Noël, 'allow a child to put more thought and energy into learning in its broadest sense – noticing, experimenting, making inferences, drawing conclusions and applying knowledge to new situations. Routine is helpful for all children, but it is essential for those who have difficulty organising themselves. There will be fewer conflicts over what a child may or may not do if he knows in advance what to expect.'

That mother has come to think quite differently about her difficult child; she now sees his energy as a bonus, not a burden. Noël corroborates that view: the nervous child is often creative, the child who won't sit still has boundless energy. Many dyslexics, once they have mastered the aspects of learning that don't come easily to them, come to feel pride in the lateral workings of their minds. 'Even AD(H)D doesn't seem so trying,' says Noël, 'if you view the child as a tireless experimenter and adventurer rather than as someone who is failing at being "normal". Of course, it is much easier for parents to view children's annoying characteristics in a positive light when we have used the sixteen skills to significantly reduce the amount of annoying behaviour that we have to put up with.'

I fought my mother at times when I was young because I just wanted to be loved.

Nicole Farhi, fashion designer

How can I help a child with a learning difficulty to do better?

Better organisation at home, Noël believes, will lead to increased success at school. 'A very important thing a parent can do for a learning disabled child is provide structure in his life,' she says. 'Structure can be established and maintained by making the daily routines very consistent; the more familiar and stable, the better.'

She also recommends that parents train such a child in the microskills of which every complex skill is made up. 'For example, one of the microskills of handwriting is pencil control. Another is being aware that the tall letters are meant to be tall (many children don't realise this). And as you train, of course, you give masses of descriptive praise as well as listen reflectively to the child's feelings.

But, she warns, 'Even the most positive, firm and consistent of parents cannot salvage the ego of a child who is continually failing at school, in the neighbourhood and at sport. Sometimes a special school is needed because it is hard for a child to develop a positive sense of self when he is constantly defeated. With such a child it is best for the parents not to dwell too much on the future because there are too many variables, too many unknown factors. But do remember that children will rise to meet parental expectations when they are given the tools to do so.'

One child I watched Noël teach was a ten-year-old with AD(H)D with, among other problems, a tendency to twitch involuntarily. He understood his situation well enough to articulate why he had had to leave his school. 'They weren't helping me and I was always being told I wasn't trying when I was. And I was always shouting out irrelevant comments like, "When's lunch?"' At home, too, he was in constant trouble: 'My parents would yell at me to do my homework, and sometimes they would smack me. I would shout at them to bring me my gym kit.'

With the help of clear and copious rules, constant watchfulness to see he kept to them, and a tick chart divided into fifteen-minute sections so that he could be praised for doing as required for manageable periods, he was beginning to gain more control. You could see the pride in his face when he was given approval.

Sitting in on lessons with his class, I saw that it would be easy for a parent to act in ways that seem only natural, but would not have been helpful. When I spoke of a child being 'naughty' I was reminded to avoid moral judgements and to talk only of 'misbehaviour'.

On another occasion, I helped a child who had tried three times to answer a question. 'He can do it,' I was reproved. 'Don't do his thinking for him.'

At another point a child said that he had a backache. I would have rubbed the child's back or been sympathetic, but Noël stopped me: 'I tell all the children that I couldn't care less about their aches and pains, unless we need to call an ambulance.'

That sounded a bit brutal, I protested, but she explained: 'I keep the focus on the task by descriptively praising children for working even though they don't feel well. I'm not ignoring the backache – I'm fostering perseverance and self-reliance.'

Once a child learns to concentrate and feels more confident, she finds, all kinds of achievements – once unthinkable – come within their grasp.

TIPS FOR CREATING STRUCTURE AT HOME
- Provide order in a child's space. 'There needs to be an easily accessible space for everything in his room,' says Noël. 'Shelves are preferable to drawers because the child can see things in their proper place.'
- Be specific on giving directions: not 'Clean your room' but 'First pick up the socks and put them in the washing basket.'
- Better still, since children don't learn nearly so much when we are doing the talking, prompt the child to use his own brain to work out the sequence of events: what happens, first, next, last.
- Expect lapses of memory, so prepare for success by having frequent talk-throughs, with the child doing the talking, before the child starts the task.
- Let the child make decisions, but only in situations in which you can live with whatever choice he makes.
- Find out the child's actual level of mastery in academic and practical tasks – not the one you would like to think he has reached.

How does a difficult child feel?

A child with difficulties, whether learning or behavioural, can grow up feeling that everything he does is a mistake and a disaster. 'What's wrong with me?' he thinks when he is responding as best he can but meets with rebuff and ridicule. He then becomes angry with himself and the world that expects him to behave like other children of his age.

Reflective listening is a way to help a child feel understood rather than blamed, and Noël taught the parents of a five-year-old with an attention problem to employ it to good effect. The boy, his mother remembers, was always in trouble, always in the wrong place at the wrong time at school – problems typical of such a child: 'His self-esteem was suffering, and it didn't help that his younger brother was in and out of hospital with asthma and bandaged from head to foot because of his eczema. He needed so much attention that we weren't nearly as positive, firm and consistent with the elder one as we should have been.'

Noël 'revolutionised' the way those parents operated at home. 'We learnt to notice the things he was doing right,' says the mother. 'As we did so, it became more fun. We learnt to operate as a team and got the school involved in creating a quiet corner, burning calming lavender and allowing him to run around the playground when he needed to. Friends sometimes laugh when they come to our house because we have rules, consequences and routines stuck up on the walls so that he knows what he needs to do, but they have found the change in him so dramatic that some have asked if he has been hypnotised.

'Once we understood more about how he felt, he was able to say if he was bored or needed to release energy. At school he had been labelled a naughty boy, and he's no angel now, but he's happier, calmer and more aware of himself.'

Is it a good idea to take a child to a psychoanalyst?
I asked Luke if he thought it was useful to take a deeply troubled child to a psychoanalyst. 'I'm pragmatic about psychoanalysis,' he replied. 'Basically anything that makes a difference is a good idea, but before going to those lengths it might be worth discussing with other parents the circumstances in which you are intervening and why. If a child is self-harming, then obviously it calls for action at that level, but if you have an eight-year-old who is not enjoying maths home-work, then it is overkill.

'The danger of sending a child to a therapist is that it can reinforce his feeling that he is the trouble in the family. When I am called in to help a troubled child, I always want to meet the whole family so that one child does not perceive himself as the problem.

'A difficult child is usually like that because of what the parents are doing – and I can see the relief flood over a child when I say that the parents will have to do a lot more work than the child. Children take everything personally – from their father losing his job to their parents getting divorced – they see it as their responsibility. That's how children who've been abused feel – and if they can blame themselves for their circumstances, any child can.

'Whatever kind of help you seek, I would be more interested in the person who is doing it than the methods being used. It doesn't matter whether a child talks to the gardener, the head teacher or a psychoanalyst: all that matters is if it makes a difference.'

Noël points out that professionals do not have a good track record in helping children. 'That,' she says, 'is because they don't focus on getting parents to change their habits; they focus on getting children to talk about how they feel. This, in itself, can cause problems because children are, by definition, immature and often very confused and inarticulate. Another difficulty is that focusing on problems can keep people stuck in the problem. I think it is far more constructive to focus on solutions.'

How can we help the siblings of difficult children?

Brothers and sisters often have intense, complicated emotions in relation to a difficult child. Like parents, they want a sibling they can be proud of and they feel blamed for the child's unacceptable behaviour. They don't want other children saying, 'Your sister's weird,' and they feel put upon when asked to include that child in their games.

Often they hate having her along, as she has to be watched all the time. In emergencies they come through – they do understand – but mostly they are irritated. All these emotions can be difficult to express, so a parent's best tactic is to employ reflective listening, not occasionally but frequently. 'It always takes longer than you imagine to help a child work through feelings,' says Noël.

Should I be concerned about an easy child?

On a home visit, while I was battling unwisely with a combative child, Noël was paying more attention to another of my children who was playing the role of Miss Perfect. She was offering to help, chatting charmingly and, Noël observed, getting away with doing exactly as she pleased because she did it with a smile. 'Start requiring the easy child to toe the line,' advised Noël, 'and you will find the difficult child becoming less angry and more compliant.'

TIPS FOR HANDLING DIFFICULT CHILDREN
- Reflectively listen to the child when you sense that he may feel upset. What deeper thoughts drive the difficult behaviour?
- Difficult children force you to work out what's best in the long run and act strategically. Less difficult children also benefit from the same approach.
- Where possible, view the behavioural and neurological problems separately.
- Help the child to get the basics of cooperation and self-reliance right. Descriptively praise every wanted action or even the attempt to do something right. Often the child knows what to do, but is not yet in the habit of doing it.
- Look for the flashpoints and work out ways of preparing for success so that those moments become less explosive.
- Humour. When something goes horribly wrong and a child explodes, laughter – so long as it doesn't involve ridicule – can defuse the situation. It delivers an important, unspoken message that life is basically sunny despite its difficulties.
- Treat the child the same as the others. It will help the child and decrease sibling resentments.

Do boys present more problems?

Many parents these days commiserate with each other for having boys as they seem to get into more trouble and be harder to handle.

They fight (especially two brothers close together in age), don't seem able to sit still, break things, make a mess, get angry, find themselves in trouble at school and, more often than girls, have learning disorders.

I wondered whether Noël and Luke felt that parents of boys deserve sympathy, or if boys need to be treated any differently from girls. Boys are Luke's specialist subject: his parents' divorce when he was nine left him without a constant male role model, and he was wayward for many years before he found a sense of purpose. 'I don't think boys are more difficult,' he says, 'but our society throws up more problems for boys.

'The symptoms of this are multifarious, from suicide rates to educational results. While the women's movement has had a huge effect on what we expect of girls, the men's movement has not yet had the same impact. Men at the moment don't know their place: some are still John Waynes, some are wet, sensitive, new age guys. I know innumerable thirty- to forty-year-olds who don't take responsibility because they weren't trained to do so when they were young.'

Noël, as a teacher, is aware that the school system doesn't suit boys as well as it does girls. 'They are seen as inferior to girls because they are behind in language, social skills and fine motor skills, such as handwriting,' she says. 'Because of that, they are more often nagged, punished and unintentionally made to feel stupid, and not helped to learn the skills that they need.'

But, she explains, there is a good reason why boys develop more slowly in some areas: 'They have 30 per cent more muscle bulk, and a large part of a boy's brain is devoted to managing those muscles, so it is not available for developing language, social skills and fine motor skills. Naturally, then, boys talk louder, grab, snatch, push and pull and, equally naturally, parents and teachers get very annoyed, especially mothers and female teachers.'

Boys who aren't allowed to make enough use of their extra muscles will misdirect that energy into being 'naughty'. They will develop the habit of seeking and getting attention for disruptive behaviour, and the behaviour will become more extreme. Equally, if they aren't helped to develop social skills and don't find safe ways to express their anger and humiliation, they can become bullies – a far more prevalent problem among boys than girls.

'The danger is that the culture of under-achievement becomes entrenched,' says Noël. 'The strongest and most aggressive set the standard. These boys, often with learning difficulties that have not been addressed, set the tone for the others and make it cool not to work. Although boys enjoy doing well, they don't want to be seen to put any effort into it and they would rather scrape through than be uncool. Their ideal is to get three for effort and ten for achievement. Although boys want to please their parents, they feel torn and as if they are failing themselves and those they love. Parents don't know how to shift that culture.

'When parents use the sixteen skills, boys, even teenage boys, become less enslaved to imitating the laddist culture. They become more confident, self-reliant and considerate. They start to take pride in doing their best. Of course, the older your son is when you embark on this programme, the longer it will probably take. But it is never too late to make a difference.'

> *. . . when I recall childhood pain . . . I recall the pains of lone-liness, boredom, abandonment, humiliation, rejection and fear.*
>
> Stephen Fry, actor and author

Do boys need men to guide them?

'Boys need men around,' says Luke, 'because men are usually much more direct. A woman seeing a boy whacking a tree with a stick would probably stop and tell him, "It's not a good idea because . . . " A man would say, "Oi, stop that." Boys miss out if they don't experience that direct approach. They don't like to have everything explained to them because they get so ashamed and upset.'

'People often say that boys will be boys,' says Noël. 'When they say that, they are usually noticing only the bad bits of their behaviour. Sometimes it seems as if half the human race is in the wrong, but it may just be that we aren't handling them sensitively or appreciating their strengths.'

A problem for boys is that women are largely responsible for bringing them up, even when there is a father at home. 'Mothers often don't know what to do with boys' energy and tendency to risk-taking,' Noël notes, 'so they try to control them, and containment is not a very effective strategy. Female teachers may not understand boys' need to be physical. Research shows that boys learn better if they are allowed to move around more; few schools allow for that because they assume it will lead to mayhem. But it needn't.'

How do you help a boisterous boy?

When disruptive boys excluded from school come to the New Learning Centre they are asked to bounce on a trampoline during some lessons. Exercise helps them get rid of their fidgets and provides useful practice for the rest of the class in learning to tune out distractions and concentrate on their work. Noël suggests that parents and teachers schedule in numerous energetic activities each day for children whose high spirits could easily spill over into behaviour that annoys others. 'Don't just offer opportunities to let off steam: require it. Children may not know that this is what they need right now, so if you phrase it as a suggestion, the child might decline. Insist.'

Why are boys so useless around the house?

Many women I know sigh about how useless men are around the house, but Luke and Noël point out that women are often responsible for making them that way by doing too much for them. Girls are much quicker to copy their mothers than boys – especially if their fathers don't do much – and mothers tend to assume it is less effort to pick up after their boys than endlessly tell them what to do.

'Often boys are nagged because they are not as organised, tidy or conscious of what they should be doing as a girl of a similar age,' says Noël. 'If we see them as disorganised, we may issue streams of instructions, and they learn to be helpless. If we find them uncommunicative, we may assume they can only express their feelings by kicking things. They seem to have almost a biological need to fight, so parents nag, cajole and eventually smack them.

'Then boys become even more convinced that they really are naughty and incompetent, and it becomes a badge of honour not to be helpful. So they wander through life waiting for instructions or for someone else to pick up the pieces. They become so used to everything being their mother's responsibility that they get angry when one day you tell them to find their own PE kit. Then they get into trouble because they can't, and their outrage is justifiable because suddenly you have moved the goalposts.'

Luke adds that 'Fathers often take the boys' side against mothers because it is annoying hearing the mother nagging about doing homework or tidying up. I've heard fathers say, in earshot of their sons, "He's not doing anyone any harm," or "I was like that myself." If the boy thinks that being helpful or organised is just something Mum is going on about and that it doesn't matter to Dad – who doesn't do much tidying up himself – he will not see the need to change.'

Everyone would be happier, Noël and Luke say, if both parents took responsibility for their boys' determination not to lift a finger and put more effort, optimism and humour into training them in good habits rather than vacillating between indulgence and annoyance.

How do you help a boy to become more efficient?

Parents frequently turn to Luke for help with listless sons. 'Motivation is a function of habit,' he tells them, 'and it is never too late to learn new habits.'

He himself is a case in point: an under-achieving eighteen-year-old who failed his A-levels yet is now running more than one business, having acquired new skills as an adult. 'I had to do it for myself. It is easier for children if you help them find motivation when they are younger. It takes energy but perhaps less effort than many parents imagine.'

Noël agrees. At one parenting class there was a mother who was wondering if she had it in her to make her tantrum-prone son do his homework: 'You probably think, "Am I being mean? Should I be doing this?"' said Noël. 'On the contrary, it is mean to let children drift into unproductive habits. It is loving to insist. You may have to wait hours the first time for him to pick up his book, but in three or four months he will do it without protest. If you don't tackle the problem now, it could last a lifetime.'

Another mother spoke of her son who was in constant trouble at his boarding school. 'He was being told off all the time,' she said, 'and came to feel he was a bad person in a good family, so he was living down to his reputation. His marks were very low because he was giving his homework in late and it wasn't being marked.'

Encouraged by Noël, she told the school that she was going to take action. 'I got my son to ring me at eight o'clock every morning to say he had given in his homework. He didn't find it easy to organise himself, but having to be accountable to me helped. Soon he was getting As, and he went from the bottom of the class to the top.'

'Sometimes parents react like children and get angry when they receive a litany of complaints about school from their child,' says Noël. 'But this mother reacted by becoming an advocate for her son. She set clear expectations and prepared for success by making it easier for him to do the right thing. As soon as he got a taste of success, he realised it was more fun to get approval instead of vegetating at the bottom of the class. Boys get cool points for not caring, but underneath they do care.'

TIPS FOR DEALING WITH BOYS

- Don't leave it to the child to create the turn-around. There is a tendency to think, 'Why should I care if he doesn't? He'll learn soon enough from his mistakes.' He may, however, learn the wrong lessons.
- Boys take longer to acquire certain skills. Have realistic expectations and remember that boys' greater muscularity at an early age is not a problem but an asset.
- Descriptively praise boys for what they are doing right, which may not come as easily to them as it does to girls. 'With rowdy boys,' Luke says, 'notice when they talk in an "inside voice", when they walk instead of running indoors, and when they sit still and don't grab. Whatever you notice and praise you will get more of.'
- Women are more indulgent of boys, but also more irritated by their irrepressible energy; men may understand boys better. Where the father is not around much and there isn't a male teacher, find other role models.
- Boys may have bad feelings about themselves if they are constantly told they are 'naughty'. Reflective listening helps them express those feelings. 'Boys don't talk about feelings as readily as girls,' Luke warns. 'The best way to help them open up is to do something together, such as washing the car. If they feel useful, they feel better about themselves and more able to open up.'

- Show them safe ways to express their anger and frustration. Punching pillows, jumping up and down or going for a run. Help them to acknowledge their anger but to separate emotion from action. It's the acting it out that gets boys into trouble.
- 'Modelling,' says Luke, 'is the best way to help a boy learn how to be gentle, courteous, generous and helpful.' (He means emulating role models, not tripping along the catwalk.)
- Parents who disagree on how to treat boys should sit down and decide on the rules. If homework has to be finished, Dad mustn't let him off the hook to play football. The same goes for helping around the house.
- Boys are often angry because they don't have a strong relationship with their fathers. They need frequent, predictable times together doing something they both enjoy.
- Rough and tumble play teaches boys how to handle getting hurt and how not to hurt others. It also helps let off steam.
- Competition with others is not unhealthy, but it can create anxiety. Help them focus on competing against themselves to do their best.
- When boys get into trouble, listen reflectively without blaming or giving advice. Let them come up with their own solutions: sorting something out increases their confidence.
- Don't take difficult, insulting or even threatening behaviour personally.

What about girls?

Girls don't get into trouble nearly as often as boys, I notice. That doesn't mean they always do as their parents and teachers want, but they tend to be more subtle about their disobedience and so avoid the consequences. They are constantly praised for being pretty, well behaved and articulate, so if girls have a problem in contemporary society, Noël and Luke believe it often stems from living up to the high expectations at home and at school.

From an early age, girls copy their mother's or their teachers' behaviour, and are often like mini-adults on the outside when they are still impulsive children, ruled by their emotions, on the inside. 'Girls keep being told they can do everything, but aren't being taught how,' says Noël, who was considered gifted as a child but found it a strain to live up to expectations, especially when her parents didn't realise that she needed help or encouragement.

For Luke, as a man, the chief problem of bringing up girls is the over-protectiveness that fathers feel towards daughters. 'The number of child abductions has gone down over the past twenty years,' he notes, 'but that's not our perception.

'And, even though in other ways we treat girls and boys equally, there is a different attitude to morality – especially among parents who missed the sexual revolution. It's OK for an eighteen-year-old boy to get drunk and fall over, but we may not have caught up with the idea that it is also OK for a girl to behave like that. It's the same with sexual behaviour. Ask me in twenty years' time and I'm sure I'll find it hard to watch my daughter ride off on the back of a motor-bike with someone unsuitable.

'Also, we still live in a male-dominated society and girls can legitimately ask, "How come we're performing better at school yet the vast majority of the top jobs are filled by men?" There are issues for girls too of balancing home and professional lives. The best we can do there is show them by our own example.'

5

DIFFICULT CIRCUMSTANCES

Isn't it hard to be in charge when you are the only adult
around all, or part of, the time? How do you handle illness
or divorce? How can you be in charge when your children
are looked after by others?

Even if children are not particularly difficult by temperament,
circumstances can make them so. The calmest children can go
haywire or get depressed when faced with death, divorce or even far
more minor disruptions to their lives.

My first-hand experience here is limited, but it was illuminating.
Three years ago one of my daughters fell down our stairwell and for
two weeks her life hung in the balance while the doctors tried to
work out which internal organ had been damaged by the twenty-foot
fall. During that time, when I wasn't changing her drips or mois-
tening her lips, I imagined what might happen if she were to die. It
would not be a self-contained tragedy, but one that would have
repercussions on the whole family. My husband and I would, I knew,
grieve differently, and the likelihood was that we would end up
divorced, like so many other couples who have had to cope with
tragedy. The lives of our other children, too, would be blighted.
However hard we tried not to let them feel our despair, I knew they
would be forever burdened by the feeling that they were falling short
of some impossible standard set by a child who would always be
remembered as a saint.

Fortunately, our injured child recovered, but from then on I was
far more aware of the fragility of happy family life. So I asked Noël
and Luke how they helped families coping with difficult circumstances. Each of them began by discussing the common element that
links sad events – change.

Children do not cope easily with change: they are creatures of habit and find reassurance in the familiar, even if the familiar is a strife-torn household. They take all change personally, and have a tendency, therefore, to blame themselves for circumstances outside their control. Whether permanent or temporary, impending or sudden, change throws children. They are dominated by their feelings, and less able to reason their way through situations since reasoning is a mature response based upon experience, which children don't yet have.

The outcome of illness or divorce is often the same: a parent who has to cope alone. But before looking at how that can be handled so that children don't miss out on the training they need, Noël and Luke spoke to me about the emotional backdrop to particular situations.

Divorce and separation

Luke and Noël see many parents who are concerned about the way the failure of a relationship has upset children. They believe that the disruptions can be handled so that a child is not burdened by guilt and anxiety. 'It depends on the parents and the situation,' says Luke. 'Some divorces are messy; some parents are more aware than others of how it may affect children.' Noël agrees: 'Even in relatively amicable divorces, children tend to blame themselves. If the divorce or separation is messy or acrimonious, children suffer even more, as they get the usually unspoken message that they should choose sides. When they do take sides they feel very disloyal and guilty, and angry with both parents.'

Luke's first concern is that the parent who is no longer at home, usually the father, does not lose contact with the children, as happens in 50 per cent of cases. Sometimes, unintentionally, fathers divorce their children as well as their wives when they get caught up in their new lives and possibly new families. Then the children have to cope not only with the distress of disruption and with the difficulties of growing up with only one parent in the home, but also with feeling abandoned and unloved by the parent whom they rarely see. 'Many fathers lose contact because they think visits upset the children. Dads don't like emotional fuss, but even if there are tears, it is important to be there. Keep up a regular contact time so the child doesn't have to think about whether he wants to see you on each occasion.'

Noël adds, 'I believe that children should not be given the choice of refusing to see a parent: it gives the child too much responsibility. It also gives the child more power than is healthy. Sometimes the mother decides that the father is so unsuitable that he should have very little access to the children. I disagree. In such a situation I would continue with frequent, predictable visits, but always accompanied by a neutral adult, definitely not the mother.'

It can happen, too, that when the mother becomes involved with another man, she unwittingly puts him before the needs of her children. In these and other related situations the sixteen skills help both parents to make the best of an upsetting situation.'

I have always wanted to live with my dad and have him to myself, and now that I have, I don't want to lose him.
Kimberley, daughter of rock star Rod Stewart

Illness and death

With illness and death, a child is often expected to assume a prematurely adult role, to listen to, understand and respond to adult fears and worries, and sometimes even to look after a distraught parent. 'Loss is a form of change and hard to deal with,' says Noël, 'and children often don't want to upset their parents by giving them the burden of their own feelings, especially the uncomfortable guilty feelings.'

She prescribes reflective listening and, with a withdrawn child, time spent alone together doing things without speaking. 'We must make the child feel that it is not wrong to be sad when someone dies, that all feelings are acceptable, whether they are of guilt or anger. The best way to deal with distress is through expressing it. Once a child has expressed a feeling and it has been heard, accepted and understood, he can begin to let go of it. The only way out is through.'

Often what worries a child is his own mortality, a fear that parents can guess at and reflect back. Telling a child the facts is useful; reassurance is usually not. It generally makes a child feel worse and clam up. Noël explains why: 'Often parents reassure a child because they are anxious themselves, and the parents' anxiety is felt by the child. Reassurance also makes the child feel she shouldn't be worried, so suddenly the child has two problems: the original worry plus the added problem that it is wrong to worry about it.'

Guilt is also common among children dealing with illness or death in the family. Many bereaved children resent a sick parent for not being available to them, or, in the case of a sick sibling, for getting most of the attention. Whatever the feelings gripping a child, Noël and Luke don't believe it should be allowed to become an excuse for behaving badly. 'Indulgence and too much sympathy can set up a pattern of getting lots of the wrong kind of attention,' says Luke. 'Afterwards the child will behave badly to continue getting it and become locked in a vicious circle.'

People think that [my childhood] must have been a bed of roses. Don't get me wrong, it was a happy childhood, but it also seemed as though I was spending every spare minute in hospital visiting either my father or my sister.
Tony Blair, whose father Leo had a stroke when he was ten and whose sister, Sarah, suffered from a form of rheumatoid arthritis

Coping as a lone parent

Luke knows from childhood experiences how hard it is for a single parent to manage children without day-to-day support. Noël, however, was a third-generation single parent and therefore did not think there was anything unusual or difficult either about growing up with divorced parents or about bringing up children after a divorce. Whatever the difficulties, neither Luke nor Noël thinks that they should be an excuse for children to grow up without proper training. That both boys and girls who grow up with only one parent in the home are more likely to under-achieve or go off the rails seems to be linked, not to divorce per se, but to poverty and to lack of supervision while the parent is at work.

Single parents face predictable difficulties: they are short of time and money and they have too much to do, especially if they are working as well as looking after a home and children. They may feel

dumped on and sorry for themselves, and often the failed relationship has dented their confidence. Noël, who suffers from depression, knows how hard it is for children having a mother under a
black cloud, but she believes it is always possible for parents to look
for the best in their children, even if they can't always find it in
themselves.

'Often there's a sense of guilt,' says Noël, 'about not being able to
provide the perfect family, which the child, who views everything
personally, takes on board. Many children feel they have to assume
adult responsibilities and worries at an early age, and, because they
feel responsible for their lone parent's anxious state, they are reluctant to put their own needs forward.'

The lone parent, meanwhile, feels she has to become both father
and mother, and that involves learning skills that may not come
naturally. As one mother said at a parenting class, 'When my
husband and I separated, I felt I had to be disciplinarian, and the
atmosphere at home got worse and worse.'

'What usually happens,' Noël observes, 'is that lone parents veer
between fierce control and over-indulgence, and end up feeling out
of control. Depending on individual temperament, they may go to
extremes. Many lone parents try so hard to make up for the absentee
that they do too much for the child. Rather than let the child have
extra responsibilities, he isn't required to take on the normal responsibilities for his age.'

Perpetual worry emerges as constant hurrying and leads to friction. If the atmosphere at home is not good, the parent justifies it by
saying that she is doing the best she can in the circumstances. As
Luke and Noël point out, the best you can do as you muddle through
is not the best there is.

'With the best motives,' says Noël, 'we do things that are counter-
productive. Misguided parents are so keen to help their children
develop good habits that they resort to nagging and criticism. There
are better ways.'

How do you stop a child feeling responsible?

Children feel that they are the cause of everything in their world: 'If
only I'd done my homework, if only I'd been better behaved, this
wouldn't have happened.' 'When a child is feeling guilty, the way to
deal with it is by dismantling the situation,' says Luke. 'There is a

need for sitting down and talking, not explaining, but listening reflectively.

'How it works is that the parent imagines what the child is feeling and reflects it back to the child. Often it is useful to home in on their thoughts by making suggestions such as, "It might be that you think this has something to do with you," or by putting it in the third person, "Sometimes children think that . . . "

'Or you can turn it round and ask the child a question. In the case of divorce you might try: "Why do you think couples split up?" You could then explain that people can still love each other but not want to live together. You can also say that the child probably doesn't understand that, but it is true. This reflective listening is useful in helping children understand the way relationships and emotions work.

'What is not useful is to go into details of the situation – children don't need to know about the affair two years ago. A stoical line is better: "Sometimes it doesn't work and right now it probably feels like hell to you and you probably think you'll never feel better, but you will."'

Noël adds a caveat that parents, while they should help their children with any feelings of guilt, should not give them the impression that it is wrong to feel guilty. 'We tend to label certain feelings as bad. If we say to children, "Don't feel guilty," they have the extra burden of feeling something that they have been told they shouldn't feel.'

The only unforgivable thing my mother did was to die. She was the gauge by which I defined my whole life – her pride and joy in my triumphs, her pity for my failures. She made existence home.

Imogen Stubbs, actress

What if the parents stay in touch?

If the relationship between the divorced parents is not good, the parent who has care most of the time can feel pushed into the role of meanie, while the one who sees the child occasionally takes on the role of treat-giver. Many women find it hard to be both tough and compassionate. Then, of course, there are the tensions and jealousies between step- and half-families, which are like an intensified form of sibling rivalry. Noël reminds me, 'When parents learn and practise the sixteen skills they become positive, firm and consistent, neither a drill sergeant nor a pushover.'

So what should a lone parent do for the best?

There are plenty of reasons – Luke and Noël would say excuses – for lone parents losing charge at home, but they would have parents look not to individual problems but to universal solutions.

'What are the qualities you are hoping to impart to your children?' Noël asks parents. 'Usually the answers people come up with are cooperation, confidence, motivation, self-reliance and consideration. Training children to have those qualities is in some ways more difficult for lone parents, but in two ways it is easier. Two parents are more likely to have the time and energy to do too much for a child, so the child of a one-parent family is better placed to learn self-reliance and motivation. Also, a single parent does not have to struggle to become a united front about values and discipline. You can speak as one voice because you are one voice.'

Parents whose confidence has been battered, whether by divorce or other circumstances, are more likely to feel that they are pushing a rock uphill and that life is too hard even to contemplate making significant changes. But, Noël says, 'The way it has been doesn't have to be the way it will continue to be. Even a small change makes you feel more confident and positive. If that seems hard without the support of a partner, a single parent has to build up her strength by taking care of herself. Among other things, that means taking regular breaks to remind you that you are not just a mother.

'Even if you can't afford babysitting, you can arrange to have someone else's children one evening a week if they take yours for another evening. The same goes for weekends and holidays. Single mothers, particularly those with children who have special needs, tend to be over-protective and imagine that they are the only ones able to give the appropriate care. Rarely is it the case – as they discover when they do hand over.'

Arranging swaps brings single parents into contact with other adults. Noël believes this is good for the children as well as the adults: 'Children may be deprived by death or divorce of hearing you talk with a partner, but you don't have to deprive them of hearing conversation between adults. It's easy to get depressed and isolated as a single parent. Entertaining can seem daunting without someone to share the work, but there's no reason not to invite people over for a simple meal.

'It is also important to have time alone. Make sure that the children are in bed relatively early. It will be good for them and good for you. After the children are in bed, find something to do that makes you feel replenished. Leave the housework for when the children are around to help. It's not good for them to feel that you are serving them when they are capable of doing things for themselves.'

'Besides,' adds Luke, 'sharing tasks is a good way to learn useful skills and to spend time together. Boys who have single mothers need to learn that housework isn't women's work. If they protest, you could explain that you don't always enjoy it either, but the work has to be done.

'Reflectively listen to their feelings, let them have their say without interrupting and arguing, and when they have finished they will often be far more cooperative. If they won't address an issue, call a family meeting and ask for their ideas on solutions. It may sound formal if there are only two of you, but it will show you mean business.'

TIPS FOR COPING WITH BEING A SINGLE PARENT
- Take one day at a time.
- Firm doesn't mean angry: it means setting rules and following through. It's not being a meanie to stick to those rules; the rules convey your values.
- Notice the effect of consistent actions, rather than mere good intentions. If a consistent tactic isn't working after three months, try something different.
- Think about and tell your child about what's going right, not what's going wrong.
- Listen to a child's worries; don't let your own crowd his or hers out. Listen reflectively to help the child feel confident or safe enough to voice uncomfortable thoughts or ones she thinks you won't want to hear.
- Teach, train and require the child to help you more. Descriptively praise all efforts.
- Find a mentor for the child of the same sex. Boys need

---

regular (not necessarily frequent) contact with adult men. Sports coaches can be ideal: they show boys how to channel aggression and work in teams. Girls need mentors too, as it can be stifling to be constantly under a mother's eye.

- Take regular breaks. A sense of humour thrives on time and space.
- Don't dump emotions on a child because you don't have a partner. Instead, talk to a friend, keep a journal, ring the Samaritans or pray.
- Give yourself credit for the things you've done well; it will help you to keep making small changes.

How do I handle a temporary absence?

My whine that when my husband is away discipline goes to pieces met with little sympathy. Noël and Luke understand that the parent left at home can let routines and rules fall apart without a partner's support, but letting things go is not going to help the children feel OK about the parent's absence or about themselves.

Some children take temporary absences in their stride, but the more sensitive can get hysterical. Reassurance that Daddy will be back doesn't seem to cheer them up. Noël is not surprised. 'When you jolly children along by telling them what they already know,' she says, 'their real feelings of distress get magnified.'

Parents, she believes, should talk less and reflectively listen more when their children are unhappy. 'The child may be worried that he won't come back or that he likes it better in other places. If there was an argument before he went away, the child may think that he's gone because she made a fuss about brushing her teeth.

'Children are often unwittingly encouraged to be upset by parents who say things such as, "I'm going to miss you dreadfully." That can lead the child to feel he should miss the parent, and to feel guilty if he has a good time and forgets to miss the parent.'

The blow could be softened, she believes, if parents put more effort into preparing children for separation. 'Explain that you enjoy your job and enjoy travelling, but that sometimes it is inconvenient. Don't expect to have just one conversation about it. Prepare for success by having many such conversations, and don't wait until your child brings it up. As you reflectively listen, the children will gradually move through their upset and begin to think about what they and you could do to make the separation easier. But don't rush into problem-solving while your child still wants to talk about the upset. It will only make the child more upset. Be patient!'

None of this, however, is a guarantee that a child won't howl down the phone at the absentee. Often it seems kinder not to put the child on the line, but Luke says that is misguided: 'Don't give children a choice,' he says. 'It puts too much pressure on them. It's important to keep in contact, especially if a parent is actually living elsewhere.'

Gruelling though those calls may be, they are a parent's opportunity to find out what a child is thinking and feeling. But not, he warns, to tell the child how miserable it is being alone in a dreary hotel room. 'It's a 1960s' hippie mistake to burden a child with adult feelings. Children are not our equals in emotional development. They can't understand. As far as the child can see, Daddy has a choice – which he does.'

Action, he believes, is a better way to show that you care. Every Friday night, after he had been away all week, Luke's father would tiptoe into his sons' bedroom with a toy soldier for each of them. 'The size of the present wasn't the point, it was the consideration that went into it. That little ritual made saying goodbye on Monday much easier.'

He speaks approvingly of a busy man, who works at weekends but makes a point of attending his son's football matches, even if only for five minutes. 'He always wears a hat with antlers on it so his son can spot him in the crowd. It makes the boy feel really important to see that his dad has made the effort; it doesn't matter that he can't stay.'

He laughs, however, to hear of my friend, who once sent her children a tiny present each day when she went abroad. She is now so trapped in the habit that she collects a bag of toys in England to post home, just in case she can't find anything between meetings. 'It's great that she's still doing it,' he says. 'If she wants to stop, she is going to have to give plenty of warning.'

As for the parent who stays at home, the tendency is to compensate by taking over the missing partner's role. 'Don't,' says Luke. 'A mother can't be a little girl's daddy. Accept it.'

Nor should sympathy lead to indulgence, I am firmly informed when I mention that one of my children is too upset by her father's absence to do her reading. 'Tell her that you know she is missing her daddy,' suggests Luke, 'but that she still has to do her reading. The two things aren't connected. Being upset doesn't excuse her (or anyone) from life's regular responsibilities. Dealing with a parent's absence is a useful lesson in learning that life is hard, but that you have to get on with it.'

And if a child claims to be too upset to tidy her room, Noël would reflectively listen and cuddle the child, letting her cry it out, but be firm. 'She must do it, even if only in token form. It may mean she goes to bed late but it's important to prove to her that she can get through misery and get on with normal life.'

TIPS FOR COPING WITH ABSENCE
- Don't look back with regret over past periods when you haven't seen your children: build upon what you have now.
- When you are around, make regular times to share one-to-one activities with each child. 'Children don't need to see their parents all the time,' says Noël, 'but they do need frequent, predictable times when you do things together away from the other siblings.'
- While away, spend a few minutes each day sending messages. It means more than two hours at the airport buying toys.
- Leave the children with something to keep near their bed to remind them of you.
- Make your work seem less mysterious and threatening: show the children your office, let them play on the computer and meet your colleagues.

Isn't it hard to train children when you work long hours?

This bid for sympathy was no more successful than any other. Once children are past infancy, most parents nowadays work and pay for childcare, whether a nanny, child-minder, nursery or after-school care. Some of those children behave well, others don't. It usually has nothing to do with the childcare, Noël and Luke point out.

Of course, they admit, leaving children with a seventeen-year-old au pair who doesn't speak English, isn't interested in children and locks them in their room as soon as you go out is not going to help the child's development or training. But most childcare is far more responsible than that.

Nor is it good if both parents work so hard that they barely see the children except to give them a morning kiss as they leave home. Most parents soon realise that it is impractical – and unsatisfying – to give their children so little attention. If they don't, Noël has little patience with them. 'Rarely is it economic necessity for someone to work too hard and not see their children,' she observes. 'It's to do with keeping up a lifestyle. If relationships are going badly, everyone is happier when one parent stops work, or both parents decide to work part-time, even if it means moving to a smaller house, having fewer exciting holidays and less expensive clothes.'

Of course, if you are at home, you have more time to train children. One woman at a parenting class said that she had given up work because she found nannies 'too rigid, too dictatorial, too ready to hem the children in with endless rules and not respectful of them as people'. Since she had been home and training them in good habits, she had noticed that the children were more outgoing, relaxed and responsive.

Isn't the parent/helper relationship a snake-pit?

We all hate to think that someone else could be better at looking after our children than we are or, even worse, more loved. In their desire to remain Number One, parents often either undermine the helper or spoil the children. 'Parents shouldn't feel threatened,' says Noël. 'They are more loved whether they are indulgent or the opposite.

'Often those who have the most difficult relationships with their helpers,' Noël observes, 'are the guilty parents who know they shouldn't be spending so much time away from home. If they are away a lot, the children are likely to become clingy, irritable or demanding; that's not nice to be around, so the parent spends even less time with the children and it becomes a vicious circle.'

Ask a parent about the relationship with a helper and usually you will hear that it is good; when you ask the helper, you get a very different story. All sorts of resentments arise, often because parents fear the helper is more in control and so, instead of giving praise, they look for shortcomings. There is also a tendency to undermine the helper's authority by giving in on an issue where she has taken a stand. My own children, I have found, are adept at exploiting any inconsistencies.

Another mistake I have made is to be unrealistic in my expectations of what a helper can achieve with tired children. Homework, practising instruments and seeing friends is too much for any one post-school evening. The child subjected to too much pressure and constant rushing will not behave well. It is only when I have been at home for a while that I have seen how hectic the schedule is that I expect others to keep.

None of this, however, means that when parents have to delegate the children can't be well-behaved. 'Working is tiring,' say Luke, 'but it gives parents the opportunity to see life outside the home and should mean they return refreshed and better able to be positive, firm and consistent.'

How do I manage the transition when a familiar helper leaves and a new one arrives?

Friction invariably occurs when one helper leaves and another arrives. Children hate change, so whether the previous helper has been loved or disliked, the next one is made to suffer. Those who have known a stream of different carers often lay bets on how long it will take them to dislodge the latest.

Au pairs and nannies are made welcome at the New Learning Centre parenting classes. I've seen helpers arrive harrowed after receiving a torrent of abuse. Usually the child's script reads: 'I hate you. I'm not going to do anything you ask and I'm going to tell my parents to sack you because you are mean.'

Noël won't allow the nannies to take the children's hurtful words personally. '"I'm going to get Mummy to sack you" is just something that kids say, like they tell their mothers "You are the worst mother in the world" when they are angry. They know it will get a reaction and it might work to get their own way. You can listen reflectively to a child who has had a change of carer, but that shouldn't mean being inconsistent. Far too often sympathy turns into making excuses and giving in when what parents should be is firmer.'

Helpers, like children, thrive within the security of routine. If they can be told the rules of a given situation, it is easier for them to please the employer and there is less change for the children to cope with.

But many parents have a strange attitude to those who care for their children. They assume that working for them is a privilege rather than a job, and neither make rules nor behave predictably. They don't want to treat helpers like servants, so they treat them like friends (doormats) who won't mind if they are back late or if there is no food in the house. The help will either take out her resentment on the children or leave.

TIPS FOR DELEGATING
- With a new helper it is kinder to set out your rules clearly rather than let her do as she feels best and then find fault with her. The rules should be written down so that there is no room for confusion. The helper doesn't have to agree with your rules: she can think what she likes, say you are daft and talk behind your back, but rules take the problem out of her hands.
- Discuss with the children the instructions you have given to the help, and post up the rules, rewards and consequences on the fridge. If children know what is going to happen, they are more likely to comply, need less policing and are less frequently criticised.
- When something occurs that needs discussing, don't leave it until hand-over time when the help is desperate to get away, the parent is longing to relax, and the children are

running around butting in. If it's important, discuss it on the phone earlier in the day, or wait and discuss it on the phone the following day.

- Parents should have the helper learn the same skills they use, especially where there is a difficult child who needs careful treatment.

- Be seen to endorse the helper's decisions. If you disagree with an action, discuss it when the children are not around.

- Helpers, as well as children, deserve, and thrive on, descriptive praise and reflective listening.

6

SIBLING SQUABBLES

How do I stop the children squabbling and fighting? How do I handle favouritism? What do I do about the cries of 'That's unfair'? Should children be treated as a team? How do you treat twins?

Sigmund Freud in his *Interpretation of Dreams* wrote: 'I have never yet met a woman patient who hasn't dreamt of murdering a sibling.' Surely Noël and Luke must agree that sibling rivalry is one of life's givens?

Luke does: 'You have only to look at a litter of puppies,' he says. 'They are always scuffling, biting and making one another yelp with pain. My brother and I were no different, we used to fight all the time. But that doesn't mean parents can do nothing to make it better.'

Noël takes a similar but more radical view. She believes a certain amount of sibling squabbling is not only natural, but also beneficial – for learning to share, take turns, give and take, be patient and tolerant, handle disagreements and get knocked about without minding. She also believes that the typically high level of squabbling between siblings can be significantly reduced.

When she studied anthropology, she was fascinated to learn that there were cultures in which sibling rivalry did not exist. 'Having studied their practices,' she says, 'I decided to try and bring up my children not to be rivals, and 90 per cent of the time I was successful.'

I find that hard to believe. There seem to be such profound differences of character between my own children that I cannot see how friction might be avoided, but I am keen to learn. It may be, as Noël says, that a lot of what I take to be jealousy is merely a bad habit. Sibling rivalry, she explains, is mostly about attention – if I pay

attention to squabbles, I shall get more of them; if I pay more attention to the children when they aren't squabbling, they will have less
need to fight for my attention.

I would love my five to get on, but it seems inevitable that three
girls close together in age will be constantly comparing everything
from their figures to their Christmas presents. All I feel I can do is
try to be fair, lecture them about being nice to one another, and beg
them to 'Just stop it' when they needle one another. When none of
those ploys does much to reduce the bickering, I revert to the opti-
mistic/passive line of assuming that, over time, the rivalries will sort
themselves out.

Worryingly, that doesn't always happen. Sibling rivalry appears
to shape how adults behave in later life, outside as well as inside the
family. Those who seem most eager to find fault with others, and
take keen pleasure in their discomfiture, seem to be playing out a
form of sibling rivalry against everyone else in the world. They
appear to believe that someone else's loss is their gain, as if there
were a finite quantity of love and success available, and it doesn't
help them make friends. 'What can I do to avoid this dismal
prospect?' I asked Noël and Luke.

'Stay out of the squabbles,' they replied.

How do you leave children to fight?

The trouble starts, in Luke's view, when parents get involved. 'When
you look at a litter of puppies,' he says, 'however much they fight, the
mother does not intervene. Parents should do the same: if you step
in and punish the elder child, the little one will never learn that the
consequence of winding up his big brother is that he gets thumped.'

It was the elder brother whom, he assumed, would be punished
– with good reason. There is a universal tendency to side with the
younger, weaker, seemingly hard-done-by sibling against the older,
stronger, more visibly angry one. The elder one, because he always
feels blamed, is then out to get the younger one at every opportunity,
while the younger child soon learns to be more cunning and manipulative, as well as agreeable to the parents to get them on his side.

'It took my own parents a long time to realise that,' says Luke.
'When my younger brother and I fought it went like this: he would
tease me; I would hit him; he would run to my parents crying; they

would tell me off and I would feel angry. But one day they happened to be watching from an upstairs window when we had one of these fights, and they saw my brother winding me up until I retaliated. For once, they didn't take his side and afterwards they stayed out of it.'

But, I pointed out, fights usually happen under a parental nose and involve so much screaming and shouting that you feel you must intervene. 'No,' says Noël, 'you don't have to get involved, and the easiest way not to is to tell children to take their squabble somewhere else. That sends children the message that they have a perfect right to squabble if they want to, but you have a right not to have to listen to the unpleasant noise and commotion.

'I strongly recommend that all parents set aside a squabbling area to which warring children must go. It should be out of your earshot; it might even be the garden. You must be firm about sending them there as soon as they begin to bicker rather than giving them a warning or reminder. It will take the heat out of the fight because, usually, the point of squabbling is to get your attention.

'Then, next time, instead of saying "Stop it," which is rewarding the squabbles with attention, all you say is, "Where do you need to go?" And if they won't get out from under your feet, you remove yourself from the scene.'

However, she adds, staying out of the fights is not in itself sufficient to stop them. 'It may help lessen the severity of the fights, but the only way to reduce the rivalry is to change the whole emotional climate in the home so that siblings are less driven to squabble.'

What if the fight looks vicious?

Parents are scared that siblings are going to hurt one another, but Noël has found that children hurt one another much more when parents are regularly intervening: 'It almost seems to egg them on.

'Obviously, if children are in danger, you have to do something. There you have rules – such as nothing to be used as a weapon – and consequences for infringement of those rules. The rules must be realistic: you cannot expect children never to hit, scream, snatch, shove or call names. And anyway, it's often one child's word against another's. But you can outlaw throwing, which transforms any object into a weapon. That rule must be enforced but, I promise you, if you stay out of their fights, children will find squabbling much less interesting.'

What makes children fight?

'The bond between siblings is strong and biological,' says Luke, 'and if a child feels slighted or wronged within the family, it goes very deep. It is possible to sort out these tensions later in life, but it is far better to address the problems at an earlier age.'

To do that, first you have to make sure that, as a parent, you are part of the solution and no longer part of the problem. The way in, Noël suggests, is via the mind of the eldest child. For him, everything was perfect, or at least normal and predictable, until his younger sibling came along; he had enjoyed his parents' undivided attention and probably had far too much done for him. Then, suddenly, everyone started saying, 'Isn't the baby sweet?' and had far less time or inclination to dote on him.

Parents know they should not get cross about temporarily immature behaviour, but even so it is likely that he felt he was often in trouble for waking the baby or being too rough with it, and was often frustrated because he wanted to go out when it was having a rest. The baby was monopolising Mummy's lap (and breast) and he had to wait longer for his cuddles than he was accustomed to. He may have discovered then that if he threw a tantrum, everyone paid attention to him. As Noël says, 'Almost all children discover that it is much easier in a busy household to get negative attention than it is to get positive attention. As far as children can see, bad behaviour works, and the most effective way of getting the parents' immediate attention is usually to annoy the younger child.'

Her solution is to be careful to pay not just as much attention to the older child as to the younger but – and this surprised me – more. As she explains, 'The first child is born into a world of adults and will always need more adult attention than a younger child, who is born into a world of children.'

Even before the second child is born, parents can plan for the avoidance of sibling rivalry. 'If you do too much for your first child – and most parents do – when the next one comes along and you have less time and inclination to do things for him, he will feel deprived of what he believes love to be – people doing things for him. Naturally, he will blame his sibling. The key is to make the first child as self-reliant as possible.'

At a parenting class, I met a mother whose sibling rivalry problems were history. Her eight-year-old son had deeply resented the arrival of his baby brother, and when the younger child was eight months old he flew off the handle and kicked him. 'Usually I would have told him off and made him say sorry, but this time I tried a different approach. I held him tightly and tried some reflective listening. 'I think it's really hard for you,' I said, 'that your brother is crawling now and playing with your toys. It must make you very frustrated.'

She also took a guess at the root of the problem. She had noticed that her husband always kissed the baby first when he came home from work, and she checked out her hunch. 'Before your brother was born, Daddy always kissed you as soon as he came in. It must make you very angry that the baby gets first kiss,' she ventured, and even though he didn't respond, she carried on: 'But in this house we don't kick or hit, even when we are angry.'

An hour and a half later the child came and told her, unprompted, that he was really sorry. He hasn't attacked his baby brother since.

How do you make children feel individual without making them rivals?

Parents are always being asked what their children are like, and because the emergence of personality is so fascinating, we tend to give them labels. 'X is very lively and outgoing, Y is much calmer,' sounds harmless enough, even if the children are in earshot, but Luke warns that they quickly pick up on labels and feel pigeonholed.

Constantly being told that you are the 'naughty' one could obviously encourage a child to behave badly, but I was surprised when Noël and Luke told me that it was equally damaging to give children labels such as 'good', 'clever' or 'pretty'. The child given a positive label, they explain, often feels compelled to live up to it, which is a strain; meanwhile, the other children assume they totally lack that desirable quality and behave accordingly. Besides, children change: looks can go off, shy children become outgoing – and labelling gets in the way of change.

Noël, who was considered clever and artistic, fought with her sister, who was considered beautiful and poetic, so she knows how sensitive children are to being pigeon-holed, and she drummed this lesson in so hard that I didn't know what to say the next time someone asked about my children. 'Describe what they do,' she advised, 'but not how they are.'

> *My father was close to all of us. He wasn't the kind of fellow to have favourites; he was able to find the originality in all his children.*
>
> Ophelia Dahl on her father, Roald

Are some relationships more likely to lead to rivalry than others?
'Girls mature more quickly,' says Noël, 'so a sensitive and intense boy may resent a younger sister who can do everything better.' It can be tempting to chide the boy for not sitting still and doing his home-work when his sister is doing hers but, like all comparisons, it makes matters worse.

Illness, genius, learning difficulties, looks – all contribute to rivalry, but what really lies at the heart of it is the way parents treat each child. As Noël says, 'When a child is angry at a sibling, it is often not really about the sibling, but about the child's emotional needs not being met consistently. The child may not dare to be directly angry with her parents for fear of getting even less approval.'

Most eldest children are upset for a while when the second child arrives but, if their needs are being met, they soon settle down again, accept the new situation and learn to love the baby. Contrary to popular opinion, children don't mind at all if their siblings are loved, so long as they feel uniquely valued themselves.

Favouritism and bonding
My children seem to have their radar permanently switched on, sweeping for signs of favouritism. Partly, Noël tells me, this is born of the natural human tendency to feel deprived, partly it is a habit, and partly it is how children typically react when they aren't getting enough one-to-one time with each parent. Sometimes my children make such an issue of favouritism that it makes me wonder whether I do have preferences.

Many parents, I find, are quite blatant about having favourites: often they single out the child most similar to them in temperament or interests, their 'mini-me'; others adore a child of the opposite sex who flirts with them. Sometimes they even say to their other children, 'Why can't you be more like . . .' As a technique for improving a child's behaviour, it is not effective. Comparisons tend only to push the child further off to an extreme, which parents might think the child is doing out of spite. 'Children aren't usually so devious,' says Noël. 'When children behave badly it is either from habit or on impulse or because the child has become hooked on negative attention. He thinks it's what he deserves, and he knows how to get it better than he knows how to get positive attention.'

Luke would have parents step back and analyse their supposed preferences. 'Do parents really have favourites?' he asks. 'I don't think many of us would know who to choose if we really had "Sophie's Choice". Isn't it just that we prefer certain kinds of behaviour? We find it easier spending time with a younger child, for example, who often has a more conciliatory approach.'

His advice is to separate out the child from the behaviour, and then train the child in the behaviour you like so that she can please you.

> *Siblings don't have the same parents. Each parent treats each child so differently that they might as well have been raised in completely different families.*
>
> Oliver James, clinical psychologist

Can bonding problems cause behavioural difficulties?

When parents are blind to a child's merits, Noël and Luke believe it may be because the bond in the very earliest days of infancy was not strong. A weak bond can arise for many reasons – the mother may not have been well after the birth, the child may have been premature or ill. Even something as minor as an infant's sticky eye can interfere with the falling-in-love sensation.

'A disproportionate number of violent boys were premature,' says Luke, 'and it may be significant that they spent the first few days, weeks or even months of their lives in incubators where they couldn't be cuddled. It could be that, not having a strong initial bond, they lack a certain responsiveness, an early awareness of boundaries.'

One set of parents he knows was so keen to avoid any attachment problems with their premature baby that, 'as soon as the child was out of hospital, and throughout his first year, they made sure that he was always being held by one or the other of his parents, and very little by anyone else.

'Bonding is a function of time,' he explains 'and it works better the longer you spend with an infant. In some cultures babies are strapped to their mothers for their first few months – something that parents ought to think about when they hand them over at an early age to nannies and child-minders. But we need to be careful not to rush into the belief that if a relationship doesn't start out right, it can never be good.

'Where bonding is weak, parents should try to do something about it because it has a profound impact on our ability to sustain relationships in adulthood. The initiative can't come from the child: no child can say "I want to be closer," so the parent has to demonstrate that it is what he or she wants. I've known parents sort out a relationship with a child who is already grown up, but while a child is still in your care, you can do much more.'

Noël is also interested in the issue of bonding. She has observed that when parents had difficulty bonding, they frequently favour that child to compensate, and she finds, 'What often happens is that they don't bond in a loving, relaxed way; they bond in an anxious or annoyed way.' She believes such situations can be remedied, although it will take time and determination. 'The answer, of course, lies in the sixteen skills.'

To this prescription Luke would add one more: 'Physical contact is extremely important. If we can't spend huge amounts of time with our children, we should try to make the time that we do spend with them intimate. Fathers and sons should play rough-and-tumble games. Mothers should cuddle their children, especially those who seem not to want physical affection. If your child is pushing you away, it is often because that child feels pushed away himself.

'If you feel estranged from a child, cancel a business trip and go off together, just the two of you. Don't be stopped by the child's cries of "No". He may be quite fearful of criticism from that parent, but it is not a good idea to allow the child to decide: that would put him in charge of the relationship. Children don't know what's best for them.'

Is each child getting enough attention?

When children squabble a lot,' says Noël, 'it is usually because they have a need that is not being met. Most often, the need is for positive attention and appreciation.'

Children, she explains, blame their siblings, unconsciously, for the lack of parental attention, so they take out their frustrations on each other. That is why spending frequent and predictable quality time with each child reduces the number, duration and intensity of the squabbles.

Quality time, in her view, is not about going on expensive expeditions. Nor is it, she tells stay-at-home mothers, about being with your children while focusing on something else. When parents protest that they are giving their children lots of attention she finds that too often it takes the form of doing things for the children, fussing over whether they are wearing gloves, or playing with them in a way that keeps the children dependent on the parent to provide the entertainment.

Instead, Noël tells stay-at-home parents as well as working parents that children don't need attention constantly, but they do need to know that at some point each day, maybe only for fifteen minutes, they will have the parent all to themselves, doing something that they both enjoy. 'That time must be regular, predictable and shouldn't involve watching television,' she says. 'The only exception to the no-screen rule during quality time would be if you have a hugely disaffected teenager who won't agree to share anything else with you. Of course, one-on-one time is a perfect opportunity for tons of descriptive praise.'

Luke is equally adamant about the need for one-to-one time with each child. When I tell him that I am often too busy cooking to play, he rejects that excuse. 'Quality time should be given as much priority as mealtimes,' he says, 'if not more. Children can handle missed meals but they can't be happy unless they are getting individual attention.'

Those who are getting individual, positive parental attention, without having to fight for it, will be much less aggressive to their siblings. Ideally, if you give the attention as soon as you see a child, there will be no need for fights later. It works with the puppy: she stops jumping up if given attention immediately. It isn't so easy to do with several children at once, but Noël told me to prepare for success by telling each child that I was going to spend some special time with him or her. 'You could even write it down,' she says, 'so the child is in no doubt that after you have played trains with the younger one for fifteen minutes, it will be her turn. One way to create this special time is to stagger children's bedtimes according to their age so that each gets fifteen minutes of individual attention.'

She looked at me shrewdly when I protested that I tried to do something similar when I came in from work. 'Were you giving them time but connecting it with homework and music practice?' she asked. 'That won't work. It must be time when the child doesn't feel that he must measure up. If you are very busy, you might not be able to do it every day, but I don't think a child can get by on quality time only once a week.

'If there is so much to be done that you can't easily find the time,' she continued, seeing me look despairing, 'an excellent strategy is to require one child to come with you when you are doing something that has to be done anyway, such as going to the supermarket or walking the dog. Or you could make sure that time you spend over breakfast or stuck in traffic is not wasted. Any of these occasions will give you the chance to chat, tell jokes and play little games, as well as listen reflectively to feelings and praise the child for being helpful.'

One mother at a parenting class said that she lets her daughter choose how to spend their special time, and the child always wants to play with her Barbie dolls. 'I hate Barbies,' the mother said, 'but I told myself that I could play with them for fifteen minutes a day. Any more than that and I would die of boredom; one lesson I have learnt about being a mother is that it can be boring.'

Noël commended her grit but felt, if she really couldn't enjoy playing with Barbies, it was inadvisable to pretend. 'I hate them too and I tell my granddaughter that if she just wants company, I will be glad to sit in the same room and read my book while she plays with her dolls, but if she wants to play with me, we have to do something that I like too, such as reading, doing a jigsaw or going for a walk. It does a child no harm to learn that not everyone likes the same pastimes.'

How can you pay special attention to one child when the others are milling around?

'You can train even a very young child to play alone,' says Noël, 'just as they do at Montessori nurseries. Start with a few minutes and build up. Bring out just one toy, put it on the mat and let the child play with that while you appear to be paying attention to something else. Of course, you need to praise descriptively almost non-stop at first. If you get too many toys out, the child may get over-stimulated and restless.

'It's very important to teach children to play by themselves,' says Noël. 'It makes them more self-reliant at school and, later, at work. Another way to teach this skill is to play next to a child, chatting about the activity, descriptively praising and reflectively listening, but not doing any of it for them. Having you there, also making something out of Playdough, enriches the experience for the child; she learns self-reliance and self-feedback by watching and copying.'

'Older children usually know how to amuse themselves, but only do it when they feel like it. Requiring them to leave you alone when it suits you, the parent, is a very important habit to establish. Otherwise, parents can feel that they are at the beck and call of their children, which is very stressful. And parents often take out that stress on the children by being irritable and impatient, and by not wanting to spend any extra time with them.'

How do you give positive attention to a child who rejects you?

In a calm moment after a jealous scene, I suggested to one of my daughters that we find some time to do something together of her choice. 'When you first make the suggestion the child may say, "I don't believe you," Noël warned, 'or "You've said that before and then you didn't do it," or "You won't like what I want to do." If the child is angry, parents often feel they shouldn't push it, but I believe they should persist. If the child refuses to spend half an hour with you, spend just a few minutes together to begin with.'

In my case, the suggestion alone had a miraculously calming effect. But Noël was determined that I should follow through. 'If the child is feeling so negative that she can't think what she might like to do with you during this special time, the parent can give some ideas, but expect a grumpy or angry child to shoot down your suggestions.'

Had I received the response, 'I don't want to and you can't make me,' Noël wouldn't have allowed me to give up. 'Parents feel rejected and hurt, so we say "OK" and don't insist. Or we become fierce and say, "Yes, I can make you." Another alternative is to say, "Come to me when you are ready," but that doesn't give the impression that you really want to be with the child. A better approach would be reflective listening and making the expectations absolutely clear: "I can see that you are so angry that you don't want to spend any time with me, but we are going to do it because it will be good for both of us, even though it will probably be uncomfortable at first." We have to be clear about what we are doing and why, and children have to learn that there are some things that they just have to do even though they don't really want to.'

Luke advises against expecting too much. 'If you go off together and have two hours in the car, you will probably imagine having an intimate chat. You can't make a child do that, but you can prepare for success by not putting the radio on. If we tend to avoid the times when we could be intimate, by turning on the radio or the television, we don't give children enough opportunity to talk. Normally, parents can bear silence for longer than children, who will eventually initiate a conversation.'

He has had to steel parents of teenagers to attempt bridge-building and he gives them this advice. 'Obviously the child will be resentful if you turn off the TV and say, "Now we are spending time together." Instead, pick a quiet moment. "From now on," you could say, "we are going to spend forty-five minutes together every week." If the child asks why, as he probably will, you can ask him to guess – you mustn't do his thinking for him. If the guess is facetious, don't get annoyed – join in the joke. If he can't think up an activity, you can tell him it doesn't matter, you have lots of ideas, and set a time.

'Then warn the child on Friday that on Monday at six o'clock you will be having your special time. Warn again after school, and again five minutes before you are due to start. You could make suggestions if the child doesn't. If the child says they are all boring, you could say, "Then, we'll just sit here".'

Luke says that he has never known a determined campaign by a parent to get closer to a child not to work. 'There are a few teenagers so far gone in apathy that watching TV is the only possible joint activity at first, but it is rare. If parents are doing the rest of what I suggest – not criticising or nagging – the kids will soften fast. Positive attention is what they all desperately want.'

How do you know what your child is feeling?

Listening reflectively sounds like a good idea but it can be hard to know where to begin. Parents assume they know about their child's inner life, but if a child is fighting with siblings, it is often a sign that he is struggling with an uncomfortable emotion that he doesn't know how to express or resolve.

During the one-to-one time with a child, Luke and Noël recommend starting with a guess as to what may be going on. Usually anxieties come tumbling out, but Noël also suggests that parents might like to find out how much they know about their child by setting themselves a questionnaire. She gave me the following checklist of questions:

- What is your child's favourite food?
- How does your child spend his/her pocket money?
- Who are his/her best friends? Why does he/she like them?
- What/who frightens your child?
- What upsets your child?
- What would your child most like to do better?

I knew the answers to some of those questions for each child. Where I was stumped, the questions proved useful starting points for a conversation. 'Sometimes,' Luke observes, 'we may not pursue reflective listening because we are nervous of finding out that the child is troubled. That is cowardly. Don't feel guilty or that life is unfair if your child has difficulties. All children have difficulties or weaknesses, but they need not be crippled by them. When we go about it the right way, we can help children build up their weak points. For example, if your child is small and scared, you might find a course in martial arts or rock climbing – something, anything they are good at – to boost their confidence.' Noël adds, 'But you may well have to insist that the child attends the classes. Otherwise his fear will stop him. We must not be afraid of our children's fears and worries.'

Another of Luke's key pieces of advice is to 'notice what you notice' in a child: 'It is easy to spot and praise academic or sporting success, but maybe not so easy to notice a child who talks nicely to Auntie when she comes to tea. If you look for the good in each child, you will find it.'

'That's not fair'

I can't bear to think how many times a day one or other of my children utters the words, 'That's not fair.' It's an exhausting complaint that always leaves me feeling guilty and justifying my actions at great length.

'Fairness is a major concern for younger children,' says Luke. 'As they get older, trust takes over.' Parents, he knows, are agonised by the need to be fair, and find they are constantly accused of not being so. 'Everyone must decide for himself what is fair, but there could be agreed fair and unfair ways to behave, about which the children should be clear. For example, hitting, kicking, grabbing and pushing might not be allowed, nor might swearing, arguing, name-calling or telling tales.

'What parents also have to grasp is that fair is not the same as equal. If you are handing out biscuits, you should give each child two. That's fair. But you cannot, and should not, treat them equally when it comes to bedtimes or pocket money. Elder children must be allowed their privileges. They need to feel that there are advantages that come with age, otherwise the older children will take out their resentments on younger siblings.'

I then told Luke about a solution that Elisabeth Luard, author of *Family Life*, had come up with. Exasperated by her children's refusal to admit who was responsible when something went wrong, she instigated a scheme called 'Victim of the Week'. One week in each month was allotted to each of her four children, and during that week the nominated child was held responsible for the misdemeanours of all four. She claims that the beauty of this technique is that it is manifestly unfair, minimising the guilt as well as the blame. Better still, it has its own fail-safe: the victim knows that if he behaves badly in someone else's week, one of the others will do so in his.

Luke laughed, saying that the idea was fine as long as it could be kept up consistently, but he doubted that it could.

One of Noël's pet hates is when parents respond to complaints of unfairness by saying, 'Well, life's not fair'. 'It is quite true that life isn't fair,' she says, 'but our children are the lucky ones, at the top of the heap according to every measure – except their own, understandably immature perception of their lot. So I suggest that parents don't rise to the bait. Just prepare for success, listen reflectively for the feeling below the complaint and descriptively praise children for every microscopic gesture of generosity, good will and teamwork.'

Is it fair to have to share?

The constant moans of 'That's not fair' can so get on parental nerves that Luke and Noël both feel the need to remind me that the wails about injustice are sometimes justified. It is unreasonable, for example, to always expect children to share. Some family possessions, such as the computer, have to be shared, but there are also personal possessions, favourite toys, that a child should be allowed to keep to him or herself. The same goes for private space.

Noël would be very clear about what is private and what is communal and make firm rules governing the two (see the suggestions below).

PERSONAL VERSUS COMMUNAL
- Any toy left out on the floor or table must be shared.
- A toy that is not for sharing has to go on a child's special shelf in the playroom or be taken up to a bedroom (which may only be entered by another child with the owner's permission).
- If a private possession is 'borrowed' without permission or a private space invaded, Luke suggests a clear consequence thought out in advance. If the situation is unclear, he would call a family meeting at which everyone has to put forward their case and their solutions. The idea is to help children learn to sort out their differences using negotiation, a vital skill for later life.
- Perhaps one child could be helped to explain to the other that she doesn't want her to come into her room when the door is shut, or that her dolls are private and are not to be

---

touched (unless she forgets and leaves them lying around). The other child will have equally precious private toys and will agree that the same rules apply.

How do you treat twins?

Twins present a special problem when it comes to fairness. Both Noël and Luke are firmly of the view that encouraging individuality is more important than treating twins the same. 'All children compare, and twins compare themselves to each other more directly; they also get lumped together more than other children because parents are often so overwhelmed by their arrival that they don't arrange the time to give them separate attention.'

Luke notes that parents often find that their twins want to do everything together. 'That means the parents should make greater efforts to help them become more separate, more self-reliant. All parents have a tendency to talk about "the children" collectively; with twins, it is even more important never to do that.'

Noël's advice for encouraging individuality begins with clothes: 'I would not dress twins alike, even if I wanted to. I would also give them names that don't sound at all similar or even begin with the same letter [so no Bill and Ben] I would put them in different classes and, later, in different schools.'

Maybe there will charges of unfairness, but she would weather them. 'Children learn,' she finds, 'to complain of unfairness before they even know what the word means. All they are really saying is that they don't like something.'

Luke has friends with identical twin boys: 'One thinks life is easy, one thinks life is tough. That isn't because they have been treated differently, because most people can't tell them apart.' To him those twins act as a useful reminder that 'However closely we watch ourselves and however fairly we try to behave towards children, they will turn out differently.'

Can a family be treated like a team?

I can see that children need to feel like individuals, especially in large families. But sometimes it seems like a good idea to treat children as a team so that each is held accountable for the actions of the others. I tried, for example, to make the right to watch television in the evening contingent upon the whole family getting up in the morning without making a fuss.

Noël advised me to prepare for success by saying to the children: 'Now, tell me how you can act as a team . . .' Once the children have voiced their ideas, they are more likely to follow through and put them into action, she said. Of course, she wanted me then to descriptively praise them for even minor or misguided attempts at teamwork and to listen reflectively to their feelings about it, with remarks such as: 'It's not easy getting everyone to help . . .'

'If it works, teamwork can be very good,' says Luke. 'Children tend to pick each other up on things in a way that they won't take from adults.

'One problem is that children of different ages will have different levels of competence over keeping rules, so your individual expectations must be made clear. Then all you can do is try it. It will work if the older, more sensible ones support rather than criticise and blame the younger, scattier ones. If it doesn't work, drop it, as it can be fraught with friction.'

But give it long enough to stand a chance of working, advises Noël. 'And don't give up too soon.' 'Instead,' Noël suggests, 'start by having the team effort earn rewards rather than lack of team effort result in a penalty. The rewards should be easy to earn at first so that your children experience for themselves the benefits of pulling together.'

What do I do when the children disagree over something important?

We had an explosion at home one day when one of our children barged into the sitting room and started making a noise when another was listening to music. It resulted in a screaming match. Here Luke described to me a technique known as conflict resolution. This is how it works:

Get the children together. Ideally you would begin by saying there have been mistakes on both sides, but now we are going to resolve this.

Find out what happened without laying any blame. Each person should then be allowed their say with no interruptions. If the stories are long and convoluted, try to tackle them in chunks. You could then recap to make sure that everyone agrees on what is being said: 'So he did that and you felt that . . .'

Ask each of them, 'Can you see what you did that made X happen?' We are all great at saying what the other person could do differently; it is more useful to say what *you* could do differently yourself. One child might say, 'When you barge in when I'm listening to music I feel you don't care about me.'

Ask them to phrase as a request how they would like the other person to behave in future. No blame, no 'You made me feel . . .', no right or wrong, but 'I would like . . .'

There are three responses to this: you can accept a request, decline, or make a counter-offer. If a child won't agree, say, not to come into the sitting room when another child is listening to music, you could suggest that she might offer to come in quietly.

Noël warns that this process may work better in resolving rows between friends than between siblings. 'With siblings,' she says, 'there is usually so much going on under the surface that the conflict is rarely clear cut. Often it is about one child believing that another child is getting away with bending or ignoring the rules – and, usually, the child is right. There is generally so much unresolved resentment intruding on the current conflict that siblings have a difficult time focusing just on the matter at hand, and it is all too easy to get bogged down in the "Find out what happened" stage, with one child flatly refusing even to consider the other child's version of reality.'

She suggests reflectively listening until both children seem ready to embark on problem-solving, and at that point guiding them to frame their requests. 'Remember to write down and read back all agreements, and then have all parties sign the "document", even a child too young to write properly. Parents should then use this document as an aide-memoire for regular descriptive praise until the new habits have been established.'

How do you deal with telling tales?

Telling children that you are not interested in hearing tales does not work because, to the child, it is not a tale, but a terribly urgent problem. Noël suggests instead saying that you are interested in hearing how the child feels but not in what her sister did. 'Say, "If the two of you have a problem and would like my help sorting it out, then both of you must come and see me." But obviously, if someone has got hurt (and is not just crying for effect), or if something is broken, you have to go and take a look.'

When you can see that a child is complaining about or 'telling on' a sibling in order to get her in trouble, you can thank the child for showing an interest in the smooth running of the house, but again do nothing. 'Once you are really consistent about not reacting, they will complain to you less and less. You need not worry that you won't then hear about the important problems. The children will still come and tell you about those. But the petty, jealousy-induced tales will dry up.'

My problem, I say, is that I often feel a child is justly aggrieved because, say, her sister is in her room and won't leave. I am still not to take sides, Noël says, because I never know the whole story. 'In any case, you would cast it not as telling tales but as asking for help. You could give her the benefit of your experience in finding solutions. "When that happened to me I . . ." But don't give her advice; she probably won't follow it. Or she'll try it and be annoyed with you if it doesn't work. Even if it does work, you will have robbed her of a chance to test and hone her own problem-solving skills. So concentrate on reflective listening.'

But what if the child is telling a tale on a sibling who is doing something expressly forbidden, such as watching television before doing homework? 'When you set a rule, it is up to you to manage it and not to leave the monitoring to the children. If you go and turn off the television after the tale has been told, you give the child an incentive to tell tales again. So you could say you were aware that the other child was illicitly watching television and you were just about to turn it off. Then you could add, "However, since you told me about it, I am going to let her have an extra fifteen minutes of TV." It may seem unfair but it will stop the tale-telling.

'Whatever you do, don't lecture children about other people not liking them if they tell tales. Lecturing only breeds resentment and "selective deafness".

What if children don't fight, but just don't speak?

While I was attempting to solve our sibling rivalry problems, a teenage visitor said that his parents would love it if he and his sister still bickered. Six years earlier they had stopped speaking and had barely exchanged a word since. At family meals they referred to each other in the third person and spoke only to their parents. Finally, now, he said, they were beginning to talk but it was embarrassing since they knew so little of each other's lives.

Luke felt the parents could have nipped the non-speaking in the bud. 'Not by saying, "You are both behaving badly," but, "We notice that you aren't speaking and we wonder if there is a reason." It might be, since they were teenagers in close proximity, that the embarrassments of puberty lay at the bottom of it. You could then talk about embarrassment and suggest that they probably want locks on the bedroom and bathroom doors. These kinds of tension are a normal part of growing up. We can't make siblings be the best of friends, but we can require them to be civil around the house.'

Noël suspected that the parents of the non-speakers might have regularly rescued one of the children, probably the younger one. 'Even when parents stop interfering,' she says, 'the other child can carry on feeling bitter. It has become his or her way of looking at the world. To that child I would say, "What do you wish that Daddy and I did differently?"

'The child will probably say something vague like, "You never listen." You can then suggest that you listen to the child for half an hour a day. She will probably say, "I don't really need that much time," but you have started to focus the child's mind on possible solutions and she may come up with other ideas about what would help.

'You must, of course, follow through. Deluge both children with reflective listening and clear the air so that they eventually become ready to think about solutions, but be aware that the listening stage will take much longer than you think. Parents tend to rush on to problem-solving, but if you try to move on too soon, the child will end up complaining for much longer.'

TIPS FOR REDUCING SIBLING RIVALRY

- Discuss strategy; stick to it for three months.
- Remember that children are evenly matched. Older is stronger, but younger can wind up.
- Stay out of squabbles – no reasoning, telling off, punishing or threatening. The fights may look dire but partly they are just habit. Siblings have to find their own ways of resolving these battles. If you have to interfere because a child is in real danger, back off again as soon as possible.
- If a child complains, listen reflectively to her feelings but don't try to solve the problem.
- Ten times a day, descriptively praise children for not squabbling, for example: 'It's nice to see you aren't hitting each other, even though I can see you are angry.'
- Give each child 'sacred' places for their belongings. Anything not in those places must be shared with whoever picks it up.
- Both parents must spend quality time with each child at least several times a week; the times must be predictable. A child who feels not only loved but liked is less disposed to fight.
- Give the older child special privileges.
- Have a squabbling place and insist children go there whenever a squabble breaks out.
- Address a child's individual needs, otherwise he will take out his anger and frustration on other family members.
- Train children to entertain themselves so that they don't annoy each other for fun when they can't think of anything better to do.

7

CRIME AND PUNISHMENT

How do I discipline a child? Is it always wrong to slap?
What other ways are there to get children to behave better?
How do I teach a child to control his temper? What's the
best way to treat a mistake? How do I resolve a dispute?
How do I stop the children swearing? Should they have to
say they are sorry?

There are moments when children seem to be spoiling for a fight. If
mine bait me for long enough when I am tired, I shout, snap and
sometimes even give them a slap. Then I feel so guilty that I burst
into tears, apologise profusely and completely forget that the child
was doing something she shouldn't have been doing in the first
place.

In this I am, I believe, a typical parent of today. We are keen to
be friends to our children, to treat them as equals, but there comes a
moment when they seem to exploit our niceness, push us too far and
we explode. Then we don't know what to do for the best. We try
reasoning. We try reproaches. We mutter dark threats. And none of
it makes any difference.

Too right, say, Noël and Luke who meet streams of parents who
can't understand why their homes are beset with constant friction.
Before they tell them how to manage flare-ups better, they make
them aware of what doesn't work. 'If nagging worked, we'd all have
perfect children,' says Noël. 'And if noticing and mentioning
mistakes worked, we would be perfect too.

'Entertaining nervous breakdowns don't work either: of course,
it is hard not to screech when a child is deliberately winding you up
– it may even be what the child is hoping for. But bellowing, "Stop
that immediately," although it may satisfy the child's thirst for drama

and may be a temporary relief for the parent, is not going to solve the problem. You are never going to get children to behave better by reacting emotionally.'

Reasoning, both Luke and Noël point out, is not the answer either, since children are creatures of impulse and ruled by their emotions. Even deliberate misbehaviour, they believe, is not the result of a reasoned, rational choice. Parents, they observe, only try to reason with children when they are being unreasonable, and the result is always a row.

As for my standard remark to a rude child – 'How dare you talk to me like that!' – I am, they tell me, not only wasting my breath but also weakening my position. 'The child does dare speak to you like that because he already has,' says Noël. 'Your words justify the child in further angry behaviour, so he will hurtle out of the room thinking, "I shall never do anything she says again."'

Threats are also useless. 'No one likes to punish, so instead they say "If you do that again, I shall . . ." Then the child, who has already got away with the misdeed once, does it again. And, usually, parents don't want to carry out the threat as it was over the top in the first place. No pocket money for a month. No television for the rest of the week. Or even no visit to Disneyland when it is already booked and paid for. So the deterrent effect is nil.'

My usual way of dealing with a scuffle or a screaming match is to bellow or beg, 'Don't fight!' If anything, it seems to egg children on. Luke is not surprised. 'It's like saying "Don't think of a pink elephant",' he says. 'What then springs to mind?' Noël is not so bothered about the reminder factor, but she does worry that negative messages do not let a child know what a parent *does* want.

I know they are right. It is not as if the negative approach works well in other fields of communication. Bosses who bawl at their office juniors soon find they have a miserable workforce preoccupied by a longing to find another job. Nor does it work with the puppy. When I tell mine off for a misdemeanour, she has no idea what I am talking about – unless I catch her in the act – so she slinks off into a corner and makes me even more cross by nervously leaving a puddle.

We wouldn't dare be constantly critical of our partners for fear they would leave, yet we appear unaware of the ineffectiveness of shouting at and criticising children. Why are we so dim about this?

Noël thinks it is because we tell ourselves that we are acting in the child's best interests: 'Parents who tell children off, criticise or even slap them usually do so with the good intention of wanting the child to do something better or be something better. Luckily, there are other, more effective ways to train children in good habits, but in order to know what and how, it is important to understand why children behave as they do.'

My father tried to train me to be obedient using the same method he tried with Lumpi our dog – including soap in my mouth, hairbrushes, belts and locking me in my room with no food. He never got the dog to stop peeing on the floor and he never got me to behave.

Ruby Wax, TV presenter

Why do children misbehave?

If children, as Noël and Luke believe, yearn to please their parents, it is useful to work out why they often do the opposite. Provoking parents is not a rational choice, although it may be deliberate, Noël believes. Children usually act up because they want attention. In fact, attention seeking is deliberately irritating so that it is difficult for parents to ignore. If a child is in the habit of throwing a tantrum, it may be because that is the most effective way to divert you from your computer screen/telephone calls/cooking. 'Most children do know what they are meant to do,' she says. 'They've been told a hundred times. If they are not in the habit of doing it, perhaps you are asking them to do something that is too hard, but it is probably because they get more attention for not doing as they are told than for cooperating.'

Of course children would prefer positive attention, she explains, but negative attention is better than none, and, as experiments have shown, animals and people would rather have an unpleasant experience than be bored. So if you ignore a child when it is being good – tempting because you can get on with other things – and shout when they behave badly, because you can't ignore it, you are rewarding the bad behaviour. Then, of course, you will get more of the bad behaviour. You will also have a guilty conscience and a child who, if it happens often, feels unable to do anything right and resentful of the critical parent.

'It is a terrible burden,' as Luke says, 'to grow up with the idea that you are impossible.' And yet we go on yelling and losing our tempers, even though it doesn't get us the behaviour we want. Maybe that's how our parents treated us: probably we don't know what else to do that might be more effective. Rather than allowing guilt to paralyse us, he and Noël would rather parents viewed these counter-productive ways as bad habits. Like all habits, they can be changed – with training.

How do you train a child not to behave badly?

With dogs, appreciation of the right behaviour – pats, praise, regular walks so that they don't get caught short or excessively boisterous – works better than punishment. With children, I complained to Noël and Luke, the solution never seems so straightforward. 'Nonsense,' they replied, outlining tried and tested ways to train a child to behave better. Here they are:

1. Descriptive praise

When a child is behaving badly Noël remains positive, looking for and descriptively praising all the good things the child is doing. 'This includes behaviour that is barely acceptable,' she says. 'To a child who often swears I might say, "I'm really glad you didn't swear at me, even though I can see that you are really angry."'

A concerted effort to do this – even making it into a game you play with yourself – will make it easier to see the good things in an exasperating child. It will also give the child the positive attention he deserves. 'Within a fortnight or a month,' she promises, 'you will see a huge difference in the child's willingness to please, as he finds that the parent is more pleased with him.'

I spoke to one mother whose three-year-old had been very diffi-cult following the arrival of his sister. She had tried reasoning with him, taken away his privileges by sending him to bed and even smacked him; none of those tactics had worked. Then she tried descriptive praise: 'At first, it was hard work finding good behaviour to praise,' she says, 'but now he is much calmer, I don't go to bed feeling guilty every night and we are a happier family. Looking back, I think he was naughty because we had a new baby and he wanted attention.'

I was brought up with praise lavished upon me by my parents.
It made me feel good and I have done the same with my chil-
dren. Kids know when they have done wrong and do not need
it rammed down their throats.

Sir Richard Branson, business mogul

2. Action replays

Noël loves action replays because they prevent a situation escalating into chaos. 'A child doesn't go from zero to sixty in five seconds,' she says. 'There will be little acts of annoying behaviour that you have chosen to ignore, either because each act in itself seemed too trivial or fleeting to focus on, or because you don't know what to do about it once it has already happened. If you ignore a series of minor misbehaviours and then finally explode, the child will feel unfairly punished and lose respect both for you and for the rules that are not applied consistently.

'Let nothing go,' she advises. 'Just as I am asking you to notice and mention all the tiny good – or just OK – things your child does, I am also asking you to notice every grab, every nasty tone of voice, every whinge. Instead of scolding, repeating, reminding or lecturing, do an action replay. Ask the child to do or say whatever it was again, but this time in the way they know they are meant to. To begin with, if you have a difficult child, or one who is in the habit of being very impulsive, unless you are doing between ten and thirty action replays a day, you are letting too many tiny misbehaviours slide. That's exhausting, so before you start, you and your partner must agree on the policy so that you can keep each other at it.'

'Also,' Luke adds, 'you have to warn a child that this is what will happen. Tell her the day before what behaviour you expect and build in enough time so that you can ask for the action replays and still get to where you have to be on time. Action replays cannot be done in a rush.'

But, I objected, when I ask my children for an action replay they often ignore me. What do I do then? 'You can say,' Noël replied, "I see you're not yet ready to do the action replay. I'll ask you again in a few minutes." It is very important that nothing else happens until the action replay is completed to the parent's satisfaction: no food, no screen, no requests granted or even discussed, not even a chat. You can say, "I'll be glad to talk about that after you finish the action replay."

'Parents may assume that children will interpret action replays as losing face or giving in. But since there is no shouting or criticising, just a clear, calm, firm requirement, children are usually only too happy to wipe the slate clean by doing the action replay and getting descriptive praise at the end of it. Plus, their life can resume only after the action replay is out of the way.'

Refusals or mucking about, she promised me, were much less common than parents fear.

3. Firmness

Often disobedience arises, Noël believes, because parents don't ask firmly and calmly enough for the behaviour they want in the first place. 'They give attention to the struggle by arguing back, repeating and justifying. They react with more emotion and negativity than they would like. They may also be scared of their own anger, so they repress it and eventually explode.'

It is hard work standing by a decision when children are moaning, sulking, wheedling, nagging or drumming their feet on the ground and I have often given in to a child who has asked for something ten times, just to shut him up. 'You can only be firm,' says Luke, 'if you believe in the possibility that things could get better. They can.'

Rather than give way or compromise, Noël advises parents to think before they speak. 'Compromise involves a measure of retraction. Of course, we should not say "No" to something that we are likely to say "Yes" to a little later.' When you decide to start sticking by your decisions, she recommends announcing the change of policy to your children thus: 'You think that I will give in if you go on and on repeating yourself. I know I have given in a lot in the past, but from now on I am going to practise being firm because I have learnt that changing my mind is not good for you or for me.'

If a child then sulks or lies on the sofa and looks suicidal, don't rise to the bait. 'Don't cajole him out of his mood; he's entitled to his feelings,' says Luke. 'He may not actually be that upset, but sulking may have got him some of what he wants in the past.'

Children act up when they want attention. I don't respond to the acting up. Mostly I ignore them, leave the room and shut the door behind me. But when they are behaving well I give them masses of praise and attention.

Jerry Hall, actress and model

4. Teach temper control

Eighty per cent of men and 60 per cent of women admit to fantasising about murder. 'The rest,' says geneticist Stephen Pinker, 'may be lying.'

Noël and Luke accept that everyone gets angry. Bottling it up is not the solution because it always leaks out – in irritability, martyrdom, comfort eating and a host of other counter-productive habits. Instead they advocate looking at safe and unsafe ways to give vent to emotion. Fighting, shouting and so on have undesirable consequences; going for a run, drawing a picture, punching cushions or pillow-fighting do no harm.

Parents can model temper control for their children, says Luke. 'A parent can say to a child, "In the past I used to lose my temper with you, and you used to wallop your sister. From now on, when I feel like shouting, I'm going to try to leave the room. What are you going to do when you feel like hitting your sister?"

'You could even get the children to help you with *your* temper,' he suggests. 'Ask them why they think you are getting angry and if they have any ideas on how you could avoid the blow-ups. When you lapse, apologise – you don't want the child to feel it is his fault – but say what you intend to do to prevent it happening again.'

5. Change the atmosphere

When children are repeatedly acting up, Noël and Luke believe there is an unmet need, usually for appreciation and for frequent, predictable, one-to-one attention. Other needs may be unearthed by reflective listening, but the child won't talk and you won't feel like listening if there is an atmosphere of blame at home.

Of course there will still be times when all parents are just itching to tell a child what he is doing wrong and why. Eager to follow Noël and Luke's advice, I've tried to do this in a positive way. So instead of saying to a child who won't turn off the radio, 'You are being so selfish,' I have said, 'I feel unhappy because you don't seem to care that you are giving me a headache.'

Noël awarded me only half marks: 'That can still feel like criticism, especially if the child has received a lot of criticism in the past. It would be better if, whenever possible, you notice the child's tiny acts of thoughtfulness and give a clear instruction when you are tempted to criticise.'

6. Rewards and consequences

'Children learn from experience far more effectively than from parental advice,' says Luke, 'so the best way to teach self-control is to set rewards and consequences. If, after hitting your sister, you are grounded, you are less likely to do it again than if you get a lecture about ending up in prison if you carry on like that.

'Make sure the consequences are proportionate: when they are too grave, we don't carry them through. Then you have a rule without a consequence, which is only a nag. And don't forget positive consequences for good behaviour. There is nothing like earning a privilege that you weren't expecting.'

Noël would make the process as positive as possible. 'Rather than taking away privileges when children behave badly,' she says, 'organise their lives so that they have to earn them in the first place. To get the things they want – money, television time, designer clothes, sleepovers – they have to behave calmly and cooperatively, help around the house and do their best at school and with homework.

'Many children are accustomed to getting most of what they want regardless of how well or badly they behave or do in school. So they may be understandably outraged when you change the rules and suddenly they have to start earning what they grew up thinking was their birthright.

To help children accept this new policy, make it easy, at first, for them to earn the goodies. 'As they see that they can succeed at earning, you can gradually stretch them further. At first "Keep your room tidy" might mean only that your child must put dirty clothes in the laundry basket and papers on the desk. After a month, it might also mean vacuuming weekly, and after yet another month, cleaning the windows on the inside.'

7. Slow down

Parents often don't notice whether a child is obeying them or not because they are too busy trying to get the next thing done. 'Slow down,' advises Noël. 'Once you recognise that it is your job to train a child, you won't be in such a rush, and fewer problems will arise.'

Is slapping a child really harmful?

I can't imagine that any parent these days doesn't feel eaten up with guilt if they ever raise a hand to a child. There have been so many campaigns telling us that it is very wrong. Equally, everyone knows how tempting it is to give a really exasperating child a slap, especially when they appear to be 'asking for it'.

When I admitted to the occasional lapse, I was relieved to be told by one of the New Learning Centre teachers that she once kicked her eight-year-old daughter who wouldn't get up (this was, of course, before she learnt better methods). But, although Luke and Noël know that parents resort to violence only in desperation, they still don't approve. 'Do you want to teach children that hitting is OK?' asks Luke. 'It will damage the trust between you and your child because children expect their parents to keep them safe.'

As for those parents who say they were smacked a lot and it did them no harm, they are often, in his view, 'walking evidence to the contrary'. Even those who think the odd slap is harmless wouldn't dream of hitting a baby or a teenager, he points out, but there is a period between the ages of three and ten when many parents think a slap seems acceptable. 'Shouting, slapping and all other signs of bad temper, show loss of control. When that happens, you lose the respect of the child.'

But, I tell him, sometimes I am driven beyond endurance by a particularly irritating bit of behaviour. 'Would you hit a child in front of an NSPCC inspector?' he asks. 'If you really do feel a red mist come over you and cannot control yourself, please seek professional help immediately.'

Chastened, I turned to Noël, saying that sometimes a slap seemed the best way of calling a halt to an escalating situation. 'A slap may seem to work in the short term because it temporarily relieves a parent's frustration, just as screaming at the child might,' she says, 'and unless you know something more effective to do, you will revert to it when you are at the end of your rope.

'The thing to remember is that a slap or bellow is ineffective in the long term because it doesn't motivate children to want to please, and, in fact, it is often ineffective in the short term because the child may just cry and cry instead of doing what you want.

'Teachers can keep order without physical punishment, and so can parents. There are more effective ways to get a child's attention, and more effective ways to stop a child doing something undesirable.'

But surely it's right to slap a child's hand away from the gas controls?

'There is no point in feeling guilty if you slap a child's hand away from the cooker,' she replies, 'but if you have time to do that, you also have time to take the hand away calmly. Then you can do an action replay and end the scenario with descriptive praise and smiles all round. That little bit of training would take only a minute or two. If you don't have a few minutes to invest in training, you need to rearrange your schedule, and probably your priorities too.'

But, she says, parents should not get hung up on guilt if they do administer the occasional slap because that is not the main issue these days: 'Most children don't get smacked regularly. Parental criticism, nagging, irritation and fault-finding can be much more injurious to a child's self-esteem and to the parent–child bond because the "verbal smacking" does happen frequently, often daily, in many families.'

> *My father was the opposite of a disciplinarian. There were no rules in our house. It was not as if you could be grounded. You wouldn't have your toys taken away. You would just be beaten occasionally with strap or fist. My father would say quietly, 'I wouldn't do that if I were you.' And I would do it anyway and he would beat me. I don't bring up my children that way and they, as a consequence, are sweet-natured.*
>
> John Malkovich, actor

What do you do if the child is lashing out?

There are times when children get so worked up that they are a danger to themselves and others. 'Then is the time,' says Luke, 'not for explaining or reasoning, but for action. I would hold him so he can't damage himself or anyone else. The hold needs to be gentle but firm. You want to stop the behaviour without hurting the child.'

Holding a child contains their anger, but touch is also calming. (The parenting teacher who admitted to kicking her daughter found that containing hugs worked far better with her next child.) So it's OK, I check, to bundle a screaming child into the car? 'I have no problem with that,' Luke replies, 'but you know when you shove harder than you need to. At special schools a teacher who feels wound up leaves the task to someone who isn't involved. If you feel angry, let your partner do the bundling.'

What if I am in a foul mood and likely to explode?

Rather than take out the bad humour on the children, he advised me to be open about my mood. 'Saying "Don't talk to me now," or "I advise you to keep out of my way," is better than confusing a child by trying to pretend that you are cheerful and then exploding over some minor issue.

'However, an angry child may not be able to keep a distance, and is likely to provoke further angry exchanges. That's the time,' he says, 'to say that you're angry too, but it is not OK to talk to anyone like that.'

'Of course,' adds Noël, 'if you can bring yourself to, weigh in with lots of descriptive praise and reflective listening. It will help the child and probably calm you down too.'

But, she added, if you notice in yourself a tendency to explode frequently she would go to a doctor. Many mothers who lose their tempers are suffering from PMT or, in these days of late motherhood, menopause; they need help, possibly from relaxation exercises, medication or improved nutrition. Or it may be that you aren't getting away from the children enough, so you feel overwhelmed by their demands and see perfectly normal episodes of disobedience as total loss of control.

What should I do if my child threatens to report me to Childline?

I have paid dearly for the occasions when I have been slightly rougher than necessary. My eldest daughter now routinely offers to ring Childline at the first scent of anger.

'Let her,' says Luke, 'and suggest she calls the police too if she really thinks she has a case. But,' he continues, more seriously, 'the only justification for being rough is that you don't know what else to do.'

Don't smack unless you want your child to learn that hitting solves problems. If you'd rather your child learnt to express him or herself in world, try talking.

Dr Penelope Leach, child-raising expert

TIPS TO AVOID EXPLODING
- Look at the circumstances in which you lash out. Is a slap or a bellow really the most useful response, or is it that you are upset already and at the end of your tether? Parental anger is rarely to do with the children, but they bear the brunt and receive the punishment because their actions are usually the last straw.
- Agree on appropriate consequences for misbehaviour with your partner. Usually one parent is relatively lenient and one is stricter, and when things go wrong we tend towards extremes. Children spot that and play their parents off against each another.
- Accept that training takes time. No one would slap a child for a lavatorial accident; other behavioural problems may also be signs of a child's immaturity.
- Avoid fraught scenes. A slap in the supermarket occurs when the parent is trying to do too much too quickly. Prepare for success so that you have the time, as Noël says, to 'move at the speed of life instead of the speed of light.' Go to the supermarket earlier in the day when neither you nor the child is tired. Give the child items to fetch to keep him busy.
- Don't try to be a saint, be consistent. If a child is being irritating, you will end up exploding anyway, and in the meantime the child will be developing a gambler's taste for excitement: 'Will it work this time?' And, of course, the child who watched a sibling get away with the same

behaviour five minutes earlier will feel aggrieved if he gets the rap.

- Hug, smile and descriptively praise the child, even when you don't feel like it. Watch closely to notice the good – or just OK – things your child is doing even when the situation is tense. That way you won't get so wound up.
- Often a particular child induces rage. Why is that child so badly behaved? Is he unhappy about something at school or at home? Or is he particularly sensitive or immature? Time for some reflective listening.

If you hit your child, you know you've failed.
Lord Puttnam, film producer

Ploys for avoiding blow-ups

Can star charts work?

Star charts are a useful way of motivating children. Earning stars that eventually add up to a reward is fun, and they focus minds on the desired behaviour. The art of using them well, Luke and Noël know from long experience, lies in being clear and realistic about what is required to earn a reward and choosing suitable rewards – not sweets and toys. Noël suggests daily rewards as well as weekly ones: more playtime, staying up a little later, an extra story at bedtime, or a choice about something that the parent usually decides.

Some parents give each child an individual star chart; others prefer a whole family star chart for which parents, too, can earn stars by not getting cross, etc. The goals for each member of the family should be equally easy to achieve; if one child is not earning stars, it may be that the goals are too high. Reset them before the child gets discouraged or resentful.

One mother who tried a whole family star chart for good humour was amazed by its success. Not only did it make the children behave better, it also stopped her losing her temper. 'It made us all aware of having a choice in how we behaved,' she says. The reward at the end of the week was a trip to the pizzeria: 'I hadn't imagined everyone would get so much satisfaction out of such a simple thing.'

Teachers at the New Learning Centre use charts to encourage those behaviours they want to see more of, and divide lessons into fifteen-minute slots so that a child can be constantly earning. 'That approach can work on car journeys,' says Luke. 'Each fifteen minutes must start with a clean slate, no harking back.'

The hardest part with charts, says Noël, is keeping them going. 'Like diets, they only work if you stick to them.'

Is counting a good idea?

By counting to ten you can give yourself a few seconds to simmer down before reacting. It takes the heat out of the situation and gives you back your self-control.

Some parenting experts advise counting to three in front of a child when you want a child to stop doing something. 'It only works if you can count without sounding cross,' Noël warns, 'and if you definitely know that you will take decisive action after you reach "three", with no warnings, reminders, second chances or lecturing.'

'It sounds very simple to do, but it requires the parent to be absolutely firm about the consequences if the child doesn't do as she is told within the required time.'

Does time out work?

This is recommended as the great non-violent punishment for the parent who has had enough. You can either send the child out of the room – which may mean pushing her out as gently as possible and holding the door closed – or, if that is impossible, removing yourself from the scene.

Time out, Luke observes, has more impact if 'time in' is a joy from which a child would not wish to be excluded. 'Another problem with time out,' Noël notes, 'is that parents tend to use it only for big misdemeanours, so they often allow tension to build up because they are not addressing the many tiny, but infinitely irritating, misbehaviours.

'I suggest using time out for every deliberate disobedience, even very minor ones. With disobedience that is impulsive rather than deliberate, I would require an action replay every single time. Don't worry that you will be spending your whole life dealing with misbehaviour. It will work.'

What do you do with a child who shuts himself in his room?

Luke advises leaving him alone to work through his feelings. 'The good thing is that children tend to do so more quickly than adults. If you say, "Take as long as you like – you don't have to come out until it is time for school on Monday morning," that tends to take the steam out of it. Usually there is nothing you need to do with the child right now, and it is important not to let him manipulate you with bad temper or give him any juice by getting upset and arguing.

'If there is a real problem, he'll want to talk about it eventually, and then is the time to listen reflectively.'

Is the occasional row healthy?

Luke's parents had only one row in front of him, shortly before they split up. As a child he connected the two events, so he grew up subconsciously afraid of rowing, thinking that conflict would always lead to the breakdown of a relationship. Since then, he has had to learn when confrontations can be beneficial. 'Rows are fine so long as they move things on,' he says, 'but usually we use them just to endlessly restate our own position and grievances.'

He finds that many people avoid confrontation with their children, as well as their partners, often by telling untruths. We say, 'It's not that I don't trust you . . .' when the truth is that we *don't* trust the child. We are then surprised when the child gets angry or confused.

His advice is to be straight with children, tell them what you think, and then listen reflectively to their feelings.

How do I stop a child swearing or being rude?

Presuming that there is a rule about rudeness and swearing, there should also be a consequence. The swear-box is the traditional solution to this, and not a bad one, says Luke. 'One family I helped,' he says, 'went one better and set up a Foul Emissions Box to cover other uncouth habits, such as burping.' Noël, predictably, suggests descriptive praise, action replays, reflective listening, leading by example, clarifying exactly which words are not allowed, and making children earn their treats.

When my son was repeatedly being rude to one of his sisters, I asked Noël what consequence I might set. 'Should I ban him from having a sleepover?'

'It's not immediate enough,' she replied. 'What does he really care about?'

'His guitar and skateboarding,' I told her.

'Tell your son that he can have his guitar and skateboard after school on any day that he hasn't been rude before school.'

'But that's cruel,' I said, aghast.

'Why? You seem to be assuming he can't control himself and that you will end up having to impose the ban. I believe he can change his habits. Don't you believe that?'

I do, but I still find myself lost for strategies when a child swears at me. It is very hurtful being called an idiot (or worse). Luke suggests that a more effective way to stop them than bleating 'Don't' is to tell the child how you feel. 'It hurts me when you call me an idiot' will help the child to see things from your perspective.

Noël adds, 'Children's rudeness is often a reaction to parents' rudeness. The more rigorously we cultivate the habit of an unhurried, friendly tone of voice, the sooner our children will respond in kind.'

I told her that I really tried to do that, even when a child was being rude to me. 'Then you are not setting a good example,' she replied. 'You are advertising your role as doormat. That might sound contradictory, but it's true. I advise parents to make a very important rule for themselves: answer children (or adults, for that matter) only when they are speaking to you politely (by your standards, not theirs). You may find yourself not talking much during the first few days. Since most rudeness is impulsive, you wait a few seconds after the child stops, and then descriptively praise her for not being rude now. You can then say, "I'll be glad to discuss that, as long as your tone stays polite." If you practise being consistent, it won't take long for children to see that if they want you to respond, they'll have to be respectful.'

TIPS FOR REDUCING BAD LANGUAGE
- Set a family rule about it. No one is allowed to use certain words, and that includes parents. You can't expect children not to think swearing is cool if you storm in moaning about the 'f . . . ing traffic'.
- Explain that it is fine to think whatever we like, using whatever words we like – what goes on in our heads is our own business – but that doesn't mean you can say those things out loud. If you like, allow words that sound a bit similar to swear words, 'Shoot,' etc.
- Descriptively praise (aim for ten times a day) all instances of irritation expressed without swearing. Notice good use of vocabulary.
- When there's a lapse, require an action replay.
- Set rewards and consequences.

What do I do about a child who ignores my instructions?

During one of Noël's visits, my husband was in bed with flu, and one of our daughters had offered to get him a drink. Since Noël was present, I was extra careful to descriptively praise the child for being so thoughtful, but, nevertheless, this perfect scene went awry. The child snatched the kettle, and when I told her not to take a boiling drink upstairs, she ignored me and took it anyway. What should I have done, I asked?

'The action replay,' said Noël, 'because it gets the child to think about what she is doing and why.'

Her sympathy was, however, entirely with the child. 'Of course she ignored you,' she explained. 'You often don't sound as if you mean what you say, and quite often you don't follow through. If you want to be obeyed, you have to make everything stick, not just some things.'

How do you deal with a child who is feeling guilty?

'If a child is feeling guilty about something he did,' says Luke, 'if he pinched or lied or hurt another person, then it's OK to feel bad. It's part of the teaching mechanism: we want children to care. There's a balance and a natural rhythm in the situation. You hit your sister, she is in pain, you feel bad, eventually she forgives you and you forgive yourself.

'And if you feel cross about something big the child did wrong, you should say so, adding that you still love the child. If you button your lip and don't admit to your own upset feelings, the child can sense your upset and becomes very confused. That makes it harder for the child to work through his own feelings and then forgive himself.

'A child who can't stop feeling guilty about one misdeed may be blaming himself for something outside the immediate situation – the break-up of the parents' marriage, for example. Then there is a need for sitting down and talking, not explaining but listening reflectively. We shouldn't tell children not to feel guilty: it's part of allowing them not to be happy all the time.'

> *Feelings are what children know about. They often feel they are frightful and wicked and hate people and want to kill them; it's surprising how rarely they do.*
>
> Nina Bawden, author

Should you ask a child to say sorry?

As soon as one of my children hurts another or breaks something, I tell him to say sorry. Rarely does a child do so with good grace. Luke and Noël sympathise with the children.

'Of course, it may be that the child is sorry but is not in the habit of saying so, in which case a simple reminder will be sufficient,' says Noël. 'If the child isn't yet sorry, you are asking him to lie. When parents ask a child to say sorry, it is almost always because the child *isn't* sorry. One of our jobs is to help children feel remorse.' For that you need the mistakes process.

How do I handle mistakes?

Every day someone in my family – often it is me – makes a mistake. Usually I have forgotten to do something or falsely accused a child or committed some other heinous crime. I then apologise copiously (even excessively) in the hope that the children will pick this up and copy it. It doesn't seem to work like that.

When the children make mistakes they tend to do one of the following:

Tactic 1: They hide it, distancing themselves from the mess or screaming sibling, like a murder-in-the-dark suspect, so when the mistake is revealed, they can then pretend it has nothing to do with them.

Tactic 2: This occurs when the mistake is so obvious – a broken vase, perhaps – that the noise and mess bring instant parental attention. The child then instantly shifts the blame on to a sibling: 'He made me.'

Tactic 3: This involves blaming a parent: 'You should have told me that I had to have my homework in on Wednesday.'

Each tactic is followed by several people screeching at once in self-justification. So I asked Noël and Luke how I might handle such moments better. 'You need The Mistakes Process,' they both said. This is a technique they learnt when working with young offenders. Before that, however, they reminded me of what I was doing wrong: my first mistake was to lecture.

'Parents often think that a child will not learn unless he feels bad about whatever he did wrong,' says Noël, 'but it is important to take guilt, which often paralyses, out of the equation. If children feel bad, they will tend to repeat the thing they have done wrong, whether it is hitting a sibling or not doing homework, because they see themselves as bad. Children are far more likely to learn and behave differently if we help them to feel true remorse and also to see how they could change.'

Luke backs her up. 'If you sit feeling bad, you miss the opportunity to discover that there's a way you can clear these things up.' But first he told me to watch my words: 'Don't talk about a child doing something wrong – even if it was deliberate – but about making a mistake. Take out the moral dimension.

116

'A mistake is something that doesn't work to get you what you want,' he says. 'If a child hits his sister because she took his toy, we could talk about it as a strategy that didn't work. After all, what happened? The child's game was disrupted because he became angry and his sister ran to Mummy. If you talk about it like that, you are more likely to help the child explore ways of preventing it happening again. It may sound a bit pious, but mistakes are an opportunity to learn.'

THE MISTAKES PROCESS
It happened. Acknowledge the mistake has been made. There's the broken vase or crushed fingers as proof. All those involved can state the facts as they see it.
You did it. Even if a child isn't wholly responsible for the broken vase, he can acknowledge his part in the mistake.
Clear up. That may mean picking up the pieces or even going to the doctor.
Make amends. There are logical consequences to every action, and if clearing up the mess has meant that you haven't got time to empty the dishwasher, the child should have to do that, or at least help.
Make sure it doesn't happen again. Here's the real learning. If your sister comes into your room, takes your doll and this makes you so angry that you slam the door on her fingers, how could you set things up differently?
Move on and cheer up (parents included). That mistake is history and not to be brought up again as a reproach or a nag.

Yes, but how do I get a child to admit responsibility?
'This,' Luke acknowledges, 'is the hardest part of the mistakes process. It may take time. A child won't want to admit that it was his fault, especially if he has been criticised and blamed a lot. Guilt and a desire to shift the blame on to someone else tend to consume the person who has made a mistake. Parents do it too. 'Look what you made me do!' is a common expression from a parent who has just slapped a child and feels guilty.

'The parent needs to help the child feel that it is not the end of the world to admit responsibility, and the way to do that is through descriptive praise and reflective listening.

'If the child still won't admit responsibility, then you have to look to the consequences – the vase got broken – and work backwards to how it happened.

'The child may end up taking partial responsibility but may well say that another child was also partly responsible, but that he always gets blamed (which may well be true). If you are sure that you don't always blame, say, the elder child and assume that the younger one is a saint, stick to your guns.'

'But,' Noël warns, 'most of us are guilty of assuming that one child is the perpetrator and the other is the victim, so really examine your conscience. It is wisest to assume that it takes two to tango.'

Is apologising a sufficient way of making amends?
'An apology is seldom enough to make amends, but it's a good start,' said Noël. 'Nor is it the most urgent part, so it can wait until the child has calmed down and had time to think and become truly sorry. Once the child is sorry, parents can help her to think creatively about what would make the aggrieved party feel better. Sometimes an action replay is enough. Talking about the 'mend' part of the word 'amends' can help the child to see that the relationship or friendship needs to be mended (or healed), not just the broken toy or vase.'

TIPS FOR GETTING A CHILD TO ADMIT A MISTAKE
- Don't stand over the child and try to catch his eye – that's intimidating. Some children and a lot of teenagers want to defeat their parents. It is difficult to look at someone who is saying something unpleasant, so don't expect them to. Praise them instead for staying put or glancing at you occasionally.
- If the child walks off, don't follow. Following means the child is setting the agenda. If the child looks away, stop talking. He will immediately look to see why you have stopped. Reflect the child's feelings by saying something like, 'This may be boring or upsetting.'

- Don't explain. It makes us feel rational but it has the opposite effect on children – 'Blah, blah, blah,' they think.
- Ask if the child knows what you want to talk about. Standard reply: 'Dunno.' Your response: 'If you don't know, take a guess.' If the child gets it right, you are away. If the child is wrong, you praise their courage in guessing. Most likely the child will say, 'I'm not listening.' So you say, 'Maybe you're not listening because you think I'm going to tell you off or criticise you.' Even if you are angry, you are not going to do that because it is counter-productive, so choose a time to discuss things when you aren't cross. That goes against the natural instinct. When we are relaxed we want to stay that way rather than deal with a difficult situation.
- Let the child describe the problem. Praise the child for doing so. You are then ready to return to the mistakes process.

8

CHORES

How do you get a child to tidy her room? Why is the whole house such a mess? How do I get the children to help around the house? How do I make them more independent?

Children are exhausting because they generate so much work. There are the rooms to be tidied, the washing, the cooking, the packed lunches, the shopping . . . The list goes on and on, I sometimes moan. I should have known better than to expect sympathy from Noël and Luke.

One evening Luke came round to my house and, by talking to me, clamped me to my seat for two hours when I would normally have been scurrying after the children. I discovered then that my twelve-year-old could cook his own dinner and my ten-year-old could iron her own shirt. The eight-year-old willingly took a message to a neighbour, while the six-year-old washed her own hair and the three-year-old put himself to bed. I ended the evening considerably less tired than usual, mystified as to how I had landed the role of maid of all works – and determined to shed it.

Noël and Luke are familiar with this kind of parental martyrdom, which can sometimes be a form of surreptitious control. Keeping children helpless is one way of hanging on to our babies, even when they begin to tower over us. Unless they are required to use public transport, cook, wash, iron and clear up – even if they don't want to – it will make the process of growing up to be responsible and independent harder than it needs to be. Although I gag when I see a six-year-old in a pushchair, who could perfectly well walk, or a teenager being ferried around by a parent, I know I do far more for my children than I should. If there weren't five of them – and the dog to walk – I'm sure my husband and I would do even more.

If you are doing too much, the only way to get it all done is by being in a perpetual rush, so my next mistake, I learnt, is to expect my children also to be able to operate at top speed. 'Children operate much more slowly than adults,' Luke reminded me. 'They don't know how to organise themselves. They are only learning. A parent's job is to train them, and that means teaching them step by step how to do all the things that an adult does without thinking.'

Although it might seem quicker to carry on doing everything myself, he reminded me that I needed to train the children in self-reliance for their sakes, not just for mine. 'Children who are too dependent on their parents often have a tougher adolescence as they adjust to coping on their own. I see many students arrive at university feeling helpless and disorientated because they have had so much done for them right up until they leave home. They get into deep trouble: who is going to want to share a flat with someone who never clears up the kitchen?'

No wonder, he observes, that we are seeing the growth of twenty-something 'boomerang babies', who return home after they have been to college because no one else will either tolerate them or wait on them hand and foot. 'Parents think they are being loving when they do things for their children, but it teaches children to associate love with people doing things for them. Children come to expect it and see it as their right, and if parents feel taken for granted and resentful, how will flatmates or girlfriends feel? You don't want their main training for life to consist of ordering around a willing slave.'

Although it is hard to disagree, it still seemed to be beyond me to get children to learn the basics of looking after themselves. The official rule in our house is that children tidy their own rooms, but they do it by sweeping the mess under the bed, where it festers. As for the playroom, that is such a pigsty that a piano teacher on his first visit denounced it as a 'health hazard' as he picked his way across the floor.

Mortified by that, I turned on the children as soon as he left and shrieked that I was going to throw all the toys in the bin. They completely ignored me, until I turned off the television, whereupon there was a chorus of groans, followed by self-righteous complaints of 'It wasn't me, it was her'. Discussion descended into argument: 'If you don't want us to play with toys,' asked the seven-year-old, 'why did you buy them?'

At that point, I learnt from Luke and Noël later, I made my first wise move – I stomped out and took the dog for a walk. 'Zip the lip' is one of the key pieces of advice they hand out: there is no point getting involved in debates that will only descend into disputes. Here is the rest of their advice on training children to do chores or, as Noël puts it, changing the master–servant relationship into one of team-work.

1. Begin early

'It's a good idea to get children doing some chores by the time they are three or four, before they realise that they are expected to hate housework,' says Noël. I have noticed that while the older ones complain about tidying their rooms, the three-year-old thinks it's a hoot.

'If you start when they are young, it won't take too long to train them,' says Luke, 'if you wait until they are fourteen, expect war. The whole issue will become mixed up with rebellion.'

As it is, many parents let children slide backwards as they get older, saying that they cannot stomach the battles. There may be another reason too. 'When we were little,' one teenager told me, 'our parents treated us as older than we were, but now we are older, they want us to be babies again.'

Whatever the age, there should be one rule for the whole family: if the youngest gets away with doing nothing, it will create arguments.

2. Have reasonable expectations

I represent one common problem when it comes to tidying up: sluttish tendencies. Noël and Luke are familiar with another, equally unhelpful, attitude: perfectionism. 'Some people are so tidy that you wonder why they ever had children,' says Luke.

There are couples whose homes are so spotless that it seems impossible they actually live in them, or that children play among the carefully arranged *objets*. Even making toast is banned because it creates crumbs. They advise such parents to set aside part of the house as a child-proof zone but to relax the rules elsewhere so that they don't always have to be nagging about not touching things.

Nor will the children of perfectionists ever be able to do chores themselves to an acceptable standard. 'Expectations that are too high,' warns Noël, 'create friction, and friction leads to criticism, which won't achieve anything.'

Perfectionists may drive themselves and others mad but, she pointed out, at least they show children that chores are worth doing. 'If we take an upbeat line that chores are something that have to be done to make life better, it isn't so hard to persuade children to do them too. Of course, if you complain about chores, the children will pick up on that too.'

As for the slobs, our expectations may be unrealistically low: 'Keep an eye,' she advises, 'not just on what the children can already do, but on what you would like them to be able to do. Once they have mastered one task, train them to do the next one.'

3. Prepare for success

If you have let children be slobs, Noël says, 'Give them a few days' warning that you are going to set new rules. Don't announce these in the heat of the moment when you are cross. And not when they are watching TV. If you have allowed them to be plugged into their favourite drug, trying to talk to them at that time will only create resentment.'

If you are going to teach them how to tidy their rooms, allow enough time. A young child cannot restore order like Mary Poppins with a snap of the fingers. Five minutes is not enough either.

4. Get everyone's ideas

Chores are a whole household issue, so everyone should be involved in deciding on the who/what/when/where of the distribution of tasks. Luke recommends a family meeting and, to prevent interruptions, he suggests all children should go to the loo beforehand.

'Discuss what needs to be done,' he says. 'The children will know, but they won't be used to thinking about it. We shouldn't do their thinking for them: they can come up with a list of tasks, from putting away toys to emptying the dishwasher. Without their involvement, you won't get far.'

My children's ideas were largely facetious. 'Put us in the bin,' said the six-year-old. 'Throw away all the toys,' said the ten-year-old.

'Stay with it,' is Luke's advice. 'You could write down all the ideas and then review the list at the end of the meeting. Usually, once the children have been silly, they come up with more sensible ideas. If they make out that they can't see the need for a discussion of chores, throw the question back to them: "Why do you think we need your help?" Putting it like that gives you a position of authority and the child a role to play. It also helps the child to see things from your point of view.'

5. Set clear rules

Many children will start out by doing the minimum necessary, so if you say 'Tidy your room' and they put all the mess on the chair, they will feel aggrieved if you don't approve. Objectives, says Noël, should be clear and detailed: books should be on the shelf, clothes should be in the drawers, folded, or in the washing basket. 'If the rules aren't clear, the children will get them wrong, feel criticised and annoyed and then give up.'

Writing down the rules or steps ensures there is no ambiguity. When going through them with a child, she advises weaving them into a narrative so that they feel less like the barked orders of a sergeant major.

'The clearer the rules, the less you need to do the child's thinking for him,' said one woman at a parenting class, who had got her children into the habit of tidying up. 'Now I don't have to say, "Pick up your pyjamas," which can cause a row: I just say, "I see pyjamas on the floor." My son knows what to do and doesn't feel blamed. Sometimes all I have to do is give a look or make an agreed secret sign."

Parents need to stick to the rules too, Noël reminded me when I complained about untidiness. If I ignored the mess for long periods and then spasmodically exploded with annoyance, I was not being positive, firm and consistent, was I?

6. Do it together

If a child doesn't instantly get the hang of a new rule, show exactly what you mean by doing the work with her. 'You have to put some energy, thought and time into making things happen,' says Noël, but she reminds parents that doing something, even a chore, with children can be an opportunity to have a nice time together and reinforce the message that chores can be enjoyable.

During the training phase, when the parent does the tidying with the child, she advises parents to watch their tone of voice: 'Often what feels horrible about clearing up is that children are told to do it in an annoyed voice, as if it were a punishment. Chores need not be a bore, remember. Creating order can be a pleasure. You could help children think about the task by saying in a light voice, "Would you like me to help? What would you like me to do?"

'If the child says, "You could put the Lego in the box," you could ask what they will be doing while you do that. "Maybe it would be better if I helped you with the puzzles, as they need sorting," you could say. It all gets them thinking.'

7. Keep it up

If their rooms are allowed to get too messy, children won't be able to face doing the tidying. Noël recommends making tidying a twice-a-day habit, before school and before bed, then things can't get too bad.

'Making something happen is about follow through, not reminders,' she says. And in the holidays, when there is more time, teach new skills to add to their repertoire – how to fold a shirt, for example. 'Don't forget, these skills are just as useful as long division.'

8. Teach step by step

Children can't pick up the skills of self-reliance by watching a parent demonstrate them at a speed that must seem as rapid as time-lapse photography.

Every chore can be broken down into a sequence of steps. With complicated operations, Luke and Noël recommend starting at the last stage. Bed-making for very young children could, for example, consist of putting the duvet straight. Once that has become a habit, you can add in the preceding step, putting the pillow straight, and so on until they can do the whole thing.

To teach organisation, label drawers so that the child knows what goes where.

9. Praise descriptively

Always descriptively praise what the child has done – not just the results, but the efforts or even, in the early stages, not running away but watching what you are doing in order to learn. Mastering a new domestic skill and being praised for it builds not only self-reliance but confidence too, especially in children who aren't feeling successful at school.

10. Listen reflectively

Requiring a child to do something that looks like hard work is unlikely to be greeted rapturously. There is bound to be a storm of 'Why?' questions. 'One mistake is to feel we should answer children's every question,' says Noël. 'But there is no point in answering "Why?" questions until the child has taken a guess first. You can say: "Maybe you really want to know why, or maybe you are telling me that you really don't want to do this."

'It helps,' she says, 'if we can guess at their feelings. You could try: "Maybe you would rather I just did it all and you could watch television?" Acknowledging feelings is not the same as giving in to them; nor do we always have to find a solution to a moan – the child might not even need a solution. Often a child just needs a parent to listen while she lets off steam by complaining for a while.

'For maximum effectiveness, combine descriptive praise and reflective listening, as in: "You probably don't want to do this now but I am really pleased that you aren't making a fuss."'

'As children get older,' Luke warns, 'you have to help them get into the habit of doing more listening and problem-solving. One strategy is to hold a weekly family meeting so that the children can have their say about whatever they think is not working well. It may be difficult clearing up, for example, if someone else throws crisp packets at the bin and usually misses. We can't protect children from frustration, but we can give them the tools to cope.'

Sometimes complaints require responses . . . One woman at a parenting class listened to her child moan about making his own breakfast and said, 'I don't always feel like making my own dinner, but it has to be done.'

Sometimes no response is required . . . When a child says something like, 'X doesn't have to walk back from school, his mum collects him, so why won't you collect me?' Luke advises against jumping on to the defensive and giving a long justification. 'Children usually know the answers; they probably don't need to be told.' Often, after they have had their say, they will later come to the conclusion that 'X is spoilt' or 'X's house is much further away'.

11. Put the idea in the child's mind

Once you have set the rules and made sure each child knows what has to be done, it is not necessary to say ten times a day, 'Flush the loo.' Tempting though it is to keep telling a child what to do, the child is more likely to remember in future if you make him do the thinking by saying, 'And what do you have to do now?'

Let circumstances do the reminding. One mother at a parenting class found that her children never remembered to put their clothes in the washing baskets behind their bedroom doors, so she plonked one in the middle of the bathroom. They couldn't avoid noticing it. Instant results.

12. Inject humour

A light touch helps with all age groups, but with older children humour is essential to prevent them going into revolt against being bossed about and treated like babies. One mother whose messy children were driving her mad wrote little poems about the bottle top begging to be put back on the bottle. When she found her son's trainers in the hall, she left a note in them that read like a plea from the trainers themselves to be allowed back into his room.

13. Use rewards and consequences

I once wailed to Noël about how my children didn't put their towels on the rail, pick up their clothes, prepare their school bags or shut doors behind them (unless with an emphatic slam). 'They know they are meant to,' I moaned. She was patient. 'Unless you attach a reward or consequence,' she pointed out, 'your rules are not rules, they are wishes or nags.'

'Rewards are the key when it comes to chores,' Luke believes, 'and the biggest reward for a small child is parental attention and praise. With older children the rewards and consequences have to be subtler. Attach them to pocket money or other things they make choices about. The point is to make them aware that they do have choices, and that some choices have better results than others.'

He would tell children that the only things they are entitled to by right are food, warmth, shelter, love and basic clothes, and that everything else has to be earned by good behaviour. 'This is much less likely to lead to friction than removing privileges when work isn't done.

'When you have to set a consequence, make it logical so that *it* does the job of reminding and *you* don't have to. If clothes aren't in the washing basket, for example, they don't get washed; no one eats until the cat has been fed. And if a child who rarely helps around the house notices that you cease to be available to drive her about, it might get her thinking.

'The child might not like to think the events are linked, but if she asks "What's going on?", you can throw the question back by asking, "What do you think is going on?" It is always good to get them doing the thinking.'

Noël would make sure that children are kept aware of the link between doing chores and earning privileges by often saying, 'I'll be delighted to do that for you when you have done what you have to do.' But don't add, 'And if you don't, I won't.' Stay positive; stick with the implication that the child will, eventually, do the right thing.

Sometimes it is hard to be tough about consequences, I said to the teacher at one parenting class. She agreed. A rule in her household was that shoes left lying about on the floor would be impounded; this meant that one morning her daughter had no footwear for school. 'I could have let her go in trainers,' she said, 'but instead I agreed to release the school shoes provided she agreed to do a chore later. She emptied the dishwasher before dinner.'

What if some children are helpful and others aren't?

Noël advises parents to notice which children are expected to help most: usually it is girls. 'Mothers often let boys off the hook because they are more disorganised and it is easier to do the task for them. Some girls too get away with not helping as much as they should by being charming but quietly evasive. That's not good training for life. It may take some children longer to learn to look after themselves, and come less naturally, but they still need to learn.'

With several children, I find that they moan (with justification) that they didn't make a mess in the playroom, so why should they clear up. Noël suggests that I make my expectations absolutely clear. A useful rule is to have a set time when all members of the family have to tidy up, either the playroom or their bedrooms or, if they haven't made a mess recently, a kitchen cupboard. It could be that the next meal happens only after the tidying is finished. She says, 'I would insist on everyone at least being in the playroom during the tidying. Then you can descriptively praise those who are actually doing it, while ignoring those who are twiddling their hair.'

I was thinking of creating a rota. One child at a time would help with the chores and I would try to make this a special one-to-one time. Noël was doubtful about the scheme. 'There will be days when you have to change the rota, but that isn't a reason in itself for not starting one,' she said. 'My real reservation is that rotas involve management.' After a few minutes' discussion I decided that running the rota would be a chore for me, so I abandoned the idea.

No wonder they (boys) have a reputation for running about like headless chickens, leaving a trail of dirty shoes and socks . . . This has nothing to do with the testosterone running through their veins, but something to do with being given permission.

Jenni Murray, broadcaster

What do I do about all the toys?

One reason why I ignore the children's mess is that it upsets me to go through the toys and realise how many of them were expensive, useless mistakes that held the children's attention for no longer than the television advertisements that created the craving. Frankly, they could almost all be thrown away, but that seems tantamount to staggering out to the dustbin with a sack full of £20 notes.

Noël knew exactly what she would do. She would limit the toys in circulation at any one time to five per child. This was not puritanism, she explained, but sound developmental policy. 'No one is saying that you shouldn't give your children lovely things, but having too many toys out at the same time encourages children to have short attention spans. They rush from one to the other as they do in a toy shop and may not play with anything properly. Also, toys get stepped on, bits get lost and tidying up is more daunting and takes far longer. Children become accustomed to living with confusion and clutter. This is not a habit we want them to develop. And children come to believe that more is better, and new is better.'

Chucking out the toys would cause ructions and be wasteful, we agreed, so instead I could set many of them aside in boxes with stickers giving the date on which they would be brought out and others put away. I would probably find the children never mentioned them again but, if there were hysterics, they would be less violent than if the toys had gone for good – not, of course, that avoiding hysteria should dictate policy.

Having toys in storage, Noël pointed out, provides a good opportunity for children to earn the reward of exchanging one toy for another. 'Make it easy for the child to succeed. The way to earn a swap could be going to bed without making a fuss. You want the child to feel successful at earning rewards.'

An additional way of whittling down the toys would be to announce before a birthday or Christmas that we need to make space for the fresh influx by giving some of the old ones away to charity. 'That way children learn about compassion *and* sharing *and* recycling,' she announced triumphantly, 'and there isn't so much to tidy.'

I am deeply opposed to plastic of all kinds, and even more opposed to plastic in primary colours, so, for me, confronting the world of children's toys is an aesthetic and moral nightmare. The average child brings into the world fifty times his own weight in non-biodegradable goods. I can't prevent other people giving plastic toys, but I can cull them regularly by putting them in the barn, and if they forget about them, I throw them away.

Roger Scruton, philosopher

Is it ever too late to train a child to do chores?

My eldest child seems not to notice that his room is a smelly, un-navigable mess of dirty underclothes and discarded bits and pieces. One thing is clear: 'It is definitely not appropriate to tidy up for him,' says Luke. 'You can either decide to let him leave his room as he likes until he gets sick of it, or you can set minimum standards and help by setting the terms, not by doing the work.

'Older children and teenagers use mess as an easy way to wind up their parents. Don't fall for the trick and get into arguments. Just start setting logical rewards and consequences now. Tell him he will get the more expensive new trainers he wants only if he keeps his clothes tidy.'

But do teach a child *how* to clear up, says Noël. 'Many children don't know that you put books on the shelf and clothes on the chair. Once he has started, offer to help. That way you are making it plain that it is his job, but fun too, so you want to be involved. And make sure it is done daily – that way every day he sees the room looking tidy and feels that that is how it ought to look.

'Here is a way to accustom children to tidying up by breaking daunting tasks into bite-size pieces. Whenever a child asks for something that you are happy to agree to, for example, play with him, watch television, ring a friend, drive him somewhere, say, "Yes, as soon as you put all the Lego in the basket, or the furniture in the doll's house, or cups in the sink, etc." Another way to take the sting out of tidying is to offer a choice between two options: "Do you want to put away six books or eight? Hang up three jackets or four?" This conveys that the child must tidy, but is friendlier than an order.'

'It usually takes only a few occasions when you follow through properly to get training under way. Don't imagine that you are condemning yourself to a constant cycle of refusals and consequences and bottle out before you start,' she said, introducing me to her six steps to get children into the habit of cooperating.

SIX STEPS TO ACHIEVING COOPERATION

This strategy may seem slow but it's an investment – and it's quicker than a strategy that doesn't work.

1. Stop what you are doing and look at your child.
2. Wait until the child looks at you and stops whatever he is doing. If the child doesn't stop right away, get down on the floor and take an interest in whatever he is doing. Establishing friendly contact is vital before introducing an unwelcome subject, such as tidying.
3. Having got the child's attention, state whatever it is you want him to do clearly, simply and only once. Don't repeat yourself. If you get into the habit of repeating yourself, children will learn to respond only when a note of hysteria enters your voice.
4. Ask the child what he is supposed to be doing. If he says he doesn't know, say, 'Take a guess.'
5. Stand and wait. No sitting or slouching, no repetition, no telling off, just smiling and waiting as if you could stand there for ever.
6. While standing and waiting, notice and mention everything that your child is doing right, every step in the right direction. If the child is not doing anything you wish for, then notice the things he is not doing wrong: 'You're not arguing. Thank you.' Reflectively listen to his probable feelings: 'I bet you wish you could keep playing football instead of having to start your homework.'

Note: There is no seventh step that says give up. Keep doing Step 6.

How do I teach a child to cook without it ending in disaster?

One of my daughters is convinced that she knows how to cook, so, exasperated by her arrogance, I once said, 'OK, make a risotto, then. Here are the ingredients and this is what you do. Good luck.' The result was a charred mess, a humiliated child and a guilty parent.

'You could get her to do cooking alongside you,' Noël suggested, 'not as master and servant, but as boss and apprentice. Set out the ground rules. Get the child to explain to you what she thinks are the steps in making risotto rather than you telling her. When a child does the explaining, the experience belongs to her. You can tell her all the bits she has got right and make it into a positive rather than a humiliating experience.

'If she still insists on doing it her own way and screws up, let her, but never hark back to it. Move on. Even if a child does something and gets it wrong, you can always praise her courage in trying.'

How do I handle a child who resents having to do something?

On several occasions, one of my children has been sent home from school for having nits. Then there is panic and the child telephones me at work and tells me, usually in a none-too-polite manner, that I have to deal with the nits as soon as I get home.

One of these calls made me so angry that when I arrived home I asked the child – calmly, I thought – how she might have handled the call better. The door was slammed. My approach was sending mixed messages, said Noël. 'Even if you are blaming in a nice voice, you are still blaming. We all want to distance ourselves from someone who tells us how wrong we are, so of course she ran out of the room. It was her way of defending herself from your criticism.'

Noël is intrigued to notice that, even when parents hear children say, 'OK, OK, OK' or 'Whatever' with a roll of the eyes, signifying that they are not listening, most of us carry on lecturing pointlessly. She has come to the conclusion that we do so because we don't know what else to do to influence our children's behaviour.

'OK, OK, OK,' I said, I handled that situation badly; what should I have done? 'First off, I suggest you make a rule for yourself that you only answer people who speak to you in a friendly or polite way. Then, when your daughter telephones, you can start by being silent in response to her bossy tone. When she pauses for breath, you can say something like, "Ah, you've stopped giving me orders. That's much nicer." Then you praise her for being so keen to get started on tackling the nits. If, instead, you react with anger, you perpetuate the vicious circle. When parents stop criticising, sooner or later a child will drop the self-defence, and then you have more chance of getting to the bottom of what is bothering her. It is safe to assume that there is a valid need behind all upset behaviour. It helps if parents slow down and think what that need might be. In addition to the obvious physical needs – hunger, thirst and sleep – most children need more positive attention, less criticism, less screen time, etc.'

I said that I felt the child needed to feel in control of the situation. 'That's not a need, that's a want, but you could be right. She may well feel powerless and embarrassed about these recurring nits, and she may even feel humiliated. When people feel powerless, they often try to make themselves feel better by bossing others around. Without realising it, you are making it easy for the child to shift the blame on to you by justifying yourself. It suggests you are not sure of your ground. Instead of explaining, arguing or cajoling, stay calm and positive. More descriptive praise and more reflective listening. You'll be less upset, and so will she.'

The next episode in the nit saga occurred the following morning when I woke the child up early for shampooing and combing. She blew up at me for making myself a cup of tea before getting down to work. I got cross and said I was only trying to help her. What had I done wrong?

'You could have praised her for getting up so early, and then asked her to explain in detail what was going to happen. She may know, or she may need to guess. Either way, she is learning to take more responsibility for the procedure. She will be focusing more on solutions than on problems. She will also be focusing more and more on what she needs to do, rather than on what you should be doing for her. She was probably nervous that you would not work fast enough on the nits so she would have to go to school with them and get into trouble. You could soothe her impatience by imagining what she is feeling and saying something like, "This is upsetting for you. I wish I had a magic wand and could make the nits disappear for ever." Reflective listening shows the child that you are on her side.'

Next I was snapped at by my daughter for not having got the towel and the brush ready the night before. 'Instead of justifying yourself, you could have praised her for remembering those things herself,' Noël explains. 'Don't react as if you and she are on the same level: she is a child and you are an adult. When she is finding fault with you, you can start to reverse the process and improve the atmosphere by finding positive things to say about her.'

Then, I wailed, she dared to complain that the water was the wrong temperature. 'Of course,' she sighed, 'by this time you felt irritated and possibly even hurt by all her criticisms. You may have felt like being horrible back to her. But all that had happened is that you didn't prepare for success, so she was expecting you to wait on her, as you often have done. Without your realising it, your historical stance of appeasement has encouraged her to treat you like a not-very-competent servant. It's time to resign! Ask her to get the water temperature right as you cannot know what is right for her.'

And to cap it all, my daughter said that the child-minder is better at dealing with nits than I am. 'Don't rise to the bait and call her churlish and ungrateful. You can say that you are quite sure she does it differently because everyone has their own style. And you can add that you are willing to respond to requests, but not to complaints or commands.'

Should I make the children work for their pocket money?

Pocket money, say Noël and Luke, is an invaluable tool in training children, but I was not making the most of its magic powers by constantly threatening to dock money for bad behaviour. 'It's much more effective,' says Luke, 'to let children earn pocket money by doing all the things they are meant to do.'

When I protested that it seemed a bit harsh, he drew my attention to the fact that this is how the adult world works. If parents want to soften the regime, he suggested making half the pocket money the children's by right, and the other half earned.

'If you work it out so that it comes to, say, 30p a day for doing as you require, then you have to be absolutely clear what is expected: making beds, clearing up after breakfast, going to bed without making a fuss. Of course, these targets should be easy to hit; you don't want to spend hours adjusting each child's money or create opportunities for sibling rivalry. Nor do you want to spend your whole time arguing about what is required.'

But what if one of the children is very young? 'A father of a five-year-old,' he replied, 'once asked me if his son was too young for pocket money. I said no. Once a child knows that money buys things and that £1 is worth more than 50p, they have a rudimentary concept of money and are ready to earn it.'

This father then went to the bank and got some little brown envelopes and polished up the coins he put into them to make it really exciting for the child. Without going to those lengths, Luke thinks that most parents could work out a weekly pay packet and give it on Friday, even enclosing a payslip so that the child knows exactly what he is getting and why.

He would graduate the amounts according to age, so there is an incentive to grow up and become more responsible. 'If the rules relating to pocket money are clearly set, there are fewer arguments and it is easier to police.'

When money that could have been earned is not earned, he would ask the child what he did to earn the amount he received, and what more the child would need to do the following week to get the full amount. In between times, he would not give or lend money. If there is to be a holiday bonus, it should come with a clear explanation of what it is for and when it is to be spent.

The point of all this, he explains, is not just to give children an incentive to do their chores, but to give them a better chance of being competent with money by the time they leave home. 'As it is, far too many teenagers run into trouble because they have never had to earn money: all they have ever done is hold out their hands.'

How do I train children to be sensible with money?

'Start involving children in the money that is spent on them as early as possible,' says Luke. 'If you are going to buy a new school bag, you could announce how much money you intend to spend and get the child to do the research and find the best deal. When children show that they regularly pick up their clothes and put them in the washing-machine, they might be given a small clothes budget. "There are a few jobs you have to do to earn this," you tell them, and have them tell you what the jobs are. Kids are so image-conscious that a clothes budget can be a real incentive to be responsible.'

Of course, the parent has to separate out very clearly what will be bought for a child – school uniform, casual clothes to a certain limit, furnishings for their rooms – and what is their discretionary spending. There will be disagreements, Luke accepts, but they are all to the good. 'Useful discussions,' he says, 'can arise when you have to put goods into categories.'

To take an example close to my eight-year-old's heart, is a glass rose for a room, a furnishing (and therefore down to me to pay for) or an ornament (and comes out of her pocket money)? 'If you cannot agree, put the problem to a family meeting. It is important for children to realise that they can live without some of the things they want, so start the conversation about priorities early.'

After children have mastered weekly pocket money, Luke would move on to a monthly allowance, which calls for parents to do much more training in planning and self-control. 'A twelve-year-old is capable of learning to do most of her own clothes shopping success-fully, as long as parents are clear about the rules. By all means give advice if you have a child who appreciates your advice. You could suggest that if she desperately wants expensive jeans, she could economise by looking for trainers in the market or finding a jumper in the charity shop. But don't expect your advice to be acted on: it rarely is.'

No matter how carefully parents prepare for success, the child will make mistakes, buy things that fall apart and then beg for more money. 'At that point you listen reflectively, but don't get sucked in to feeling sorry for her or bailing her out,' says Luke. 'A child won't die of embarrassment if she doesn't have the latest and most expen-sive trainers. You could offer to buy the cheapest available if she really has no shoes, but you want her to think about quality in future. She's more likely to learn the right lessons when she has to live with the consequences.'

And what about a child who seems unable to learn to manage money? Noël replies: 'It's highly unlikely that he can't learn. He may temperamentally be more disorganised, impulsive and immature, so it will take him longer and it will require parents to be that much calmer and more consistent. A child like this needs extra coaching on budgeting, more talk-throughs, more descriptive praise. Financial competence does not come naturally – it requires training.'

Noël would approach this training in smaller steps. From weekly pocket money she would go to fortnightly before monthly. 'Once you start, don't bottle out and don't rescue them, even when things don't go smoothly. Many parents think they are on a roll because their children are becoming more and more sensible when they are aged nine, ten and eleven. Unfortunately, what happens is that many children seem to go backwards and lose that earlier good sense once they become teenagers; they become terminally embarrassed, easily led and determined to appear cool. You might think it will be easier just to give them money and let them manage it or mismanage it, and learn, eventually, from their mistakes. But it is often far from easy because of the repercussions: blame, arguments, complaining, pleading. When we neglect to prepare for success, the enduring lesson that our children can be left with is that they can't cope and that the adults they care about are fed up with them much of the time. No parents want to leave their children that legacy, so don't even start on an allowance until you are prepared to make the time to teach and train. A big part of training is not rescuing the child.'

What is the difference between a reward and a bribe?

My child-minder's husband is far better at getting the children to tidy their rooms and clear their plates than I am. When I asked him how he did it, he replied with a broad grin, 'Bribery.' Lollipops go to those children who do as he asks.

I wasn't sure how to react. Quite aside from the sugar issue, is it a good idea to give a reward other than approval or a logical consequence? I asked Noël and Luke how they distinguished between a reward and a bribe.

'In this context a bribe is something promised beforehand to persuade a child to do something that he would not otherwise be willing to do,' said Noël. 'A reward is something given for a job done well. We don't, for example, consider our salaries to be bribes. We do our work for various reasons, including money, not because we are bribed to do it.'

Luke had a different definition: 'A reward is something reasonable and designed into a situation. A bribe is something you come up with on the spur of the moment. To distinguish the two, ask yourself if you would feel uncomfortable if you had to explain it to the other children or your partner. If you would, it's a bribe.'

Whatever the definition, both are adamant that a bribe might or might not work in the short term, but that it definitely causes problems in the long term. Noël explained: 'When we bribe, we are abdicating responsibility for motivating and training our children. We are relying on the bribe to do the motivating. But what if the child does not care that much about the promised object, or knows he will probably get it anyway, whether he complies or not?'

Motivating children to do what's right by making it fun is not bribery. Bath time in my house is not usually noted for scrubbing, but one guest had the children polishing their grubby knees like angels, giving them imaginary ticks on the bathroom wall. 'She made it into a game,' explained the six-year-old, 'like Simon Says.' Clever her.

WAYS TO ENCOURAGE SELF-RELIANCE
- Don't do for your children anything that they can do for themselves (including their thinking).
- Let children have their feelings – do not rescue them. Remember, it is not our job to fix their life. Into every life some rain must fall. It is our job to teach our children how to weather the storms.
- Don't answer their questions. Make them guess, look up, remember or ask someone else.
- Remember that there is something to be learnt from every situation, whether it is the lesson you hoped would be learnt or something completely different. A child who tries to vacuum his room when the bag is full won't discover how to clean a room, but he will learn something about the vacuum cleaner.
- Don't answer your children when they call for you from another room. Don't even say, 'Don't shout; come and talk to me,' because that is still answering their shout. Instead, say nothing (having told them previously about your new rule for yourself), even if they shout louder and louder. Once they come to you, reflectively listen and descriptively praise.
- Whenever you notice something that your child has difficulty doing or is reluctant to do, teach or train one little bit of the task or skill at a time. Keep gently but persistently expanding the number of tasks that your child can and will do for himself.

9

SOCIAL SKILLS

How can I teach my children to be friendly to visitors?
How do you stop a child boasting? What's the best way to
tackle lying? Why doesn't my child make friends easily?
How do I stop games descending into tantrums?

All parents long to bask in the reflected glory of a child who is a wild
success at sport or academic work. I too would love to be the mother
in the front row of a concert where my child performs a peerless
violin sonata; realistically, this is not going to happen to most of us.

As Luke and Noël reminded me, those achievements are not
what make a child – or an adult – loveable. What matters more is an
individual's human qualities. In the end, even the most results-
orientated parents don't care that much whether their child is brilliant at trigonometry or a star high-jumper. They mind more about
having children who are at ease with themselves and others, who are
fun and caring, who laugh with and not at other people, who share
worries and pleasures, and keep promises rather than a score of
favours received and given.

Those skills, they say, are often the ones that we leave to chance
and instinct and don't bother to train children in because they seem
too vague, too much a part of what we consider to be inborn and
immutable. But these social attributes are just as susceptible to
training as reading and writing.

Once again, having a puppy made me more aware of this. I
learnt from the manuals that if I didn't socialise the dog in its early
months, it was likely to be a loner, unable to occupy itself in the park
and more likely to chase children than creatures of its own kind; that
if I didn't train her not to jump up, she would be considered savage,
however mild her intentions. The dog-training manuals also made

me aware that the easiest way to train out the characteristics that you don't want an animal to have is by training them into the good habits that you do wish them to acquire.

Children are much the same. Personality is a result of experience as well as temperament. An only child is often more at ease with grown-ups, but that doesn't mean he can't make friends of his own age. A child who demands and interrupts is tiresome, but parents have let these habits develop by being tolerant, and even charmed by them, when the child was tiny.

It is only as my children have got older that I have become more aware of their failures as communicators and social operators. At that point I, like many parents, have started to nag. 'Don't interrupt,' I find myself saying, 'Stop biting your nails,' 'Don't boast' and 'Show some manners when someone arrives for tea.'

None of this does anything to install desirable behaviour: it simply serves to make nail-biters furtive and boasters defiant. 'You must find a positive way to teach social skills, as the negative ways don't work,' says Luke. 'Set an example. Show them what you want by demonstrating the desired behaviour, and use all your skills to train them in those behaviours. Parents are sometimes nervous of putting names to their children's social problems, but diagnosing something doesn't mean that it is going to stay that way. Most of us start out in life shy, but most of us learn not to be.'

Some of my most embarrassing moments occur when I over-hear one of my children displaying gauche social behaviour, bossing friends around or telling jokes and stories that have long ceased to entertain the listener. Usually I create a diversion. 'But when we distract a child,' says Noël, 'he learns nothing about how to behave or speak more sensibly. A better policy would be to devote some quiet moments to prevention. Social skills and social confidence are far more useful than the subjects children study at school.

'These skills will also prevent children becoming either bullies or bullied. The immature or very self-absorbed child who bores others, lies or can't judge people's reactions is vulnerable to these outcomes. Also, a child who is a tyrant at home is often either a bully or victim at school.

'Children are naturally self-centred; they don't see the world through others' eyes, and they don't understand how their words and body language affect others' perception of them. They need us to help them understand why people react to them as they do.'

Before starting this training, Luke recommends some careful thought about which social skills children need to learn for their own benefit, and which are purely for the parents' glory. 'Of course we all want smart, articulate, cheerful children,' he says, 'but we probably weren't always like that ourselves and we shouldn't expect too much.'

It is easy to feel guilty about all you are doing wrong as a mother, but there is nothing more rewarding than a single compliment about your child or the feeling you get when you look at them and realise you must be doing something right.
Jemima Khan, celebrity charity worker

How do you train a child to overcome the habit of shyness?

Many children start off shy and hide behind their mother's legs at the sight of a stranger. I used to find it funny and make excuses. Noël would take action.

If a child won't greet a stranger, first she would set aside a bit of time every day for the child to practise eye contact, hand-shaking, smiling and saying hello. Once the child feels relaxed and confident doing these things with a parent, she suggests recruiting a friend. 'Tell your friend that you are training the child and ask her to wait for a greeting when she arrives.

'If the child hides, don't say, "She's shy,"' advises Noël. 'That's pigeon-holing her. Say instead, "She's feeling embarrassed at the moment and she will say hello properly when she's ready." This rolls reflective listening and clear expectations into one calm and positive sentence. You could then ask the friend to wait until the child has summoned up the courage. Praise the child when she does.' The point, she explains, is to let the child learn that she can do it and that nothing terrifying results. The child needs to do it often enough for greeting people politely to become a habit. Parents using these step-by-step teaching and training methods, she finds, are often amazed at how outward-going a previously 'shy' child can become.

But sometimes there is a deeper reason for shyness. One mother at a parenting class was anxious because her child would never even shake her nursery teacher's hand: 'I asked my daughter why she thought it was important to say hello. She gave me a sensible answer but also said that she doesn't like being kissed by strangers. I was then able to say that it is fine not to let people kiss you, but that you do have to greet them.

'She still wouldn't shake hands with the teacher at nursery, but when she moved to primary school her first report said how good she was with the adults.'

'If she had practised the greeting daily,' says Noël, 'the child would have got it right at nursery. This parent chose not to train, but to leave it up to the child to comply when she felt like it. This is tempting when your child is highly sensitive, immature or stubborn. You want to avoid battles, and you may even be worried that insisting on shaking hands will somehow traumatise your delicate flower. I would almost say that the opposite is true: this approach inadvertently gives our children the impression that we don't think they can learn to cope with the normal, everyday demands of life the way other children their age can. And that self-image is limiting and damaging. In my experience, this often leads to further shyness or anxiety. Be proactive and help children improve their skills, rather than hoping they will grow out of it.'

How do you help a child who says no one likes her?

It has broken my heart when a child comes home from school saying 'everybody hates me' and talking about break times spent alone at the edge of the playground, excluded from a gang. Short of talking to the teacher – and what can she do? – I have never known what to do except encourage children to invite a potential friend home to tea (a good idea, according to Luke and Noël) and tell them that I'm sure everyone likes them really (counter-productive).

'Why is it counter-productive?' I asked Noël. 'Because if the child really believes that no one likes him, and the parent disagrees, suddenly the child has two problems: no friends and a parent who doesn't believe him. Reflective listening is much more comforting than reassurance.'

Luke agrees, but he also recommends that parents take a step back from the situation and ask themselves whether this harrowing tale is true. As he says, 'It may be just that the child is feeling lonely and she would like to be more popular. But by making that statement she is telling you something, and this is not the time to contradict her by saying, "But you have lots of friends. There's John and Jane . . ."

'When you explore the feelings further, by listening reflectively, you may find out that there is no one she can play with this evening, or that John and Jane are next-door neighbours, so they can see each other all the time. The child's upset is not something we have to try to fix straight away, but once the problem has been uncovered, you can look for things you or your child could do about it.

'Ask the child for her ideas. She might start with, "We could move house." Now you might be tempted to say, "Yeah, right" or "Get real" to such a suggestion, but if you do, the brainstorming will be over and the child will stop producing ideas. So you could try instead saying, "That's one idea. I'll write that down. Any others?" She might then say, "Well, Jane could move house." By the third preposterous suggestion, which you duly write down, you are both laughing and the situation doesn't feel so serious. Then you and the child can come up with some other ideas. One might be, "I could go to the same dance class as Jane on Friday nights."

'When you have run out of ideas, go through the list together and work out which ones are practicable. Then together you prepare for success. "If you want to spend Friday nights at Jane's house, what will you need to have done beforehand? Yup, your homework."'

Finally, Luke adds, 'Don't sneer at the friends your child does have. They may be the only ones she can get. If you want her to make different ones then you must help her by involving her in activities where she will meet children who are more to your liking.'

But is there anything I can do to help my child handle her friendships better?
Often it doesn't surprise me when my children fall out with their friends. I cringe as I listen to them sometimes being boring or bossy or muscling in on someone else's joke. I asked Noël if there was anything I could do. 'Plenty,' she replied. She would start by reflectively listening to the child's worries about friendships. 'When you think your child is ready to stop complaining and think about solutions, you could say, "I wonder why your friends prefer to play with other people?" If she says it is because other people steal them, you

might respond, "You could look at it that way, but it still doesn't explain why your friends prefer to play with them. I wonder what the 'stealing' consists of. Your friends obviously like it."

'It will be hard for her to take responsibility for having created or contributed to the problem; no one likes admitting that. Blame is a way of shifting responsibility on to someone else, so don't expect the change to happen fast. You will need to do lots of teaching and training, over weeks and months, to change a child's victim mentality. But it's well worth the investment of time and effort. At the same time, train children in the skills that they need to be successful socially.'

Taking turns: 'Learning to take turns, not just in games but in conversation, is an essential social skill,' says Noël. 'The children who get left out or teased at school are often those who try to hog the limelight. They desperately try to get attention in ways that annoy their peers. If, for example, one child makes a joke and everyone laughs, the socially awkward child may imitate and make the same joke again. This time some children laugh but others don't. Then, instead of applying the law of diminishing returns, the child repeats the joke again. This time one or two may laugh and the others groan. When she tries it yet again, several shout "Shut up" or "You're stupid".'

Noël would train immature or over-excited children to say things only once. 'This requires parents to keep alert. When a child starts to repeat himself, put your hand up and say in a strong voice, "Sh! You said that already." Then you can descriptively praise the child for not repeating himself. With this approach, children will learn to get someone's attention before they speak.

Reading facial expressions: Being able to interpret faces accurately is important for judging how well one's presence is going down. Nothing is more irritating than a child (or adult) who won't take a hint, but often they don't because they haven't got the message. Noël would teach children to be more sensitive to others' expressions and body language by making it into a game at home and using role-play. 'First name an emotion, such as anger, then make a face to match it. Then make another face and ask the child to guess the emotion. Then switch roles. Also, you could look through a magazine and ask the child to imagine what the people are feeling. Very often children with poor social skills will get it wrong. Sometimes they can't even make an approximate guess, but you can teach them. Looking through that magazine discussing the pictures, you can extend their perception and vocabulary to reflect more subtle variations in feeling. Next, when you notice that they are feeling something, you can help them pinpoint it.'

Making conversation: To a child, making conversation with a stranger, whether another child or an adult, can be as stressful as public speaking. 'Little children will go up to anyone and chat,' says Luke, 'but from eight onwards they become self-conscious about their image, their body, their voice. One way in which adults can help children is by acknowledging how hard it can be. We can tell them that we were not always as at ease socially as we appear to be now.'

Then we can try to make it easier for them. 'Children,' he notices, 'hate talking to adults because they get grilled about school. I tell children to turn the tables by thinking of something the adult could tell them about. Most adults are delighted to give advice and not to have to think of questions.'

Luke suggests that a meal is the best time for conversational training because children are less self-conscious when they are doing something else (eating) at the same time. 'When they do have a good conversation,' he says, 'wherever it is, in the car or at the table, descriptively praise them for it, tell them they were being really interesting.'

'Starting a conversation and keeping it going,' Noël points out, 'is only part of the problem. Ending conversations gracefully is also a crucial social skill.' She suggests using role-play and conversations within the family to teach the signs of someone being bored – flitting eyes, lack of response – and that these signal the moment for the child to stop the long tale of who said what to whom, and ask another question. She would also teach children how to close a conversation, one way being, 'I've got to say hello to X.'

Be careful during this teaching and training, she warns, not to let your tone of voice sound critical or annoyed: children's confidence is fragile and they need to savour success.

Expressing opinions: 'Of course,' Luke concedes, 'sometimes children's views may be half-baked, but it is a mistake to treat children as if they were adults and contradict them. Even if there are flaws in their arguments, it is important to get them to express their views and show interest in them. Maybe they won't think the same when they are older, but don't crush them now: it is stifling and creates resentment if adults say things such as, "The world is not as simple as that".

Striving to make a child happy should not be an end in itself. Such enjoyment as a child feels should be a by-product. When you make enjoyment the goal, the process of growing up becomes a confession of failure because you are losing the thing which is most important, the childhood itself.

Roger Scruton, philosopher

How to behave at a grown-up party

'Some people are naturally relaxed and easy, but most of us weren't always like that,' says Luke, 'and there are certain little routines and conventions that make things go more smoothly. These can easily be taught or trained. Schools used to do this, but tea with the headmaster is no longer part of education, so it's the parents' job.'

Several weeks before a crucial event he would begin teaching and training by demonstrating and having the child practise the adult 'tricks' that make social life easier. In addition, Noël would co-opt a friend to act the part of a stranger.

Handshaking: Adults know that a limp or bone-breaking handshake is off-putting; children don't. 'Boys are always amazed,' says Luke, 'when I tell them that if their hand is clammy, they should wipe it before shaking. It doesn't occur to them. They often shake too vigorously and need to be warned off that too.'

Looking adults in the eye: My children tend to direct their hellos at their feet. 'Insist on eye contact and be prepared to wait,' says Noël. 'Don't let them get away with a quick glance. They have to look while exchanging greetings. Descriptively praise all progress.

'Children who don't make eye contact with strangers generally don't look their parents in the eye much either. Often this is because a child has been nagged, reminded or criticised a lot. Why would you want to look at someone who is always telling you that you've forgotten something?'

Posture: With children who slouch, show them how important posture is to how people perceive others. But showing is not enough: you have to train daily, not by reminding, but by descriptively praising every tiny improvement.

Entering a party: Explain that the first act is to find and greet the host. 'If you let them skip that and slink into a corner,' says Luke, 'it is much more difficult to come out and show themselves later.'

Introductions: Introducing a child to someone is helpful; so is suggesting something they might have in common. Having done that, parents should vanish. Don't monitor their conversation, butt in or keep glancing over from the other side of the room. 'My mother was very good at that,' says Luke. 'I remember her once finding a girl of my own age for me to speak to, introducing us and then disappearing completely.'

Suitable clothes: My thirteen-year-old likes his clothes hanging off him; my daughters favour clingy gear. None of them likes being thrust into traditional clothes for grown-up occasions. Luke's advice is to give children some choice so that they don't feel bossed. 'Don't say, "Wear the red shirt." Ask them to choose clothes that are appropriate. When they appear looking half-OK, praise the elements they got right and ask them nicely to have another go at the rest.'

But there are some lessons that can probably only be learnt the hard way. When we had two weddings to attend in quick succession, at the first our twelve-year-old was seated with a table of twenty-somethings who encouraged him to drink wine – with predictable consequences. 'I'll never do that again,' he said, and at the second he didn't.

How do children learn to behave in a restaurant?

Luke is staggered by how many teenagers have no idea how to order even a cup of coffee when they are out. He would make a point of taking children out to eat occasionally and showing them all the basics, from how to hold the menu to how to attract a waiter's attention politely.

'Let the kids do the ordering. Let them go and get the coffees. Don't do anything for them that they can do for themselves, especially when it involves interacting. Make them aware that if they've got the basic table manners right, they will be able to give all their attention to the talking, which will make a big difference to how their first date goes.'

To save time, money and embarrassment Noël advises practising these skills through role-playing at home first. In the restaurant she would not just let the children order – she would require them to do so.

How can children learn to be good winners and losers?

At parenting classes I have frequently come across parents groaning and sighing about the torture involved in playing games with children. Cheating, sobs and temper tantrums, they complain, usually make such sessions a nightmare.

One nanny arrived ragged because her eight-year-old charge had played Monopoly the night before and enjoyed winning so much that he had refused to go to school until he had played again the next morning. This second game had been a disaster: they were rushed, the child had insisted on being allowed to buy Park Lane and Mayfair, and the scene had ended in hysteria.

On another occasion, the father of a five-year-old who wanted to learn chess described his dilemma in playing with him. The man loves the game and wants to play with his son, but doesn't want to let the child win, nor does he want to beat him all the time.

The first point Luke and Noël both make is that games are a good preparation for life. They teach invaluable lessons about winning and losing, but they have to be handled sensitively because we all know how painful it is to be thrashed, and how exciting it is to feel like a champion. 'Help children explore those feelings,' says Noël, 'before you even get the board out. You might start by asking how the person who doesn't win might feel. If the child says "Sad", you could say, "Yes, you might. And what about a word beginning with D?"'

'If the child comes up with "depressed", you could say, "Well, that means sad for a very long time; what about "disappointed"?' (Introducing and discussing words helps pinpoint feelings and refines a child's use of language.) 'And if you felt disappointed, what might you do? Punch the cushions, go off to the bottom of the garden? Fine, so long as you don't punch your sister.

'And how might the winner feel? Really proud, that's right, and you know that the grown-up thing is not to go on too much about how proud you are.'

Parents should also set up the rules of the game so that a child has a fair chance of winning. 'Most people's reaction to losing at something new or difficult is to opt out and grow to hate the game,' she says. 'You don't want a child to do that, so make sure he doesn't lose most of the time. Don't bend the rules or let him win; instead, give the child a fair chance by handicapping the adult. In chess, for example, the adult might not be allowed any thinking time or might start with fewer pieces.'

Parents have a tendency, Luke observes, to introduce children to games that they are not yet mature enough to handle. Monopoly is a prime example: being bankrupted by rent demands is hard to take at any age. Uno, Connect and simpler games of chance demand less emotional maturity, as they move fast and one person's gain is not so obviously another's loss. There are also games, such as Pairs, where experience doesn't count and children can beat their parents from an early age.

'Monopoly is probably too tricky for an eight-year-old,' he says. 'Try it, but ask the child beforehand what he will do if he feels upset, and say that if it does go wrong, you will put that game away for three months until he is able to try again in a different spirit.

'As they get older, children learn to cope with losing by watching their parents. I knew a thirteen-year-old who always had to win, and wouldn't play tennis against his friend in case he didn't. When he watched his father play and lose, he was so amazed that his father came off the court and said how much he had enjoyed the game, regardless of the outcome, that, two years on, the boy's whole attitude has changed.'

What's the difference between copying and cheating?

'Copying is a compliment,' says Noël. 'We all do it and we want our children to copy as that is how they learn new skills. The only thing to watch is that they don't claim the credit for the original idea, which, of course, they often do. Muscling in like that does not go down well with the child who had the original idea.

'As for cheating, it could be that the game or the work is too difficult and that you need to be more realistic about the child's capabilities. But start by teaching the child so that eventually he can do whatever it is for himself.

'Children who cheat at games are often highly competitive, and often, but not always, feel bad about themselves. It may be that the parents are too annoyed too often. Or it could be that the school sets standards the child doesn't know how to reach, although this isn't so common these days.

'When parents react to competitive cheating with moralising along the lines of "It doesn't matter who wins", it makes no impression on a competitive child.

'What often happens when a child cheats is that parents turn a blind eye. Instead, they should treat cheating as a lie: an action lie rather than a verbal one. Use the "mistakes process". Lying is a mistake because it doesn't work to get us what we want. We may avoid getting caught, but we lose some of our self-respect.'

Should lying be taken seriously?

In Noël's view lying should not be treated as a moral issue because everybody lies. 'It's a matter of teaching and training children in which are the socially acceptable ways to lie, and which aren't,' she says. 'Lying is sometimes showing off, but mostly it's about trying to cover up something that has gone wrong.'

Children tend to cover up minor misdemeanours because they don't want to be told off, and parents who get angry about lies can make children more prone to lying. Noël's view is that it is best to treat lying as an immature attempt to achieve something. 'It helps to work out what the child is trying to achieve. Reflective listening can be very useful for this. Sometimes the lying is to get the parent's attention. When a child is caught in a lie, a parent tends to stop everything and deliver a lecture. A child may find it easier to get this kind of attention than the frequent, predictable, one-to-one quality time that is what he really needs.'

Luke's reaction to lying would vary according to the context. 'If a child lied to me at school, I would take it head-on: "Is that exactly what happened? That sounds amazing." At home it is difficult to tackle a child about not telling the truth without giving him a totally negative experience. So long as it was not a lie that was causing problems right then, it would probably be best to let it go and think about why the child was doing it.'

Noël, however, would always have a conversation, again without moralising, to find out which bits of the story are true and which are embroidered. This shows the child that parents are not gullible. And, of course, she would let no opportunity slip by to descriptively praise children for honesty and courage whenever they do own up. That helps children to develop the habit of honesty far more effectively than lecturing does.

TIPS TO STOP CHILDREN LYING
- Don't be afraid to use the word 'lie' rather than softer versions such as 'fib', but don't make it sound as if telling a lie means that you are a bad person.
- When a child backtracks, you know she is lying – both versions of her story can't be true – so point it out. If a child suggests you check with someone else, follow through. (Parents rarely do so because the occasion doesn't seem important enough to expose the child.)
- If you are going to check with another parent or the teacher, ask the child beforehand if he wants to change anything about his story.
- Praise the child who comes clean for being brave. It is important to show that honesty pays, and don't make too much of the crime.

How do I discourage excessive honesty?

I love it when other people's children cause a stir by asking embarrassing questions such as, 'Why is that lady so fat?' or 'How old are you?' I'm not so keen when my own children fail to show tact and discretion, so what do I do?

Luke would train children to keep their thoughts in their own heads and ask their parents later. The way to prepare for future success, Noël adds, is by having frequent talk-throughs about what people do and don't say and why. 'The parent should ask leading questions and make the child use his own brain to come up with sensible, thoughtful answers. Any child given to being embarrassingly blunt needs lots of descriptive praise about being considerate, not blurting, not hurting feelings and being respectful.'

How do I stop a child boasting?

Noël doesn't think parents should make a moral issue out of boasting because we are all guilty of showing off in subtle ways. 'I tell children that instead of boasting in words, they could boast in actions. It works better. If you say you can do something and on that occasion it doesn't work out, you look foolish, but when people see you doing something, they know you can. It's the difference between showing and showing off.'

But boasting, I tell her, is also about saying that your Uncle Bill has the fastest car in the world. Her way to help a child in that case would be to have several conversations in which the parent listens reflectively and eventually asks the child what she expects others to think when she says that. Noël and I role-play this together, with me playing the child, and so expert is she at reflective listening that before long I am telling her that I want people to think I am rich because I don't think I'm pretty.

Noël made the conversation go straight to the heart of a child's insecurities, but she also admitted that it would not be easy to get there that fast in a real situation. 'In fact, a child is more likely to say "I dunno", but over time, whenever the child looks unhappy or cross, you could explore her feelings, help her to understand herself. When a child doesn't feel pretty, it is often a metaphor for insecurities or worries that are deeper yet vaguer, such as not feeling appreciated by a busy, stressed parent who isn't scheduling in enough one-to-one time with that child. A child who is being picked on or criticised a lot by an older sibling often reacts by feeling similar dissatisfaction with herself. Parents need to change these circumstances as quickly as possible to allow children's self-esteem to flourish.

'You also need to descriptively praise the boasting child for every small step towards developing good habits and values, such as helpfulness, thoughtfulness, courage, willingness, flexibility, etc.'

Luke agrees, but he would tread very carefully with boasting because it is easy to humiliate a child. Except where it was causing noticeable problems, he would let the boast pass and devote his energy to thinking 'Why is the child doing this? What does he believe about himself that makes him do it? And what can I do so that he doesn't feel unconfident?'

The next time he took the child out somewhere with friends he would choose an activity at which the child could shine – maybe football – so he wouldn't have to boast. 'Then I would think about the long-term ways of creating confidence, such as special time with parents. I would also make sure that the child doesn't think that your love depends on school grades or any other achievement. You might think it is obvious, but a child doesn't have the experience and confidence to have an overview of a relationship.'

How do I stop a child being bossy?

'Why are some children bossy and others not?' I asked Noël one day after one of mine had given a fine display of telling schoolmates how to breathe. 'Do you think she has picked it up from me?'

In answer, she began by making the distinction between being boss and being bossy. 'Parents have to be boss, but they don't have to be bossy, which involves using an ordering tone of voice, telling people to do unnecessary things or things that they already know.'

Let's pretend that I never make the mistake of being bossy rather than boss, so my child can't have copied me: how else would she have picked up this habit? 'If a child is used to saying "I want" and getting it, she will be bossy,' Noël replied. She had noticed in me a tendency to appease rather than to retrain a demanding, bossy child. Typically, I did not assert my authority. 'You are talking in a high-pitched, tentative voice and expressing instructions as if they are advice. What is advice? It isn't a clear instruction, so it can be ignored with impunity. Advice can seem like a nag. It is only worth giving if someone asks for it, and even then the child often doesn't follow the advice. In future, be firm. Train the child to be polite by doing lots of action replays, to frame wants as requests, and don't give in to demands.'

To make a child more adaptable she would take the following line on what she calls the 'red cup syndrome'. 'Some children, usually the sensitive, highly strung ones, get fixated on their usual routines, and become upset by even small changes. These children appear stubborn, spoilt, determined to get their own way. Giving in to their demands perpetuates and escalates the behaviour, so whenever a child really wants something, such as the red cup, she shouldn't get it. Give her the blue cup so that she will learn, over time of course, that she can survive changes in her routine. You could give the red cup to another child, explaining that you are doing this to get her used to handling disappointment without making a fuss.'

This will cause an explosion, I protest, but she doesn't soften. 'What is most likely to cause a tantrum is the parent's annoyance or disapproval. But I am suggesting that you stay calm and friendly. Even so, the child might explode. Don't be afraid of children's reactions; focus on getting them into good habits. In life, those who demand usually don't get, and a child will learn that more effectively through experience than through being lectured. So what if the sister who does get the red cup crows? Don't get involved in the sibling squabble. The child has to get used to not having her own way.

'Of course, you help her to see herself in a new, more positive light by descriptively praising her every time she accepts or is even willing to consider someone else's point of view or agenda, and every time she makes less of a fuss when things don't go according to plan.'

How do I deal with a child who won't stop complaining?

One of my daughters has a tendency to find fault, which can be very wearing. When I mentioned this to Noël she told me how to teach her to turn a complaint into a request, and then train her so it becomes a habit. 'Complaints don't work well as a way of getting what you want,' she said, 'requests are much more effective. Often children complain because they want someone else to guess the request.

'Pick a calm moment to show her how to turn a complaint into a request. If you try when she's complaining, she will already be in a bad mood. Think up some examples to illustrate it: "Why is everything too high up?" can, for example, be turned into, "Could you please reach that book for me?" Turn it into a game. When she asks a question, praise her for not complaining.'

The next morning, when my daughter complained that her fried egg was overcooked, I asked her to turn it into a request. 'OK,' she replied, 'can you please cook me another fried egg?'

As I gave the original egg to the dog and made her another, I noticed that I wasn't as wound up as I might be by a complaint, but I wasn't sure that I wanted to cook endless eggs to her specifications. 'You have a choice, of course,' said Noël. 'When someone makes a request, you don't have to agree to it. Instead, you could teach her to cook her own eggs. Or you could make a rule that she can have fruit if she doesn't want what you have prepared.'

How do I stop children whining and sulking?

The prospect of whingeing children growing into moaning, dissatisfied adults who leave others feeling drained is a gloomy one. 'The solution is simple,' says Luke. 'Don't respond to whining. You wouldn't take it from your boss or your friends, so don't take it from your kids. Children are not going to be happy all the time, and one of the hardest lessons of parenthood is to allow children to be upset if they don't get their own way.'

Noël adds: 'If they get away with whining at home, they may do it at school or with their friends, and no one will appreciate it. One way to reduce the amount of whining is to respond only to a polite, friendly voice. A whining voice makes the whinger feel even worse, but if you ask the child to say the same thing again in a normal voice, it often becomes a reasonable question. You can say that people will like them more if they sound positive and strong.'

As for sulking, it is a way of playing on parental guilt. 'Sulking is a genuine emotion – "I'm too annoyed to speak" – that carries on after the emotion has cooled because the child has learnt that it gets attention,' says Noël. 'It usually works because parents explain themselves at great length, and often even go back on what they said, as they try to make the sulker feel better. This gives the child the power to manipulate the parent.'

'So I should try asking: "What do you really want?"' I suggested. 'The problem then,' Neil replied, 'is that you often get a whinge *and* you have implied to the child that you will provide whatever it is they want. Reflective listening is better. Often children know what they want, but not what they need. You can help them explore and understand their feelings.'

How do you stop children interrupting?

Children gain reassurance about who is in charge, say Luke and Noël, from (among other things) not being allowed to interrupt their parents. Yet mine carry on interrupting, not because they don't know they shouldn't, or even because they are impulsive. My theory is that they are worried that if they wait for the adults to finish their conversation, they will have forgotten what they want to say.

Noël felt it was far more common to find that parents have been unintentionally rewarding interruptions with immediate attention. 'Have you ever said to your child, "Don't interrupt. Now, what do you want?"' she asked. I blushed.

The way she and Luke recommend to help children interrupt much less is to have clear expectations, to prepare for success by not having a long phone call just when it is about to be the children's suppertime, and to descriptively praise children whenever they don't interrupt. If interrupting really seems to be caused by fear of losing a thought, get the child to write or draw it.

I can be President of the United States or I can control Alice. I cannot possibly do both.
Franklin D. Roosevelt, of his daughter, who ran in and
out of the Oval Office

How do I encourage a child to be polite to me?

At one meeting with Noël I was jubilant because one of my daughters had decided to give up being rude to me for Lent. In return I told her I was going to reward her at the end of a week's politeness by giving her a book.

'She needs smaller rewards sooner,' Noël said. 'When a child announces she is going to do something desirable, we shouldn't just say "Wonderful" and make it sound easy. Descriptively praise the intention and her acknowledgement that she is not as polite as she should be, but also say that you don't expect her to change overnight and that you expect her to make mistakes.

'If she catches herself being rude, praise her for doing so and ask her to make it right. Coming up with something she can do to make amends is as important as not being rude in the first place.

'If she *is* rude and doesn't realise it, of course you won't respond because you have a new rule for yourself that you respond only to a polite tone. As soon as she stops, point out that it was probably not her intention to be rude, but that it had sounded as if she was being rude. If the child says, "I didn't know," you might be tempted to say, "Oh, yeah". Instead you can say, "I'm glad to hear that you didn't mean to be rude. Let's do an action replay." And follow that with descriptive praise.'

Can you stamp effectively on ugly habits?

Nail-biting, nose-picking, fiddling with hair, sniffing, cracking knuckles, burping – these are just some of the ways in which children goad their parents. Sometimes they are even unconscious of what they are doing.

Luke's advice is to ignore the behaviour, especially if you think children are doing it to wind you up, and descriptively praise them when they are not displaying the annoying behaviour. If a response is needed, the logical immediate one is best: handing over a handkerchief, telling a child to go outside the room, or insisting that hair is tied back.

'You want a strategy,' he says, 'that will work with the minimum of hassle. None of these should become big issues. Keep a sense of perspective. Remember how many successful people were once grotty, snuffling children. Think how many bad habits you may once have had. They will change.'

Noël agrees and points out that often these behaviours turn into habits because parents rise to the bait and give attention to them so predictably. The annoying behaviours also often occur as a by-product of embarrassment when a child is asked to do something that she has not yet been taught or trained to do.

What can be done about a child who steals?

Luke would be very wary about getting too moral about children's tendency to light-fingeredness. All children, in his experience, help themselves – whether it is to biscuits from the cupboard, pencils at school or even sweets from the shop. He suggests asking other parents what their children do as the best way of establishing what is normal.

'You have to be careful about the moral dimension,' he says. 'There's a temptation to label people, and it is upsetting enough to be caught stealing without being labelled bad. But you must be clear with children that stealing doesn't work to get you what you want: if you steal, your friends won't trust you, or your parents won't let you have pocket money. And, of course, there's also the deeper level: people who steal don't end up liking themselves – but it is best not to say that when the child's fingers are in the purse.

'Later, however, you could try having a conversation about what makes people feel good later in life. What makes them feel honoured and respected in society?'

But, I protest, stealing might be a cry for attention. 'Indeed it can,' he says. 'You can ask yourself if this child needs more attention and what you need to do to provide that attention, but the stealing is equally unacceptable whether it is done out of selfishness or as a cry for attention. You could ask the child to think up a more sensible way of getting your attention next time he needs it.'

As for deterrents, the best one is a logical consequence: making reparations, so long as these aren't too punitive and likely to have the same effect as the arrangements at the end of the First World War. 'When a child has taken something from a shop, going back to the shop is a fantastic deterrent,' says Luke, 'if the child has the nerve. "Joey's got something to tell you," you can say to the shopkeeper. "Is there anything he can do to make amends, such as sweeping the pavement outside the shop?"

'People are incredibly good about these situations. A teenager who had robbed a Kentucky Fried Chicken outlet at knife-point went back two years later and told the manager, knowing that he might call the police. The manager was so impressed that he let him off. The boy then had such a feeling of pride in his action and the clear message it gave that he could forgive himself.'

TIPS FOR TRAINING IN SOCIAL SKILLS
- Accept that these skills don't usually come naturally and that children need to be taught and trained in them. If you hear yourself say, 'I've told you a hundred times not to do that,' it's time for training.

- Be patient while training. These skills that we take for granted were hard for us to acquire too.
- Break the skills into little pieces so that they can be mastered one bit at a time.
- Parents of the same gender are best for teaching social skills. Many boys won't take such lessons from their mothers. Luke suggests that fathers call it 'man's stuff'.
- Be careful with humour. Children are very sensitive to ridicule. And avoid labels, such as 'shy'. The aim is to give them more confidence, not to take away the little they have.
- Have faith, says Luke. 'Most children over the age of eight go through an awkward stage when they are trying to establish their own identity. Give them time and space to be as they are, and have confidence that by the time they are grown up they will be less awkward.'

Is there a way to prevent bullying?

'If schools knew how to eliminate bullying, they would have done so already,' says Noël. 'Teachers can drive bullying underground in the classroom, but in the typical playground they are almost powerless. They can usually prevent children being beaten up, but they often don't know how to stop, or even reduce, the incidence of name-calling, exclusive games or one-sided shoving, grabbing and pestering.'

Obviously, a school should have a written anti-bullying policy, but that is not enough. Neither Noël nor Luke believes this is a problem that parents should leave to schools to sort out, partly because schools don't have a good track record in this area, and partly because the problems usually begin at home. 'Bullying arises,' Luke believes, 'because children, like adults, are better at noticing their own and other people's bad points than their good ones. It's utopian to imagine a society without bullies; slightly more realistic to hope for one in which people don't see themselves as victims.'

Noël adds: 'Without intending to, parents and schools contribute to a "bully/victim culture" by making some children feel powerless or like failures. Well-meaning parents and teachers criticise, nag and punish the same children over and over again. These are the children who often become bullies or victims. Often the same child is a bully in one situation and a victim in another. For example, I have found that many playground bullies have a history of being teased or pummelled mercilessly by an older sibling or cousin. Conversely, a victim at school is often a tyrant at home. Parents of a sensitive, impulsive child drift into the habit of tiptoeing around him, so the child never learns the tolerance and patience that all relationships depend on. This is the child who is eminently wind-up-able.'

What do you do if you suspect your child is a bully?
'There is no point lecturing bullies,' says Luke. 'Either they already know they are doing the wrong thing but can't stop, or they have found a way to justify their behaviour to themselves. Bullies usually behave as they do because they have been bullied themselves and picking on someone else makes them feel more important. It is not helpful to tell a bully that bullying is a sign of weakness because that adds to the vicious cycle of their low self-esteem.'

Bullying, Noël and Luke believe, is usually an extension of extreme sibling rivalries or a reaction to unreasonable parental expectations (a common problem with children who are very immature or who have learning difficulties or a very sensitive or impulsive nature). 'The fact that one child feels driven to be a bully, within or outside the home (usually both), demonstrates that something in their circumstances is pretty unhappy,' says Luke. 'Rather than make an ineffectual attempt to stop the bullying, look into what is going on for the child.'

To that Noël adds: 'Parents have to make changes in the child's life so that the urge to dominate or hurt is reduced. To make those changes go back to the sixteen skills.'

And what do you do if your child is being bullied?
Some tactics Noël considers virtually useless. She does not advise nobbling the bully's parents or criticising the teacher. 'Of course the school should be kept informed, but most adults don't know how to change the dynamics, so expecting the school to handle the situation is worse than useless. It lulls both parents and child into a false sense

of relief that the problem will be sorted out quickly, it can also reinforce the child's feeling of powerlessness, and if the bully finds out that the other child has ratted on him, he may be in for it in spades.'

Nor are my standard methods of tackling distress sufficient in her eyes. 'Asking a child "What's the matter?" is the most common parental reaction to distress, but, unfortunately, it's also the least effective way of getting a child to come out with anxieties,' she says. 'And telling a child who is being bullied to stand up for herself will only make her feel worse because you are making it sound too easy to solve. The child probably knows what she should be doing, but can't bring herself to do it. Or she may have half-heartedly tried to follow your advice and now be convinced that it doesn't work.'

As for telling her to have a sense of humour about the teasing, it is useless. 'The child can't; on this point she is sensitive and unselfconfident,' says Noël. 'You have to help her become more confident, not make her feel worse by chiding her for having no sense of humour.'

Luke agrees with Noël that bullying is not random. When a child is a frequent victim, there is always something about the child that draws the fire of the bullies. Often the bullied are socially immature or they may have a learning difficulty, dyspraxia perhaps, or problems with spoken language. AD(H)D children are 'fun' to tease because they over-react and find it hard to learn to behave differently in order to get a different result.

'It is how a child reacts when bullied or teased that makes him an easy target,' says Noël. 'If, at home, a child displays rage, outrage, rigidity or makes accusations of unfairness, it is likely that with friends the child will be able to control those reactions a little better, but not much better.

'The child who feels unhappy or left out at home may transfer those feelings to school. He's developed that role at home and is playing it out in a larger arena. That child will be sensitive and ready to take offence, argue back or cry. He may think the teasing is because of his appearance. A sign of his immaturity is that he doesn't realise that he is being teased in large part because of his actions and reactions. So you have to start the change at home by creating good habits and training him in more mature and assertive social skills. We can help a child to appear and therefore to become more confident through training in eye contact, posture, body language, tone of voice and choice of words. Boys in particular also feel more confident when they know how to defend themselves physically, even though they may choose not to.'

Are battles with friends the same as bullying?

When our ten-year-old was involved in a prolonged and often savage slanging match with a classmate, we talked to her about her behaviour but left it at that. 'Was that right?' I asked Luke. 'Yes,' he said. 'It was an argument between peers; they were taking it in turns to be nasty. Bullying is when one person or group dominates.'

TIPS FOR DEALING WITH BULLYING

- Don't leap into action before gathering all the information.
- It worries children to see their parents upset. Go for the calm, mature approach.
- Listen to the child's uncomfortable feelings without trying to fix, sympathise or agree. Remain objective. Children often misinterpret reality. 'Rather than demand confidences,' says Noël, 'spend regular, predictable, frequent time with the child and let whatever she has to say come out when she is ready.'
- Take action. It gives the child the message that bullying isn't right and won't be tolerated, but confine action to the home front.
- 'It may be,' says Noël, 'that you have blamed the child too much when things go wrong. This is easy to do when a child is particularly impulsive or immature. The form of bullying a child may receive at home from parents or siblings doesn't have to take the same form as the behaviour the child displays at school: a child doesn't have to have been hit to become a hitter.'
- Role-playing can teach a child about the body language that contributed to him becoming a victim. Rehearsing can be embarrassing at first, but learning to stand up straight, look others in the eye and not to seem upset can make a big difference.

- Build self-esteem by finding something the child is good at, whether art, ballet or sport. 'Have him learn a martial art,' says Luke, 'not necessarily so that he can fight back, but to give inner confidence and help conquer fear. Rock climbing is another good idea.
- 'If a child wants to conform as a means of self-protection, let him,' says Luke. 'It will pass.'

  Noël agrees that children may need help working out how to blend in, but she points out that trying too hard to be cool or popular is often the problem. 'With girls in particular the social hierarchies are amazingly defined. A girl will be teased for trying to be part of the cool set, but that same girl will not be teased if she does not try to be included in that set. It's a matter of "knowing your place." '

10

SCHOOL AND HOMEWORK

How do I get children to go to school? How do I get them to do their homework? Can I help them do better? How do I get a child to enjoy reading? Is it possible to teach exam technique?

One of Noël's favourite sayings is 'Education is too important to be left to schools'. She has seen enough distraught parents to know that schools don't always correctly identify a child's needs, or know how best to meet them. 'Parents know their child best,' she says, 'but they don't necessarily know how to meet their child's needs either.'

As a result of personal experience and their work with children and teenagers, both Luke and Noël have formed strong – and somewhat divergent – views on school matters. Where they agree entirely is that the vast majority of school-related problems boil down to two factors: unrealistic parental expectations and children who lack motivation.

Noël, as a teacher, has helped many children who had become demoralised and rebellious because they felt like failures at school. Success or failure is not just important in itself – it also has an enormous impact on children's self-esteem and general behaviour, so she believes strongly that parents must do everything in their power to help their children be successful at school. By successful she means achieving their potential, not necessarily reaching a standard that would be right for another child. 'All children are capable of surpassing their own and our expectations,' she believes, 'if we are willing to invest in teaching and training.'

Luke, who himself put in a dismal performance at school, would not like anyone else to have to fight their way out of dead-end jobs as he did. However, he believes that not doing well at school needn't be the end of the world.

'Parents must not be too focused on grades,' he says. 'It is more important to be able to put across a passionate argument or find what you most love doing than to get straight As. Just because a child is a year behind at primary school or flunks his GCSEs doesn't mean he will never do well. Parents can be over-anxious about the future. That worry paralyses them, preventing them from doing anything useful in the present.

'One of my closest friends was a punk who dropped out of school at fifteen,' he says, 'but once she was older and had found what she wanted to study, she was accepted by Oxford with a B and a C in her A-levels because she could so obviously think for herself. Those who can do well at school will, and those who can't can find another way.'

Noël agrees that grades aren't everything. 'Parents must look for what their children are making an effort with and improving in and value them for that. Self-confidence is probably the most important thing a parent can give a child. Usually, confidence comes not from being talented in one area, but from knowing that one can meet the demands of the environment.

'A parent's job is to look for where a child might succeed, and help them do so by teaching and training them. High expectations are good so long as parents help their children achieve those expectations rather than nagging and criticising when their expectations are not met. Parents are either part of the problem or part of the solution.'

They are definitely part of the problem, she finds, if they are in too much of a hurry, expecting children to be able to tackle complex tasks before they have mastered the basics, or focusing too much on the child's eventual career rather than the challenges of the moment. But despite contemporary concerns about pushy parents who are desperate for their children to get ahead in a competitive world, to her they are a comparatively rare problem.

'I see far more parents who have unrealistically low expectations of their children. If only their parents taught and trained them for academic success, the children would learn more thoroughly and feel better about themselves. I'm not talking about parents teaching subject matter – that is the school's job – I'm talking about parents teaching and training work habits, study skills, exam strategy and revision technique. We might like to think that children will automatically develop these skills as they mature, or that schools will teach them. That doesn't often happen.

'I also see many sensitive children who find it hard to accept discipline at school because they have not experienced much discipline at home. For these children, school becomes a huge source of frustration that they take out at home, often by behaving aggressively to their parents or siblings.'

Between them, my five children have presented a cornucopia of issues related to school – from refusing to go, to being disorganised and not doing their homework. When I started taking these issues to Noël and Luke I learnt that I had added to their problems by, at some moments, being critical and nagging, and at others by sympathising too much with their feelings of distress and not requiring them to do their best.

Luke and Noël introduced me to more productive strategies. I learnt to be more consistent, to give descriptive praise as opposed to evaluative praise of the 'super', 'marvellous', 'brilliant' variety, and to listen reflectively to the children's feelings without letting them wriggle off the hook. But the greatest revelation of my advice sessions and parenting classes, in relation to school topics, was a shift in focus.

I was, I realised, in the habit of noticing results rather than efforts. I wanted the children to do well for my sake as much as for their own, so I was cheering their successes and passing over their shortcomings. It was only with Noël and Luke's guidance – and the salutary experience of some competitive exams – that I discovered I could help my children more if I left them to enjoy the subjects that came easily and focused my efforts on their weak spots, whether organisation, reading or handwriting.

Noël and Luke also taught me to look beyond the dramas of the moment and address learning issues in a more systematic and upbeat way. Once, when I moaned to Noël about the homework battles, she pulled me up: 'You don't need to see it as a battle,' she said. 'There will always be things that children don't want to do. As a parent, you are in charge. Think of it as your job to get the children into good habits. Work out whether a particular skill is one that you should be teaching or training.'

How do I prepare a very young child for school?

After the free-wheeling life of early childhood, school comes as a culture shock to many children, especially boys, who are often later developers. I remember the terror that no one will speak to you, that your uniform won't be right, that you will be in trouble for getting things wrong. It's scarcely surprising that many children cling to their parents at the door of their first classroom.

Noël has seen so many children develop a strong dislike of school that she firmly believes we are sending some children at too young an age: 'Boys, in particular, are often very immature when they are four,' she says. 'It is partly anxiety to get them on track for exams that has some children pushed through the door before they are ready. I think parents should consider the option of not sending a child to school until he's really ready to be successful with that school's curriculum.'

Once a child is going to school, however, both she and Luke believe parents have to be firm about attendance and shouldn't bribe children to enter the classroom with promises of sweets or toys. 'Don't reward a child for going to school; it's something he has to do,' they say. 'There are other, more constructive, ways to help children enjoy their first days at school.'

Noël would prefer to see parents building up children's confidence by imparting the skills that will make for success. 'Many parents unintentionally keep children unconfident,' she observes, 'by doing too much for them. Even tying their shoelaces for them whittles away their self-confidence. The more self-reliant a child feels, the more confidence he will have and the more willing he will be to face challenges.'

Luke suggests networking with the other parents, agreeing to share lifts so that a child doesn't enter a classroom full of strangers: 'It will be easier for your child to invite friends home if the classmates already know you. And familiarise a child with a new school. If you can't go in, walk around the outside, point things out. The worst fear is fear of the unknown.'

An important way parents can prepare a child for school, they agree, is to listen reflectively and non-judgementally to a child's fears. Parents should stay calm on the outside, however much distress they feel on the inside.

Very young children are often most terrified of the times when the whole school mills around – playtimes and lunchtimes. A good primary school will separate out the youngest children so that they don't feel overwhelmed, but the school my first child attended didn't do that and he begged to come home at lunchtime. 'Should I have let him?' I asked Luke.

'It's not a good idea,' he replied. 'It will make him feel different from the other children. If you listen to the specific fears, maybe the teacher can address them.'

'Bending the rules for a child,' Noël adds, 'reinforces the child's view of himself as someone who cannot cope with the routines and rules that others can cope with. By gradually and consistently requiring children to do what they think they can't do (systematic desensitisation), we can help children overcome fears and worries.'

Often it is tiny issues that colour a child's attitude. At one parenting class I met the mother of a boy who had been petrified of his new school. Only after close questioning did she discover that his fear was of being lost in this vast new place, so she got him a map, they pored over it together and when term started he bounded in.

What about the shift to secondary school?

Much as children like to feel they are growing up, each new stage brings fresh terrors. At one parenting class I spoke to a mother who recalled vividly the shock of suddenly being a small fish in a big pond. 'At primary school I had always done well,' she said. 'Suddenly at secondary school I was nothing special. It was very difficult. I never recovered my confidence and left school without going to university.' Had her parents acknowledged and helped her explore her feelings, she thinks that she might have got over them sooner.

'Even that might not have been enough,' commented Noël. 'Parents need to take action. Any distress, if not resolved, can start a sensitive child on a downward spiral. By secondary level, unpopularity is a common worry. Tempting though it may be to dismiss such fears as silly, ridicule encourages bottling up and increases the terror. Reassurance is equally counter-productive. If you say, "How could anyone not like a lovely girl like you?", the child will have two problems – the feeling of being unpopular and the worry that her parents don't think she should feel that way.'

One area where she feels that parents must be sensitive is to the higher level of organisation required of children in a secondary school. They move from being given all their lessons by one teacher in one room to a much larger environment with a whole host of teachers. They also have to find classrooms that are far apart and equip themselves with the right books for each lesson. 'Children often get in such a state that they arrive late and get into trouble,' Noël observes, 'or they are so worried that they won't have the right book for each lesson that they give themselves backache by carrying all their books around at once.'

To help children organise themselves, Noël suggests: 'You could ask every morning if they have the right equipment, but it will give the children more confidence if they make a list of what is needed each day and go over it every morning, at first in the parent's presence, so that the parent isn't doing the reminding. Descriptively praise the child for everything he gets right. This should all be done without moralising. Children often know what they have to do. We must help them view it strategically.'

I watched her help one AD(H)D child organise his book bag. She didn't do it for him: she prompted him to remember by asking questions. Every time he got something wrong she noticed the mistake but left him to work out how he could correct it. She never said 'Hurry up'.

It is easier to be patient if you are not the parent, but she believes mothers and fathers too can also be calm if they anticipate what a child needs to master and accept that training takes time. 'If a child can't organise his bag, show him how to pack it and praise him for imitating you. If tying a tie is a problem, teach him by doing it over his shoulder in the mirror.'

So strong is her emphasis on solving problems that she was able to help the mother of a disorganised child who had just started at boarding school. 'She taught me to look for solutions,' said the mother at one parenting class. 'Even though my son was miles from home, I managed to get him to his weekly clarinet lesson by putting reminders in places where he could not fail to see them.'

Should I worry if my child wants to conform at school?

Anxiety about fitting in is very common. Luke sympathises: 'When we moved to the country from London, my parents didn't have time to visit our new school, and they bought my brother and me the complete uniform. On our first day we stuck out a mile – no one else was dressed as we were. It was agony.'

He believes that parents should swallow their pride and let children conform. 'Don't buy second-hand uniform without the child's agreement; it could mean years in therapy later,' he jokes. 'And, even if you are a health nut, don't send them off with a lunchbox full of tofu if everyone else has white bread sandwiches – at least not in the first week. It may seem sad that your child wants to be like everybody else, but it is only a stage. He will emerge.'

Noël takes a tougher line. As a teenager she was often embarrassed by her mother's bohemian clothes, but ended up feeling proud of her mother's non-conformity. 'Parents should stick to their values when it comes to uniform, or anything else,' she says.

'As for kissing children goodbye in front of classmates, do what you think is right, and don't be put off by protests. To make it easier for the child, descriptively praise her for not pulling away or for hugging back, reflectively listen to any feelings of embarrassment, and prepare for success by saying what you intend to do so that the child doesn't hope to sneak out of it. At age five, my son made a fuss about my kissing him at the school gates because, as he put it, "That's girl stuff." I followed my own advice and insisted. There may be no connection, of course, but my son, now aged thirty-four, is extremely affectionate and loving.

'Giving in to a child's self-consciousness gives her the message that fitting in is the most important thing. It isn't, and anyway, children who are desperate to fit in don't. The ones who get teased and bullied are not those without the latest trainers – they are usually the ones with poor social skills.'

TIPS FOR STARTING EACH NEW TERM SUCCESS-FULLY

- Listen to the child's fears without trying to reassure or fix. As Noël says of emotional states, 'The only way out is through.'
- Get into the routine of getting up earlier at least a week before term starts so that the first day isn't a panicky rush.
- Luke would start reading with the child before term starts to wipe the rust off study skills. Noël would go further and organise short daily reading, writing and maths sessions during the holidays so that children don't forget what they learnt the term before.
- Teach children the practical skills they need. Don't undermine their confidence by doing things for them or by reminding them of things they should already know.
- Ask the child to work out a timetable of what needs to be taken to school when. 'What does your list say?' is less likely to lead to a row than 'Oh God, why didn't you say it was PE?'
- Set achievable goals and descriptively praise the child for mastering each skill, such as bringing the right books home or filling in his homework diary. Dwell on the achievement for a few weeks before looking to the next challenge. Praise previous achievements.

Why won't my child go to school?

Luke has helped children who bunk off. 'If a child is not turning up,' he finds, 'it is often because the parents are not convinced of the value of school, or cannot keep control. Some children who won't go to school are protecting a parent who cannot cope, whether through illness or depression. The first step is for the parent to accept the need for change, but to effect it they may need the help of a doctor or even social services.'

Another common reason for a child becoming a school refuser is that the parents are afraid of the child's reaction if they insist, whether it takes the form of an explosion or verbal abuse. Noël has found, not surprisingly, that children who don't feel successful, whether academically, socially or behaviourally, often don't like school. They may stoically accept it as their lot, or they may refuse to go, or they may accept it in principle but become expert dawdlers.

Parents can also put a child off school by blaming the school for not doing well by the child. 'This is most likely to happen when a child has learning difficulties that the school is not addressing satisfactorily,' says Noël, 'and it almost gives the child permission not to go to school.'

And then, of course, there is bullying. This often causes children to develop a terror of school. Once the bullying has been stopped, the parent then has the problem of getting the child back to school. This can demand great patience and determination.

So how do I get a refuser back to school?
At a parenting class I met a father whose child had been bullied. 'I had to wait outside his door until he was ready to put his shoes on, even if it took half an hour. He had to take each step of the way back to school. It was slow, but he made it.'

At bottom, says Noël, it's about parents getting back in charge of children who have often ruled the roost from infancy.

How do I get the children to do their homework?

Children who rush home from school and settle down to homework with no demur are rare. Most of mine fuss around, put it off, get into a state shortly before it has to be handed in and then dash it off or invent excuses. When the scrappy results do not go down well, loathing of homework becomes entrenched. Before I consulted Noël and Luke, my approach was to veer between ignoring the problem and screaming at the children for their lack of application.

Luke's reaction was to accept that homework was unlikely to come naturally: 'I'm deeply suspicious of a child who says he likes doing homework,' he says. 'It smacks of insecurity and a desire to please the parents at all costs. That said, it has to be done and you can tell your children that you don't always like having to work either.'

Doing homework, and doing it carefully, Noël believes, are skills, like toilet-training and saying please and thank you, that children have to be required to practise long before they can understand why they are important. To make the training easier for them, she suggests that parents reflectively listen to their children's feelings, all the while making it clear that homework is not an option, it is a requirement. 'Saying "You wish you didn't have to do these sums" conveys a parental empathy and also that the child has to do it. A child may show annoyance by making a face, but he still has to buckle down and do it.'

TIPS FOR GETTING HOMEWORK DONE

- Don't hope for the work to be done: require it. That means structure it, plan it, supervise it.
- Place. Homework should be done in a consistent setting – somewhere quiet and uncluttered where the children can be supervised. It is the parents' responsibility to prepare for success by removing all distractions – pets, toys, screens, siblings (if they bug each other), anything that competes for the child's attention. To set an example of concentration, the adult should be quietly working at the same table but not getting drawn into helping.
- Timing. Set aside a patch of time each day so that it becomes an invariable routine. This should be before a child has entered a television-induced trance, but after a child has had the chance to run around and get rid of the fidgets. If a favourite television programme clashes with homework time, have your child record it.
- Diet. 'Sugar, white flour and caffeine are known to inter-fere with every stage of learning: motivation, attention, understanding, retention, retrieval, use of information and generalisation,' says Noël. 'Give children a high-protein snack and complex carbohydrates before sitting them down to work.'
- Set a time limit. Choose a time by which homework must be started. Homework should not be an open-ended nightmare that makes a misery of the whole evening. It should last for a fixed time on the principle that there's nothing so terrible – even cleaning the loo – that you can't

---

stick if you know it will soon be over. A good principle is to require the hardest work to be completed first. Half an hour, rising to an hour, Noël and Luke reckon, is the right amount of homework for primary school children. Don't let children put off longer projects until just before they are due. Require a bit to be done every day.

- A quick child may rush through the work and finish in twenty minutes. If his work is correct, thorough and careful, give him more to do to make use of the time. A slow child might never finish in the time allotted, but should still stop at the appointed time because non-homework activities are just as important. The school may need to be told of the new policy so that the child does not get punished for idleness. Secondary schools set more homework; by then, if you have started this programme early enough, the child should be in the homework habit. Even if you start when your child is older, good habits can be established, but it will probably take longer.

- A timer on the table can keep everyone focused.

- Don't try to justify or convince a child of the usefulness of homework. If a child asks, 'Why do I have to do this?', ask the child to tell you why. Don't accept 'I don't know'.

- Supervision. The adult should make sure the child knows exactly what is to be done and how by having a daily 'talk-through', during which the parent asks questions and the child has to think. Convey authority by eye contact and sitting up straight: don't repeat, make sure that you get replies. Talk to the child politely, as you would to an adult; try to sound enthusiastic. Point out, for example, how useful take-away sums are for checking change when you next go to the sweetshop.

- Both parents should share supervisory responsibility so that one doesn't have to bear the burden of being the 'heavy one'. Fathers who are not home for weekday evening homework can take sole charge of weekend homework sessions.

- Time spent going through the instructions is vital. So are frequent checks to make sure that the child is following them; a child can't be blamed for flouncing off if he discovers at the end that he has been doing it all wrong.
- Show where the information is to be found; do not find it yourself.
- Notice a child's unproductive habits without moralising. Children may know what they have to do; they just aren't yet in the habit of doing it. If a child is disorganised, don't say 'Hurry up'. Instead, break the procedure down into even smaller steps and teach the child to master them in sequence.
- When a child is stalled or not concentrating, Noël would remove the books, paper and pen and listen reflectively to the child. Give the paper back only when the child is ready to have another go.
- Don't criticise. 'Many children hate doing homework with their parents as they are constantly criticised,' says Luke. 'If the child is staring into space, saying "Get on with it" never has the desired effect. Nor does harping on about old mistakes – "You're daydreaming again . . . " Avoid questions such as "Why do you always . . . ?" Never say "lazy", even in a joky voice; say (and think) "unmotivated" or "not yet in the habit".'
- Be firm. Trying is not doing; only doing is doing. Allow messy work in rough but not in best – children need to learn that they can achieve work they can be proud of.
- Let the procrastinating child go as slowly as he wants so that he learns that wasting time is not rewarded with parental attention. Work not finished when the homework hour is up remains so; he must face the consequences.
- Praise. Descriptive comments about anything the child has done right should be given every few minutes to keep her on track. 'There is often precious little to praise,' I point out to Luke. 'Surely you can find something?' he replied. 'There is bound to be one word that is correctly

spelt, one full stop in the right place. If you praise the good work, the child is more likely to go over the rest and spot her own mistakes.'

One mother found the key to success was starting the descriptive praise as soon as she met the child at school so that both of them were in a positive frame of mind when it came to homework time. Even if the child is fiddling and avoiding for much of the time, there will be moments of concentration to notice and praise.

- Rewards. Television time should be earned by doing the homework first. Always reward effort, whether the homework is finished or not.
- Teachers have their part to play. Tell them if your child is having difficulties with homework, and ask them to make a point of noticing any tiny improvements. Make sure, too, that they mark the work that has been done, even if it is only a small amount. Homework is not just about doing the work, it's about feedback.
- If the child is still having difficulties, the work may be too hard or the school may be unrealistic about the time it takes some children to complete the homework. Discuss all this with the teacher without blaming. Remember to descriptively praise the teacher regularly so that you and the school become allies rather than enemies or strangers.
- If the child is going out, have him do the homework in advance. 'If the child has to catch up afterwards,' says Luke, 'he won't enjoy the outing as much as if he had no worries.'

How do I supervise homework when I am home late?

I am not home from work until 6.30, by which time the younger children are too tired to do their homework, so it is often left undone. Luke and Noël have a host of solutions all of which require parents to believe that getting children into good homework habits is very important, not just for school, but for later life. 'Does the school have a homework club? Or could you set one up with neighbours and take it in turns to come home early?' suggests Noël.

'Could you get someone to come in specially to supervise the homework?' she continues. Specialist tutors are expensive, but a local sixth-former might come in and supervise.'

'It can be easier for a child to ask for help from someone outside the family, especially if he is having to do remedial work,' Luke points out. 'If you can't start and finish work earlier, could you help whoever is looking after the children to take homework more seriously by providing them with a list of rules?' Noël also suggests that parents and carers regularly sit down together to discuss how well the rules are working. Don't wait until things start to go wrong.

Even when I am at home to supervise homework, I confessed, I find it hard because the little one wanted to play. Luke suggested setting the little one some 'work' to do, such as cutting out pictures and sticking them on to paper. It will help the habit of concentration.

How do I help a child concentrate on schoolwork?

The words 'organisation' and 'concentration' crop up rather too often in some of my children's reports. Naturally I want to help a child who isn't doing as well as he might, but I also don't want to make the child unhappy by focusing on his shortcomings, so I veer between saying, 'It doesn't matter' and 'Let's do some maths together.' Noël says my anxiety is misguided: 'When a child is having problems at school he is the first to know it, so parents are unintentionally doing the child a disservice when they avoid mentioning or tackling it in an attempt, always futile, to keep the child from feeling bad.'

A more consistent approach, she says, is the place to start. Regular sessions, including thirty minutes to an hour a day during the holidays, will give a child who is falling behind the practice she needs, plus concrete proof that you care enough to give your full attention to whatever she is finding difficult. 'When there is a gap between potential and performance, even in a bright child it can usually be traced back to a weakness in a few basic learning skills. Only a few children acquire these skills by osmosis. Teachers don't know how to impart them, or don't see it as their job, so parents have to teach their children not to be slapdash and to listen without interrupting. These skills are useful outside school – for self-reliance, initiative and perseverance. Children can learn them later, but you are helping your child to be and feel more successful if you train her in these skills at an early age.'

All children, even those with a specific neurological disorder, can concentrate at least some of the time. I know (very well) boys who have no patience in class who can spend hours refining and perfecting skateboarding tricks with single-minded intensity. Rather than feel exasperated by that, Luke suggests using the example of the times when the child does focus to help him learn to concentrate at school. 'Keep reminding the child that he can focus by saying that he is just trying to do the same as he does when he practises with his skateboard. This is called neuro-linguistic programming: you are looking to anchor a feeling or habit so that it can be recalled.'

Watching Noël teach fidgety children, I have marvelled as she gets them painstakingly to perfect their handwriting. I confessed to her my doubts that I could get my own children to sit around a table applying themselves to lined paper, 'Who is in charge at home?' she challenged. Parents owe it to their children, she urges, to brave their initial wrath or indifference.

But surely, I said, a child will knuckle down and produce a decent history essay when necessary, so there is no need to make him work during the holidays when he should be relaxing? 'The longer you leave it,' she replied, 'the more likely he is to become disaffected and annoying in lessons because he is falling behind. When children have work to do or when they know they aren't able to do something well, they can't relax anyway.'

I asked Luke whether he agreed. 'I missed out on learning how to sit down and do things formally,' he said. 'I got through O-levels, but by A-levels I was in trouble as I wasn't in the habit of reading, taking notes and writing an essay. I'd have liked it if my parents had instilled those skills. The problem of building up a "bright but troublesome" image is that it can go beyond work into money and relationships. You can get to think of yourself as a nice guy with no focus, and, although nothing is set in stone, it is hard work when you are an adult to get out of it.

'But I would also look at the whole picture: is this particular problem "life threatening"? If you have a child who is twelve and he can't read or write, you certainly should be helping him, but if a child is operating at a level that will allow him to pass exams, even if he doesn't get top grades, there may be other areas where he needs more support. Is he fit? Is he overweight?'

I didn't like working because I had no concentration. Concentration was a fortress it never occurred to me to scale; and I remember gaping through hours of tuition without a thought in my head.
    Martin Amis, novelist, on failing his English A-level.

What should I do if a child blames her poor perform-ance on having a boring teacher?

Children have a tendency, Noël finds, to blame teachers for their own shortcomings. She wouldn't be put off the scent by that. 'Yes, teachers can be dull sometimes. Parents often reinforce the "blame game" by saying they had some boring teachers too. It is not a helpful response. "Boring" is an entirely subjective judgement. Ask the child or the school if everyone in that teacher's class did badly. Probably not. In that case, your child is finding some aspect of the work hard to follow.

'If you have a child who is interrupting teachers by asking unnecessary questions or is distracting himself by chatting in class, he is probably unable to do the work easily, or unable to do it quickly enough to satisfy the teacher. Children use bravado to mask feelings of inadequacy.'

Even so, I worry that tackling academic problems head-on at home might upset a child, I tell Luke. 'I'm a great one for learning things without it feeling like work,' he says. 'With little children you can give them mental arithmetic tests as a game, and the same with spellings and times tables; if you are enthusiastic, they will be too. You might get an older child to do some research on a subject that really interests him, such as what new skateboard he might get next. You could ask him to find out all the options and write them down with pros, cons and prices, and then given a reasoned report on which he considers the best.'

Noël doesn't dismiss that plan, nor does she rubbish my tactics of teaching learning skills through memory games played in the car, but she doesn't think either of those approaches sufficient to help a child who is having difficulties with learning or with classroom behaviour. 'If a child is introduced to a concept in conversation around the dinner table at home, he will be better able to understand it in a textbook,' she agrees. 'But if you really believe that all important cognitive skills can be learnt from daily life, why do you bother to send your children to school?'

'For the social life,' I ventured.

'If that is your only reason,' she said, 'there are much better ways to fulfil a child's need for companionship. And remember that it is perfectly legal not to send children to school, as long as parents make sure that the children are being educated. But most parents do think there are specific academic skills that children can best acquire at school.'

TIPS FOR HELPING CHILDREN DO BETTER AT SCHOOL

- Take the time to work out exactly what it is that the child can't manage. If a child is 'bored' or unmotivated, check that he is not being expected to do anything that is too difficult, too rushed, too abstract for his current level of understanding, too long for his attention span, or unsupervised. In science, for example, the basic terminology may be unfamiliar, so the subject becomes a blur. Once you have a clear idea of the problem, give your child frequent step-by-step practice in this area. This will lead to increased competence and confidence.

- Don't get too anxious: children pick up on that. Instead, plan what actions you will take. Let determination replace worry.

- Have realistic expectations about how quickly your child can improve work habits and academic skills.

- Meet the teachers and ask them about their teaching methods – these are almost certainly different from the way you were taught. 'Teachers can be very defensive because they are used to being got at,' says Luke. 'Praise them whenever you can so that if you do have a criticism, they won't bridle.'

- Involve the child in discussions about what needs to

change and how that can be accomplished, Noël recommends. 'Let him hear, let him speak.' But not if you take issue with the school: then, she believes, parents should uphold the school's authority when talking with the child, and sort out the matter in private.

- Talk to the child about how he might please the teachers more or annoy them less. 'What is it that makes teachers like a pupil?' I heard Noël ask one ten-year-old. Tackle at home the behaviour that is irritating to teachers at school. For example, with their parents, children often interrupt a conversation with a joke or irrelevant comment and get away with it. Announce interruption-free periods daily at home so that children can practise and get better at impulse control, focus and patience.
- Ask if the child could sit at the front of the class where there are fewer distractions.
- Play brain games at home and in the car. Learning songs or poems, painting by numbers, playing cards or draughts, or following the instructions for origami all help.
- Boost a child's listening (and ultimately reading) comprehension by reading to him (even after he can read well), by waiting for a reply in a full sentence when you ask a question, by appreciating and elaborating on the child's comments, by asking the child what she is going to do and how, and helping the child come up with detailed, thought-out answers.
- Teach accuracy and attention to detail by getting children to copy a piece of text exactly: 'When copying something, the child doesn't have to think about composing the content, so it is much easier to pay attention to detail than when writing a story or essay,' Noël explains. 'The child must work to get the handwriting, spelling, punctuation and presentation perfect. He can do a rough first, but the fair copy should have no mistakes. Underline the perfect parts in green; let him spot the mistakes. Praise his efforts as well as the results.'
- Make opportunities for a child to teach others.

How do you deal with a bad school report?

'Think and talk not in terms of results and coming top,' says Luke, 'but of improvements and goals. Concentrate on helping children with their weak spots as much as pushing their talents. Dwelling on the worst aspects of this report and harking back over the less eulogistic parts of last year's will only discourage.'

If tempted, he says, 'Examine your intentions. Do you really think the child has forgotten his past record? Aren't you just trying to shame him into higher achievement? Can you find a more positive approach?'

'Start by focusing on anything good or even just OK in the report,' says Noël. 'Slow down and make a meal of these areas. That will be far more motivating than first discussing the problems. Whatever extra practice you arrange, remember frequently to spend time doing what you and the child both enjoy, and let the child lead. Reward all improvements, even small ones. Detailed feedback – particularly descriptive praise – is more motivating than testing, and results in more improvement.

'When a child makes a real effort, don't just say, "I'm proud of you," but also, "You deserve to feel proud of yourself." It is natural for children to want to please their parents, but some may need to be weaned off working for their parents' sake.'

To that, Luke adds as a caveat, 'It is easy to forget, particularly in the highly competitive private school system, that there is more than one type of intelligence and all of them need to be cultivated. Visual intelligence, an understanding of nature, sport and getting on with other people are just as important, maybe more so, than reading above your age or being a star at mental arithmetic.'

Should I take my child to an educational psychologist?

One of my children's teachers suggested this to me at one parents' evening and I was nonplussed. She thought there was a problem; other teachers didn't. I couldn't decide whether to seek help and risk demoralising the child, or ignore well-meant advice.

'Think about it for a bit,' Luke suggested. 'Ask yourself, "Is what I am considering doing likely to help my child or am I merely giving vent to my own frustration?" Keep any anger and bitterness to your-self: whatever anyone says to you about your child, remain cool and dignified. Then, if you do think the child needs to see an educational psychologist, visit him or her first. Don't hawk children round experts. Find one you trust and stick with him or her.'

Noël says, 'If you or the school suspect a difficulty with learning, the first thought may be to get a diagnosis. Labelling the problem can help everyone concerned to stop blaming, but a diagnosis is not a solution. Effective solutions usually require teachers and parents to handle the child's learning differently.'

How do I help a child who is falling behind with her reading?

To some children, reading is a chore. Some of mine can't seem to get caught up in a story, so they avoid picking up a book. I've nagged and tried reading with them but they always think of some excuse to disappear. When one of them began to slip backwards in the class reading groups, Noël and Luke agreed that action was called for. Their tactics, however, were slightly different.

Noël started by giving me a pep talk: 'Her loss of interest may be just a blip, but it is imperative to take action before the child decides reading isn't her thing. Not being "a reader" often makes children feel embarrassed or guilty, and avoiding reading is a habit, reinforced daily, that can take years to dissolve on its own, and it may never dissolve. Children build up a strong defence system that is harder to whittle away as they get older.'

'But I have tried to encourage her,' I bleated.

'When you say "I've tried" to help the child, what you really mean is "I've given up",' she responded. 'Whose job is it to get her into good habits? If you can't make it happen, how can she? Don't make it be her fault. If she makes excuses not to try, and you let her get away with not trying, then, in effect, you are obeying her.

'A child who is not yet a fluent reader often finds reading a chore. The effort necessary for decoding distracts the child from visualising the story. When she says she doesn't find it interesting, she might mean that she doesn't feel successful. Children are willing to do things that don't interest them – they do hundreds of them every day – if they feel successful. Success is what motivates them.

Maybe initially it will be hard to make a child practise reading, but children get into good habits very quickly with daily practice and descriptive praise.'

She suggests looking at why it might be that a child has lost enthusiasm. 'Usually,' she says, 'people who don't get pleasure from books are being expected to read above their level of competence. It may be that the book contains concepts beyond her grasp.

'Young readers are often stumped by abstract words, such as "however", which show the relationships between things, whereas they can manage concrete words, even ones that are difficult to pronounce, such as "rhinoceros", because they can visualise them. Often, too, children get confused and frustrated by names that they can't pronounce and it makes them want to give up. Try some simpler but very engaging books, such as the Barrington Stoke books, written for and vetted by dyslexic children, which are designed with short paragraphs, simpler sentence construction and easy names.

'Use your common sense and persist,' she advised me.

Luke saw the issue as a test of parental commitment. 'The child may be testing you by playing hard to get,' he suggested. 'As much as anything, this is about proving that you are sufficiently committed to the child, and to reading, to devote regular time to it. I would tell the child straight that there is going to be some time spent with books and that it will be at 6.30 each evening. If it's just you reading, it will be half an hour; if the child reads alternate pages, it will be twenty minutes.

'The child will make excuses but you must be firm. "It is now 6.30," you say, looking the child in the eye. Smile all the time. Don't sound angry or annoyed: she already feels that dropping down a reading group is a disaster, but she doesn't know what to do about it. Don't worry about doing some of the reading yourself: being read to is just as important as reading because it gives children the chance to listen to the literary spoken words that they don't otherwise hear, certainly not on television.'

Children are prisoners of even loving parents, prisoners of even kindly schools. Reading, they can escape to freedom.
                                                            Nina Bawden, author

TIPS FOR HELPING CHILDREN WITH READING

- Ask the child to suggest books to share, and enthuse at the suggestions, Luke says. 'If he doesn't choose, say that you will. Don't choose long books: they are daunting. If he produces a comic strip, don't explode. Ask calmly why he thinks this one isn't going to be suitable, or if he can guess what you are going to say. If he says, "You'll think it's fine," then you respond, "I know that's what you'd like me to say."'

- Set aside half an hour a day. Don't exceed the time. Read together by alternating sentences for fifteen minutes, then discuss for fifteen minutes. Avoid questions that have yes or no answers, and questions that ask for recall of details. 'Why?' questions are the best for making children use their brains. Be creative in your discussions: you could pretend to be characters in the passage, invent backgrounds for them, think of alternative endings . . .

- If you have to miss a session, make up the time in advance, but not in one great marathon.

- Never nag. 'You catch more flies with honey than with vinegar,' says Noël.

- Don't expect enthusiasm. You supply the enthusiasm.

- Set an example. Why should a child think reading is important if you are rarely seen with a book?

- Many reluctant readers think they can't concentrate, but they just haven't learnt how; when the parent and child read alternate sentences, the child does not have time to tune out.

- End each session with a joke and lots of descriptive praise.

- Before the next day, note down what was read, what happened, what went well/badly, and choose the next passage.

- Reflectively listen to the child's feelings about reading (but not during the half-hour) so that she feels understood.

- And, of course, descriptively praise cooperation, courage, willingness, patience and not whingeing as well as progress.

Any tips for helping with spelling?

A parent's instinct is to point out an error. 'Then the child whines or sulks, doesn't he?' Noël points out. 'That is because fault-finding reinforces the child's belief that spelling is too hard and that he can't do it. Show him that he can, and don't take the moans and groans personally.'

The next time one of my children spelt 'look' as 'lok', I followed her advice. I did not say that she had made a mistake; I said, 'You've left a letter out.' It would be even more positive, Noël told me later, to say, 'Those three letters are right but there is one more letter before the 'k' – what might that be?' That way the child does her own thinking. Once again, descriptive praise goes a long way towards motivating children to care about and think about spelling. Parental enthusiasm is contagious, but children might not catch it overnight.

How do I get children to practise their musical instruments?

In my house violin practice creates regular havoc. The daughter in question chose to do the instrument, but every time she has to practise she sobs and makes excuses on the grounds that it is too hard and she wants to give up. I plead, reason and cajole, but the problem keeps recurring.

Luke advocates less sympathy and more firmness. 'Is she truly distressed? Probably not, I'm sure you can tell. Have an annual review of the situation, but in between times don't get drawn into discussions of giving up. You don't want her to get into the habit of quitting, and you do want children to develop a bit of stoicism.

'When the time comes for practice, remember: listen, praise, set rewards and consequences. Ask her how you and she can make practising more appealing. Get her ideas and act on them.'

Later I told Noël how pleased I was that this advice seemed to have worked. My daughter was now more enthusiastic about practising, I said, so I no longer had to get heavy with her. I should have thought more carefully before I spoke. 'Do you really equate firmness with heaviness?' she asked. 'Getting heavy sounds like it is linked to anger, disapproval or blame. Being firm, however, is about following through on what you think is right, and you can certainly be firm while staying friendly and calm. If you are confusing firmness with being heavy, you won't want to keep it up. But you must not rest on your laurels now just because at the moment she is more keen to practise. It may be going well now, but sensitive children's reactions come and go in waves. Don't leave it up to her to keep up the routine: that is your job. The more positive, firm and consistent you remain, the more willing the child will be.'

How do you deal with a child saying he isn't good at anything?

One of my children confessed that for years he had felt that, at school, he was no good at anything; he could admit it now that he had finally found something he was good at.

'Pay more attention to the positive than to any depressing reviews of the past,' said Luke. 'Say how pleased you are that he feels good about something now and that if he needs extra support with anything, you'd be happy to give it. It is sad if a child has been unhappy, but as parents we aren't entirely responsible for our children's experience. They have their own temperaments to contend with and all the other influences in their environments.

'Also,' he warned, 'it may be what he is saying, but not what he actually thinks. "I've never felt good at anything before" is a dramatic statement, designed to have maximum impact. Take it with a pinch of salt. By all means use it as a spur to be more positive, but not as something to beat yourself with.'

One mother with a son who felt constantly gloomy first checked with the school that there weren't any major problems. There weren't; her son was just in the habit of looking on the dark side. So each day she made a habit of asking him in the evening to tell her about three things that had gone right that day – or had even been just OK. 'It helped him focus on what was going well,' she said.

What can be done to help a child with exams?

When a very young child is being examined, Noël points out, a school is not looking so much for knowledge as for sensible behaviour, social skills and alertness – the ability to answer a question in a full sentence, to give interesting details, not to fidget, to make eye contact – all of which can be practised at home.

With older children, life's not so simple. They need to revise what they have already been taught, and they may also need to learn new information and skills that their current school has not even covered. When one of mine was preparing for competitive exams for secondary schools I complained to Luke about her moaning and groaning. Surely, I said to him, a ten-year-old should be able to see the point of trying her best to get into a good school. 'How many twenty-five-year-olds do you know,' he replied, 'who control themselves in the present in order to get what they want in the future? It's crazy to expect children to be able to do that. Normal children want to watch as much television as possible and do as little work as possible, eat what they want and go to bed when they like. They don't have to like preparing for exams; they just have to do it.'

Noël's advice was not to react to grumbles. 'Do lots of reflective listening about how revision eats into free time and the anxiety that surrounds exams. Never say, "Please, we need you to do well." It's so weak to beg – your boss at work doesn't beg – and it gives the child too much power.'

But I do feel powerless, I protested. 'You can't, of course, move the child's arm for her and make her work,' she agreed, 'but you can set her up to be motivated by keeping to a routine of short daily revision sessions, descriptive praise of course and frequent rewards. As she is doing more work, she's due more rewards than the other children. This will also show the younger children that when their time comes, there will be a definite up side to it. If an older child were to complain that he didn't get special treatment last year when he revised for exams, you could reflectively listen and then explain: "When we were going through this with you, we did it one way. Now we've found a better way. We can't keep doing it the old way once we've discovered something better just so that you aren't upset."'

WAYS TO HELP CHILDREN PREPARE FOR EXAMS
- Teach and train revision technique (see below).
- During the week before an exam stick to the normal bedtime.

- Don't allow caffeine (in the form of cola or chocolate) that could ruin sleep and concentration.
- Don't let them work themselves into a state by discussing the exam with classmates the night or morning before.
- Get the child to the exam in good time and with all the necessary equipment.
- Teach and train exam technique, i.e.
    - Read the test; see where the points are awarded; plan the time.
    - Ask for clarification if any procedures are unclear.
    - Don't stare at a blank sheet of paper: move on, but mark the question you've skipped so that you can return to it at the end.
- Train a child when stuck to say to himself, 'I'll do what I can.'
- Teach and train deep breathing and stretching.

How do you teach children to revise?

Older children are tested on knowledge, and that calls for revision, the main purpose of which is to transfer information from the short-term memory to the long-term. Learning to revise effectively doesn't come naturally. 'Left to their own devices,' says Noël, 'children tend simply to reread their notes, but that is far too passive an approach to make much of a dent on the long-term memory. The key is active repetition, with variety, at lengthening intervals.

'Say the task is to learn a poem: the way to do it is to say it out loud in a number of different ways. Surprisingly, it is important after you have memorised it thoroughly not to rattle it off every day but to leave lengthening intervals between recitals because the attempt to retrieve the poem releases chemicals in the brain that encourage storage in the long-term memory.

'A daily routine of homework done carefully and thoroughly will mean that the basics won't have to be learnt or relearnt at the last moment, but parents may have to teach and train careful reading of instructions, note-taking, making an outline, proofreading and knowing the difference between, say, a definition and a description, or between a general statement and a supporting detail. Very few schools teach revision skills; even fewer train pupils to use the skills habitually. So it's up to parents to teach and train; it really doesn't take an expert.'

Revision should also happen daily. Fifteen minutes each day is more valuable than two hours once a week. Vary the times of day. In the morning the brain is fresh, but when revision is followed by sleep or recreation, less is forgotten. Never let a child at secondary level revise one subject for more than one hour at a time.

TIPS FOR HELPING CHILDREN TO REVISE

- Start early, using an hour of every weekend to review what the child has learnt that week. Similarly, use the holidays to review the previous term's work. That's the way to commit information to the long-term memory.
- Teach the child to make a realistic timetable and how to work out the amount of time required for each subject.
- Train him to rewrite notes to make them less messy, more succinct, more thorough and easier to use.
- To test knowledge, have your child read, then shut the book and write a skeleton outline, using his own words (phrases rather than whole sentences) and leaving plenty of space. Underline key headings.
- If the child doesn't understand a topic, find a book on the same subject aimed at younger children. The vocabulary will be simpler, and only the most basic points will be covered. Have the child revise this book thoroughly before going back to the more difficult material.
- Teach the use of mnemonics.
- Go over old exam questions with your child, asking what they require. Teach the checklist of six question words: who, what, where, when, why, how.
- Give the child frequent praise and frequent breaks.
- Teach relaxation exercises.

11

TREATS AND TEMPTATIONS

How do I stop television and computers dominating the children's lives? How do I prevent birthdays becoming an expensive nightmare? Are there ways to make holidays happier? Do journeys have to be hell?

I give my children far too many treats, but contemporary life makes it hard to be more self-disciplined. We are all so busy that, with six things I could be doing at any one time, I often park the children in front of the television, or feel grateful when they play quietly on the computer. I fall into the trap, too, of buying approval because I am not around at home as much as I would like. So if eating at McDonalds or going clothes shopping will earn me a chorus of 'You are the bestest mummy in the world', it is an almost irresistible temptation.

Usually, when over-excitement leads to mayhem, I regret my permissive, extravagant ways and start shouting or asking rhetorical questions, such as, 'Why can't you just be quiet? Why are you so ungrateful?' If I were not so busily rushing on to the next event, I would be able to answer those questions by saying that the children are wildly over-stimulated.

Many factors conspire to make them so. Electronics and the media are in themselves a constant source of exciting flashing lights, whirrs and bangs. They also provide opportunities for advertisers to whip children up into a consumerist frenzy of desire for the latest gizmos and toys. Cars and planes also generate excitement, which combines with inactivity in often volatile ways. Then there are the further thrills of theme parks and holidays that lie at the end of those journeys, and the sleepovers that keep my children awake most weekends. Add in the consequences of sugar, caffeine and E-number-laden foods and drinks and you have a highly explosive cocktail.

Even for a child with a steady temperament, all this stimulation is enough to create tension; in a sensitive child the effect can be (and regularly is) catastrophic. Nevertheless, rather than work on creating more calm, I, like many parents, add to the problem by ladling on to the children's overloaded plates further dollops of demanding experience. This, I tell myself, is for their own good. We all want to give our children every chance in life, so we book them in for anything on offer, from chess club to ballet lessons, from kung fu to French playgroup. Even knowing that the child who rarely comes straight home from school to play may never learn to occupy himself hasn't stopped me. Nor, to judge by the waiting lists for these activities, has it stopped many others too.

It is hard to know how to act differently. Few homes are without television, computers or Game Boys, and it takes a very strong parent to decide to live without them for the sake of the children. It might not even be wise: nothing is so attractive as forbidden fruit. As for exciting events, such as Christmas and birthdays, they have to be celebrated. Holidays and car journeys, too, are part of life. What can be done to keep excitement under control, I asked Noël and Luke.

My stance is that of most parents, I told them: I want the children to enjoy everything that the modern world has to offer, but I want them to learn moderation. I fear that the legacy of a life lived constantly in the fast lane will be a craving for instant excitement, which in adulthood can be met only by drink, drugs, promiscuity, rampant materialism and the insecurity that comes from believing that needs can be met by fulfilling a momentary want. But the temptations are all out there and available from an early age, so I want my children to learn to deal with them in a mature way – while they are still immature.

Luke understands the problem. 'Our lifestyle makes this the most difficult time ever to be bringing up children,' he believes. 'There is a huge difference between what children want and what they need. Children these days are growing up faster than ever before under the influence of the media, consumerism and drug culture. That means they need more guidance, not less, but many parents are – or feel – unsupported, so they find it hard to take charge, and instead give children treats to show that they care.'

As Noël puts it succinctly: 'There is a direct link between guilt, over-indulgence and out of control behaviour.'

How can I limit television time?

My policy on television has been one of derision. 'How can you bear to watch that rubbish?' I mutter at my glassy-eyed children. I assume they will eventually catch my lack of interest, but in the meantime, even the three-year-old talks as if he were a character from *EastEnders*. When I confessed this to Noël she was horrified: 'The more time children spend in front of screens, the less good their relationships.'

Research and observation have convinced her that screens (in which she includes computers, console games and hand-held games) act like a drug on children, who are more sensitive than adults, and find it harder to detach themselves. Studies have shown that screens have a harmful effect on the brain development of children up to the age of three. She therefore strongly recommends that until that age children not be exposed to screens at all, no matter how excellent the subject matter. Prolonged viewing, regardless of content, increases excitement levels, making it harder for children to concentrate afterwards, and interferes with sleep patterns so that they awake tired and grumpy.

Television and computer games also provide a host of unappealing role models of sharply distinct villains and heroes who meet with dramatically different ends. And hours spent glued to a screen, of course, eat into time that might otherwise be spent running, playing imaginative games and reading. In addition, there is television's role in creating pester power.

I hadn't met Noël when my children were small, so they developed a love of screens at an early age. My hope has always been that once they start secondary school, they will simply be too busy to spend much time looking at them. This policy has worked with my eldest child, but Noël thinks it is a foolishly optimistic way to proceed. 'There's no guarantee you are right, and meanwhile your children are wasting valuable time – and it is doing nothing for your relationship with them,' she says.

Since she believes that 'childhood is more satisfactory without television', she advises parents who can't yet control their children's viewing to arrange for all their televisions to 'break' for several months. A friend of mine did that for a while, but she did not use that time to train her children into more wholesome habits. When the experiment was over, the children went back to their old habits, and the screen-free days soon became a distant golden age. But rather than approaching screen-free time in the same way as a crash diet (amazing effect but not sustainable), Noël's advice is, 'Use the screen-free months to get back in charge so that the children thereafter obey your rules. During this time the children will also learn to entertain themselves so that they will no longer be slaves to the "plug-in drug".'

Luke also had a screen-free childhood and is glad of it. 'That's almost unthinkable now,' he admits. 'Although I don't subscribe to the view that TV is evil – you get rubbish everywhere and there are some brilliant programmes – I would definitely limit children's access and certainly never allow televisions (or other screens) in children's bedrooms. Like eating pizza, viewing is fine occasionally, but not constantly. Just as we don't let children choose their bedtime, they shouldn't choose when or how much TV they watch. Where we can encourage them to exercise choice and learn selectivity is over what they watch.'

His particular concern is for vulnerable, lonely children. 'I don't buy the argument that it is hard to make friends if children miss out on popular culture. If children are not getting on well socially, it won't help not to be able to discuss what was on the favourite soap, but it is not essential. What actually happens is that vulnerable children become greedier and needier and don't develop maturity and responsibility.'

As for content, he says, 'Common sense tells us that a huge amount of exposure to violence, real or simulated, is not good. Even if a direct link can't be made between a particular film and certain behaviour, the amount and the continuous drip, drip, drip of irresponsible violence is damaging.'

So how would Noël and Luke limit screen time? They start by reminding me why my policy of ridicule has been ineffectual. 'A reproof without a consequence is just a nag,' says Noël. Luke adds that my scorn is hurtful. They advise the more positive approach of rationing.

When I followed their advice I was amazed by how readily – even enthusiastically – my children took to rationing. They compiled a timetable of favourite programmes, stuck it up on the fridge and began to trade shortfalls one day for an extra long burst on another day. When I announced that screen time couldn't be carried over from one week to the next, they accepted it without demur. Here was proof positive, to my mind, of children welcoming limits.

Other parents find the same. A mother at a parenting class spoke of her son who went 'ballistic' when she first told him to turn off the television; a week later, after she had told him that the television was to stay off while she took the dog for a walk, he did not attempt to turn it on. 'Trust is very important to older children,' observes Luke.

Referring to the parental temptation to use screens as child-minders, Noël reminds me, 'Before the electronic age, children, who have always wanted to be where the action is, hung around their parents, listening, learning, getting attention and being useful. It is not necessary to get children out of the way in order to get things done. Of course, tasks will take longer to complete when you involve the children, but surely relationships and values are more important than speed.'

If a child really wants to watch a programme you regard as pointless rubbish, a good compromise is to agree, provided that he writes a review and draws a picture to illustrate it.
Libby Purves, writer and broadcaster

TIPS FOR RATIONING SCREEN TIME
- 'Always watch television with children,' advised Noël. This surprised me, but she explained that if parents actually watched the pernicious trash that their children soak up, they would be fired with greater determination to ration it. Plus, it gives parents on-the-spot opportunities to explain concepts and clarify their values.
- Announce well in advance that rationing is to be introduced and make a big deal of it. 'You aren't going to like this. Mummy and I have made a new rule about screen time. Can you guess what it might be? Yes, starting from Monday you can earn a maximum of an hour of screen

time each day.' This hour should be after all homework and chores are completed to the parents' satisfaction, and must finish at least an hour before the children go to bed so that they have time to unwind.

- Have a sliding scale. Noël recommends: no screen at all before age three; a maximum of half an hour a day (combined total of all screens) between the ages of three and eight; a maximum of one hour a day from age eight onwards.
- Reflectively listen to their feelings if they seem at all distressed. (They will.) Don't suggest alternative ways to spend the time, as all your ideas will be shot down.
- Mention the new rule several times a day as the deadline approaches. With each repetition the children will become less upset and more accepting.
- Allow the children (within limits) to choose their hour's viewing; make the children responsible for taping their favourite programmes if these are broadcast at inconvenient times.
- If there's a programme you particularly want them to watch, allow it on top of the ration.
- When the hour is up, ask a child only once to turn off the television. If nothing happens, do it yourself. This cuts down on arguments and shows who is in charge.
- If the child screams and shouts, descriptively praise her for whatever bad things she is not doing, but don't argue. You aren't going to change your mind.
- The reward for following the screen-time rules to the letter is that the child has earned screen time for the next day.

To say his reading and concentration have improved times one hundred would not be overstating the truth.
Polly Samson, novelist, quoting her seven-year-old's school report after she had chucked out the television

How can I control what the children are watching when I'm not at home?

Luke was impressed by one father who attached a timer switch to the television and, having drilled some holes for wires, put it inside a locked box. Once the children had agreed on their hour's programmes for the day, the schedule was fixed. 'That way he found he didn't have to tell the children off about it,' says Luke, 'and they couldn't cheat.'

Noël gave full marks for determination to a father who took the television aerial to work each day. She also knows parents who sold all the televisions except for a small portable one, which is kept in a locked cupboard and brought out with a flourish on special occasions. One family has come up with a unique method of rationing screen-time that works very well for them: on odd-numbered days of the month, children can spend as much time as they like in front of screens, but on even-numbered days, none at all. Some parents limit viewing to weekends, and a few choose to eliminate screens from their homes altogether.

What do I do if the only time a child will spend with me is watching television?

Luke and Noël are always advocating each parent spending more one-to-one time with each child. When I told a daughter of mine that I wanted to do something just with her at least once a week, all she could come up with was watching television. I hated the idea of having to sit through some deadly soap, so I asked Noël and Luke for advice.

'Sometimes an older child feels so alienated and criticised that she won't agree to any other activity during one-to-one time with a parent,' Luke acknowledged. 'In that case you agree to the offer and don't criticise her choice of programme.'

'As you demonstrate that you really enjoy spending time with the child,' Noël added, 'she'll eventually accept some of your suggestions for other activities, and she will even come up with some herself.'

Is the computer really as much of a hazard as television?

Luke describes the computer games that show constant violence without any blood or pain as acting like classic desensitising programmes. 'Children can, of course, make the distinction between games and life, but the games don't help them to develop good values,' he observes.

These games are also bad for their nerves. Noël cites some research into the effects of computer games, which shows that although only a few children who are addicted to them become more aggressive as a result, many more emerge from this virtual world of hazards and enemies perceiving the real world as a more threatening place than it really is. 'Do parents want their children going around feeling like potential victims?' she asks.

They worry too about allowing children access to the Internet. 'Even speaking as a liberal,' says Luke, 'I would be very concerned. There's stuff on there that is horrendous.' When teenagers and older children have stumbled into paedophile rings while looking for rude pictures of girls of their own age, the results have been traumatic. Families' lives have been wrecked by police investigations, expulsion from school and recriminations.

Luke's advice (and Noël's) is to invest in an effective site-blocking service: 'You should be able to take the block off yourself. In any case, be careful where you have Internet access. Always keep it in a public room that people walk in and out of, not in a bedroom.'

Clothes and other stuff

Noël suggests that rather than give in to (and, in my case, simultaneously pooh-pooh) children's demands for endless new clothes and toys, parents should listen to their desires and show that they understand by reflecting their wishes back at them in the form of a shared fantasy. 'You could say, "I often wish I could have all the new things I want too, but I have to make choices. Let's imagine what this family might do with a few thousand pounds."'

What parents can no longer do, as previous generations used to, is inflict their choices on children. The frilly party frocks that I bought my girls went straight into the fancy dress drawer. Luke is on

the children's side. 'Choosing clothes,' he says, 'is essential to establishing an identity. Let a child go to nursery in a Winnie-the-Pooh
costume. Let children wear what they like to their friends' parties.

'But when it is a grown-up event, parents have a say too. Try not
to be prescriptive. Discuss what is suitable, don't bark instructions,
and then let them choose. Praise whatever items they get right – 'The
trousers are perfect' – and ask for another try if you think the ripped
T-shirt or belly-top is not quite right for a wedding. Let the child do
the thinking and come up with an outfit that will work.'

Noël makes the point that, increasingly, pre-teens are wanting to
dress like teenagers, which often means provocatively for girls and
tough for boys. 'If we complain but at the same time let them, we are
sending confusing messages and also not standing up for our values.
We can require an acceptable (to us) standard of dress, just as we can
with behaviour, homework, chores and screen time. Our children
will thank us for it, and sooner than we think.'

As for rampant materialism, Luke says, 'The world is the way it
is; kids are the way they are; we can't change that. But we can reframe
things so that they go the way we want. There's no point saying to a
kid, "You can't have those fancy trainers because I have read that the
company exploits poor workers in Southeast Asia, so here are some
sandals." But you can say, "I'll contribute £40 towards your shoes; if
you want more expensive ones, you can earn the money."'

If the child saves up for the expensive kind, then loses them on
the bus, you have to replace them because they are essential for
school sports but you can buy a very cheap pair. 'Let them learn from
their mistakes. It is an excellent lesson to freeze when they don't put
their coat on. And let them earn their own money as soon as they
can; I used to collect and sell apples from our tree.'

Noël suggests that parents make children earn any extra money
they want by doing one-off household chores. Children become
much more appreciative when they have to work for the extras they
crave.

How can I give a pain-free children's party?

Special events need celebrating, but they can become a focus of inor-
dinate fuss. Competitive parents turn birthday parties into Busby
Berkeley productions. The result, say Noël and Luke, is that everyone

misses the point. 'Parents feel that if they ensure their child has a wonderful birthday, she will feel truly loved. But by setting so much store by birthdays, aren't we making it appear that ordinary days don't count?'

Life isn't about waiting, in Noël's view, so when her children were young she took the pressure off the great day. As their birthdays both fell on the fourth of the month, she made it a routine that on the fourth of each month they were allowed a special meal with friends.

Luke takes a slightly different view: he approves of ritual and delayed gratification, and thinks birthdays should be a focus of excitement, but he too believes celebrations often get out of hand. 'Like many things in contemporary society, parties have become about excess and consumerism. There are parents who will pay $1 million for Michael Jackson to sing for their eight-year-old. That encourages children to think about birthdays as a show, and delivers the subliminal message that fun must involve sugar and mounds of presents rather than playing with friends. Especially when a child is not very confident, a celebration should not just involve money, but time and effort and care.'

I find that my children begin to plan their next party even before the balloons from the last one have gone wrinkly. I groan, but since much of the fun of a party lies in the planning, I go along with it. When a child seems more than normally preoccupied by that special day, however, Luke and Noël would find out why. 'The child may feel he only gets his parents' undivided attention on that day,' says Noël. 'If he has more of what he needs — usually positive attention — and less of what he doesn't need — usually criticism — throughout the year, after a while he won't invest so much emotion in that one day.'

Accordingly, I asked one of my daughters why she spent twelve months a year worrying about her annual party. Her reply brought me up short. Her birthday, she said, was the only day of the year when everyone was nice to her. 'Particularly in large families,' Luke reminds me, 'children need frequent, predictable times when they are made to feel special.'

Rather than being the scourge of a parent's life, Luke and Noël believe that birthday parties and other celebrations can provide a useful opportunity to instill values. Noël sees a party as a chance to learn about making sensible choices, planning, organisation, healthy food and how to please one's guests. Luke, keen that privileges should be earned, would make certain aspects of the celebrations, such as how much to spend on decorations or how many guests to invite, contingent on good behaviour: 'But don't make threats that you will never carry through, such as, "If you do that once more, I shall cancel your party."'

How many elaborations of the modern birthday party a parent takes on board is a matter of personal choice. Noël would ban party bags, so only the birthday child gets presents. Luke thinks an exchange of gifts is a nice idea but he would make the birthday child responsible for making or choosing the contents.

TIPS FOR CALM BIRTHDAYS

- Keep parties small. Noël recommends one guest for each year of a child's life. Big parties mean more presents, but also more work, more havoc, more thank-you letters, and the treadmill of a party invitation in return every weekend.
- Involve the child at every stage, from working within a budget to making decorations and cooking. Get the child involved by giving a limited number of choices that you approve of and let the child pick one.
- Entertainers are fashionable and take the pressure off parents, but Noël disapproves because they require children to sit passively. Children will have more fun, and burn off more energy, if the party involves races or a day out to remember. Also many small children are terrified of clowns with painted faces.
- Be realistic. 'Children almost always have more sophisticated tastes than parents believe,' says Luke, and it is cruel to insist on pass the parcel if the rest of the class likes disco dancing and make-up.
- Encourage self-reliance and maturity. With that in mind, Luke would leave older children alone as far as possible. With teenagers he would negotiate on weak wine cup and (fairly brief) parental absence somewhere close by, perhaps a neighbour's house. 'If you control everything too strictly, when they leave home for university they

---

won't be used to taking responsibility. Give it to them bit by bit and their mistakes will be smaller.'

- Limit the sugary options. 'You don't have to serve fizzy drinks,' says Noël, 'you can serve diluted juice. I gave a children's party where I served crudités with houmous and taramasalata, and the kids loved it because it was so different. You don't want children to grow up to equate having a good time with the over-excitement that comes from gorging on sugar.'

  When I serve carrot sticks, I tell her, they get ignored. 'That's because you have provided piles of unhealthy food as well. Give the children a proper meal and just a few sweet things afterwards. How about spaghetti or meat loaf? It's not the food that makes a party, it's the people and being active.'

- Have a quiet room for children who don't want to join in. Just as at adult parties, there is always someone who prefers to hang around the kitchen. Pop in every ten minutes and chat to them.
- Don't require children who don't like parties to stay for long; parties are meant to be fun, but some children hate crowds. However, do require them to attend so that they build up their stamina, and prepare for success by having clear expectations and giving the child alternatives to group games, such as reading a book or chatting with the grown-ups.
- Allow siblings to invite a friend each so that they don't feel left out or become disruptive.
- If there are no party bags, tell the children so nicely at the beginning.
- Don't let rules and routines go out of the window.

Sex, drugs and alcohol

Most of the big, potentially dangerous temptations used to strike at a time when teenagers were largely outside parental control. Now they loom at an earlier age, so parents feel they have to take a stand. Noël and Luke believe they should, but that they should keep morality out of it as far as possible.

'Stick to talking about which behaviour gets the result that the child wants, and which does not,' says Luke. 'You want your child to be able to think for himself and not succumb to peer pressure.'

Parents who don't know enough – either about the detailed effects of drink and drugs, or about the prevailing youth culture – tend, they find, to rely on disapproval when they are attempting to influence their children. There is less likely to be conflict and rebellion if parents are well informed and share information with the child. 'Rather than hand out leaflets, read and discuss them together,' says Luke. 'Dialogue is more memorable.

'If the child gets into trouble, it is important not to take the behaviour as a personal affront or to make the child feel bad. Praise the child for being willing to discuss the problem; children need to feel good about themselves, and they need to feel parents will listen without judging.

'And talk to other parents to get a wide view of current culture. Attitudes to sex and drugs have changed a lot since we were young. Your children may be behaving perfectly normally for this generation. Keep a sense of perspective.'

Noël would start the preparation for these teenage issues way back in childhood. 'When a five-year-old is given champagne at a wedding and he falls about, everyone thinks it is very funny,' she says. 'That is not a helpful message to give the child. But it is never too late to influence our children, even if they have already gone off the rails.'

How do you set up a harmonious holiday?

Holidays with children are wonderful when you browse through the brochure beforehand or look back through the photo album afterwards, but while they are actually taking place, they are often exhausting. 'The problem,' says Noël, 'is the mismatch between expectations and reality.'

No sooner have parents got their feet in the hammock than there is a screech of 'I'm bored', followed soon after by the sound of children squabbling. So you go out to do something the children want, spend a fortune, argue with them about eating foreign food and wanting expensive souvenirs and end up feeling – at least I usually do – that the children are spoilt and that I have only myself to blame.

'It doesn't have to be like this,' sighs Noël. She feels this so strongly – that family life really can be calmer, easier and happier – that she has fantasised about having contact cards printed with the words 'It doesn't have to be like this' and handing them out in shops, parks and on the street to parents whom she saw having a difficult time managing their children.

'Most holiday problems arise,' she says, 'because of over-stimulation and over-indulgence, neither of which bring out the best in children. Holidays usually mean junk food, sugary drinks and daily treats, which the children take for granted. Children assume that having their parents around all day will be wonderful, but often it isn't because adults and children have very different interests and tempos.'

So what should be done with over-excited children? 'It is pointless simply to hope for the best,' says Noël. 'We need to plan to avoid the worst. The solution is structure, structure, structure . . .'

TIPS FOR HARMONIOUS HOLIDAYS
- Consult the children. Find out what they do and don't enjoy before, rather than during, the holiday. Together, think about how all of you can make the bits that you and they don't like less annoying.
- Be realistic. Most children are not going to want to trail round art galleries. 'If they can't see the point, don't force culture upon them,' says Luke, 'and don't make a fuss about trying foreign food. Children are conservative. Let them order the chips; they may try the squid if you don't push it at them. Eventually they will turn into the product of their backgrounds and share your enthusiasms, but maybe not yet.'

  Noël suggests, 'Start with thirty minutes or an hour at a museum before you go off to a more typical children's activity. Structure the museum visit by going to the gift shop first and having the children choose postcards of works of art that appeal to them. Listen while each child

---

tells you why he likes that painting. Then help the children find "their" paintings.'

- Know your limitations. With five children and two adults, a trip to Disneyland where everyone will want to try different rides is going to be chaos. Frantic parents make for frantic children. Save that treat for a day when the adult/child ratio is better.

- Be clear about parental attention. You need time off and children need to practise self-reliance, so establish rules. It could be that the children have to amuse themselves until 11 a.m. and then you'll do something with them. When they are supposed to have your attention, give it fully, or they'll have every right to whine. 'It can be frustrating,' Luke reminds, 'to be around parents but not have any more attention than at home.'

- 'Holidays are a good opportunity for parents to give children individual attention,' says Luke, 'but make it casual and don't have high expectations. Nothing special has to happen, there don't need to be heart-to-hearts, just go for a walk together.'

- Don't pack too much into a day. 'Two events of no more than four hours in total is plenty,' says Noël. 'Maybe I am over-romantic,' says Luke, 'but my happiest holiday memories are of playing on a beach for hours with some bits of driftwood. Entertaining yourself is vital to growing up.'

- Watch your own alcohol intake. Parents who over-indulge on holiday don't sleep well and are perpetually grumpy.

What do you do with a child who doesn't want to go on a family holiday?

Every year I have to deal with at least one child who views family breaks with dread. He would be graciously prepared to come with us if we were going to a five-star hotel, but the thought of camping or caravanning fills him with gloom. On one half-term break he stayed behind with a friend, but that's not an option for the summer, and besides, I feel it is important for us all to be together. 'How do I handle this situation?' I ask Luke.

'He has to go with you,' he replies, 'he's far too young not to – but don't tell him he's being silly. Reflectively listen to his reasons. Maybe his real worry is that he will be parted from his favourite possession. When you know that it's his guitar he's concerned about, you can tell him he can bring it.

'If the dread is unfocused, try gentle joking along the lines of "Oh, it really is going to be hell, isn't it, being by the seaside, eating ice-creams, visiting new places . . . " Not then, but later and subtly, you could tell stories in his presence of times when someone else had to do something they dreaded and ended up enjoying it. He's old enough to learn to be responsible for his own happiness.'

Then he taught me a useful seven-step technique for letting children feel they have a say in family decisions.

SEVEN STEPS TO PROBLEM-SOLVING
1. Take time talking about everyone's feelings and needs. Parents will need to do a lot of reflective listening and descriptive praise.
2. Brainstorm together to find a mutually agreeable solution by writing down all ideas (each person must contribute three) without anyone evaluating any of them.
3. Challenge yourselves to find something positive in all the ideas no matter how impractical they may be.
4. Allow all family members to eliminate any suggestions they don't like. If all are eliminated, go back to step 1.
5. Plan how to implement all those that remain, except those that are mutually exclusive.
6. Implement them immediately.
7. Every fortnight, until the problem no longer exists, review how well the solutions are working.

Must shopping with children be a nightmare?

Most of the time I am vaguely in control of shopping: I set budgets and objectives and limit the time available. A recent holiday in

Prague was, however, wrecked by the children's constant demands to shop and total refusal to sightsee.

Talking it through afterwards with Noël and Luke, I realised I had made some classic mistakes. I had played the generous mummy by telling the children they could each have £5 to spend, but I had not prepared sufficiently for success by making rules about when to spend it, so the children had the leeway to make shopping a priority over any other activity. 'Once you have got yourself into a sticky situation,' I was told at a parenting class, 'you have two choices. You can simply accept that you made a mistake and live with the consequences. Or you can rectify your mistake by changing the rules, which may cause resentment at first, but will probably make everyone happier and calmer. But it's like trying to handle a frenzied child in a supermarket. It is actually much easier to think things through beforehand so that you avoid the problem.'

Although we learnt tips to handle these situations, Noël pointed out: 'The thing about holidays is that they are relatively rare. If you deal positively, firmly and consistently with the ordinary situations that arise throughout the year, holiday nightmares are less likely to occur because you and your children will be in better habits.'

What if a promised reward cannot be given?

Another parent at the class admitted to landing herself in a hellish situation in Rome. Her children had bellyached for some soft toys on sale at a stall, and to shut them up she had promised them they could have them after lunch if they behaved well – a good, logical consequence, you might think. However, by the time lunch was over, the stall had gone and the furious parents wasted the rest of the day haring around the city looking for another stall.

In the first place, neither Noël nor Luke would ever have made a promise that they couldn't be sure to fulfil. '"Probably" is a far safer word to use,' says Luke, 'when there is a trace of uncertainty. When you make a promise – usually to get yourself out of a hole – and can't fulfil it, a child has every right to feel aggrieved.'

Once the situation had gone wrong, they would have listened reflectively to the children's feelings. 'You must be really disappointed,' the parents could have said. When the children begged them to search for the toys, their response could have been, 'We have decided not to do that.'

If the children grumbled, 'Why do you have to have everything your way?' the parents could have asked them to take a guess and praised their attempts. When they get near the truth the parents might say, 'That's right, I'm boss because I'm the grown-up.' No further discussion from the parents, even if the children continue to moan and argue.

TIPS FOR CONTROLLING RAMPANT SHOPPERS

- Set out the ground rules in a family meeting. Explain what you will be buying for the children and what they must buy for themselves. If this prompts cries of 'Unfair', listen reflectively and let them get their feelings out in the open.
- Talk through, as opposed to discuss, the rules. 'What we call discussion,' Noël points out, 'often consists of adults talking and children nodding while thinking "Will she shut up in time for me to watch my favourite programme?" Talking through, by contrast, consists of the child talking while the parent asks prompting questions.'
- Limit the shopping time. I should have said, 'We will shop for an hour each afternoon, but only after we have done some sightseeing.'
- Limit the money. £5 is a fortune for small children; they got over-excited.
- Before the shopping trip, prepare for success by talking through the pros and cons of one high-quality item versus several cheaper ones.
- Call another meeting when something goes wrong, such as a lost purchase. 'I wouldn't buy a replacement,' says Luke. 'Your bank manager wouldn't give you back money you had lost. If the child's toy has been stolen, you might find that the other children suggest that they chip in to buy something else. Children can be amazingly generous if they are allowed to do the thinking.'

How do you deal with complaints of boredom?

Two or three weeks are all that most of us can take off for a 'proper' holiday. The rest of the time children have to drift around at home often, if the parents are busy, complaining of being bored.

Wonderful, say Luke and Noël. Boredom is good. Boredom is relaxing. Boredom is character building. When you are bored you find out what you really like doing. To help me absorb this lesson they discussed with me what children really mean when they are bored.

Sometimes a child may be genuinely under-stimulated and need to get out more, meet other children, or be taught new skills, from bike riding to reading. This situation, they find, is rare. More often the child is not used to finding or making her own fun.

'Often the child doesn't mean she has nothing to do: she means she wants you to do something with her,' says Noël. 'That doesn't mean you have to spend every minute amusing the child. When children know that they will have your undivided attention for a part of each day, they become much more willing to wait. When you do play with her, you could get her started on something that she can carry on with once you have gone.'

But, she warns, 'boring' is also a word that children use of a book, a project, a game or anything else that is beyond their grasp. So it is better to be realistic about what they are capable of doing once left to themselves, and leave that nice idea for a scrapbook on the kings and queens of England for a time when you are around to help.

'At other times,' says Luke, 'when a child says he is bored it means that he is swamped by ideas and unable to sort them out.' The worst possible response at such moments is a long list of suggestions of things he might like to do, from practising the piano to reading a book or writing a story. Every suggestion will be immediately shot down, which is scarcely surprising, he says, since what the child really means – but cannot say – is that he or she needs to unwind.

Noël agrees: 'Unless you are suggesting to a girl that she might like to go clothes shopping, there's no point reeling off ideas. All you can do is understand what is going on and listen reflectively to the child's feelings.'

A further cry of boredom used to go up when I sent children off on holiday courses. Then, says Luke, 'I'm bored' probably meant something no child is ever able to articulate: 'I'm overtired'. 'School is exhausting and so are the holidays. Even though the children don't have to get up early for school, they often get up early anyway and they usually go to bed much later.'

The best solution, Noël says, is to leave those overtired, over-stimulated children to bumble around at home and not worry about boredom. 'All children need time alone with their own thoughts,' she says. 'That means not having the TV or video on, no music blaring, nor even a constant supply of playmates – but reading, playing a solitary sport, drawing, making a model, walking the dog, writing letters, emptying the dishwasher, writing a diary, adding to and organising a collection, or sorting out their room.'

That, in Luke's view, is the main point of holidays. 'Your job as a parent is to prepare your children for separation. Learning to occupy themselves in unstimulating circumstances is the key. If the children complain, you can always remind them that no one ever died of boredom.

TIPS FOR TIME AT HOME
- Don't arrange something for every day, and certainly not for the whole of every day. And make sure children earn their treats.
- Change the routines only a little. You might, for example, want to make bedtime half an hour later, but stick to the basic structure of bedtime and mealtimes and continue to ration screen time.
- If they are going to stay with someone for a few days and will be spoilt rotten there on sweets and videos, that doesn't mean that the rest of the holiday has to be like that.
- Give children the opportunity to learn at least one new thing each, especially if the child isn't doing well at school. It could be a big ego boost to learn how to make pots or play tennis.
- Devote an hour a day (in the morning, before the fun activities begin) to academic practice. Your child probably

needs to brush up on handwriting, spelling, reading aloud with expression, mental arithmetic, multiplication tables, French vocabulary. With this plan he won't lose ground and may well forge ahead.

Can long journeys be calm?

The 'When are we going to get there?' cries start up at the first traffic lights, and there are still two or more hours to go. Like many parents, I panic as children get more and more fractious and start fighting on the motorway. Eyes glued to the road for grim death, I feel powerless to do anything other than shout, 'Shut up'.

It doesn't have to be like that, say Noël and Luke. Like any other potentially fraught occasion, it can be handled better with planning. 'No joy,' says Luke, 'is going to come of jumping into the car and shouting "Be good or else" and driving off. You have to set things up.'

TIPS FOR COPING WITH JOURNEYS
- Set out and talk through the ground rules beforehand at a family conference. Remember, the child must tell you the rules in his own words so that you can be sure they have really sunk in. Discuss what might go wrong and ask the children what you and they can do so that it doesn't.
- Agree then on a rota for the front seat – a common source of friction – and how many CD tracks each child is allowed when it is their turn.
- Give regular reviews of what is expected. 'And if the children do fight,' says Luke, 'don't get involved. Just stop the car and ask what the rules are for travelling in the car.' Noël strongly recommends stopping the car as soon as the children get noisy, whether they are squabbling or playing. 'Any distraction is dangerous for the driver. Wait patiently until they calm down, meanwhile descriptively praise any small steps in the right direction. After a few unscheduled stops, the children will start monitoring themselves and each other.'

- Allow plenty of time. A mother whose child always refused to put on his seat-belt added an extra fifteen minutes to every journey time so she could wait patiently with him until he complied.
- Set up a reward system for good behaviour and break it down into fifteen-minute bites. 'Short periods are easier to enforce and children can feel the results,' says Luke. 'Each person could get a star for good behaviour. Make a game out of it so that the emphasis is on the positive, and allow the children to be the timekeepers. Each fifteen minutes is a fresh start. No lectures about why someone is not getting a point.'
- 'If you agree to buy magazines,' says Luke, 'don't get them before you set out; let them be a reward for good behaviour at the first stop.' Pocket money could be earned by good behaviour: this isn't bribing them to be good, but making it less worthwhile to be bad.
- Avoid food that will hype children up. Take bags of cut-up apples and sandwiches. You can always clear up the mess when you arrive.
- Stop regularly and make the children get out and run or do star jumps, even if they don't want to.
- If things go wrong, interrupt early.
- If necessary, stop on the hard shoulder, which is there for emergencies. 'It's no more dangerous,' says Noël, 'to stop on the hard shoulder than to carry on driving while children are fighting.'
- 'If you are going on an outing with a difficult child,' she says, 'take two cars so that the difficult child can be taken home early if necessary, without spoiling the day for everyone.'

Note: My personal tip for all journeys is never to be without a pack of playing cards.

CONCLUSION

My conversations and classes with Noël and Luke lasted for roughly a year. That was easily long enough for my home life to be transformed but, if you visited my home now, would you find a set of perfect children living in total harmony with never a raised voice?

No, you wouldn't. The children are still tiresome at times – upset, impulsive or jealous of one another; they have problems with their work and fall out with their friends, but I have learnt how to handle the problems better, not just intellectually but practically, by each week doing the homework I set myself. After every class my task was to do one thing differently: on one occasion it was to tackle a child's reluctance to read, on another to make the mornings calmer, and one week it was to smile and not react when a child was grumpy.

At an early class I met a woman who said she had come to relish new problems in her children's lives because it was such fun finding solutions; I now see what she meant. The children have changed, but I have changed more. As Noël says, 'Most parents have to grow up and take responsibility for their children. Some have further to go than others.'

Certain aspects of what she and Luke taught came easily to me. The shift from evaluative to descriptive praise is not hard and soon becomes a habit, though I still don't descriptively praise as often as Noël recommends. Reflective listening took courage at first – it can be scary encouraging a child to reveal uncomfortable feelings – but that too fast becomes a habit.

I now accept that children cannot always be happy, but they do deserve to have their feelings taken seriously; that parents should not even try to sort out all a child's emotional problems – anger, frustration and hurt are part of life – but they can feel sure that the child will feel those pains less sorely if he can rely on regular, one-to-one parental attention.

I am more aware, too, of not trying to load too many of my own hopes on to the children and, as they get older, of helping them to become more self-reliant.

The more I look for the positive in my children, the more I find. And the more I look for the positive changes in the atmosphere at home, the better I become at congratulating myself on what has gone right rather than worrying about what has gone wrong. And when my plans do go wrong, I am soothed by something Luke once said: 'Aim for the best, but be satisfied by whatever you can achieve.'

However, I still find it hard to be firm, consistent and to plan for success. I continue to rush when I'm in a hurry and snap when I'm tired. Visiting au pairs still accuse me of being 'too soft', but now I am more prepared to admit that they could be right. As Noël says, 'Practice makes progress.'

My experience is, as far as I can tell, typical of other parents who have been through this same training. Some have told me of more startling improvements, but they often started from a worse position. I can see why Noël and Luke were so confident that change was possible, as they have seen it many times before. 'The only occasions,' says Luke, 'when there hasn't been an improvement there is always some reason why the parent is unable or unwilling to get back in control.'

As for the dog, she needs a lot more training, but now the children are easier, I have the time. And some of the children, who have caught on to the idea of training, are eager to help.

FURTHER READING

Families and How to Survive Them, John Cleese & Robin Skynner (Vermilion, 1993)

Holding Time: How to Eliminate Conflict, Temper Tantrums and Sibling Rivalry and Raise Happy, Loving, Successful Children, Martha Welch (Ebury Press, 1989)

Raising Boys: Why Boys Are Different – and How to Help Them Become Happy and Well-balanced Men, Steve Biddulph (Harper Collins, 2003)

The Secret of Happy Children, Steve Biddulph (Harper Collins, 1999)

How to Talk So Kids Will Listen & Listen So Kids Will Talk, Adele Faber & Elaine Mazlish (Piccadilly Press, 2001)

Siblings Without Rivalry, Adele Faber & Elaine Mazlish (Piccadilly Press, 1999)

USEFUL ADDRESSES

Those who want to explore further Noël and Luke's ideas can contact them directly:

Noël Janis-Norton and her staff of learning and behaviour specialists teach the 'Calmer, Easier, Happier Parenting' methods through workshops and classes at the New Learning Centre (NLC) and in schools, as well as through private sessions and telephone consultations. Their senior lecturers also give seminars for teachers and other youth professionals in many UK cities on topics such as:

- Improving Classroom Behaviour
- Helping the Atypical Learner to Thrive, Not Just Survive
- Preventing and Reducing Bullying
- Involving Parents as Partners in Education
- Raising Standards Through Effective Differentiation

In addition, the NLC also produces and sells a range of audio tapes and booklets on many different aspects of parenting and teaching. The classes for children, which are held during holidays and half-terms, teach basic academic skills, learning strategies, social skills and positive behaviour and attitudes.

The NLC's 'Time Out Programme' is a temporary alternative to mainstream schooling for children with acute problems. It is a demonstration school, where parents and educators come to observe and learn about the NLC's unique methods by seeing them in action. Anyone is welcome to book an appointment to observe (after having listened to one of the audio tapes, which serves as an introduction to the methods).

The New Learning Centre
211 Sumatra Road, London NW6 1PF
Tel: 020 7794 0321 Fax: 020 7431 8600
E-mail: admin@tnlc.info Website: www.tnlc.info

Luke Scott has been working with children, teenagers and parents for over ten years. He originally trained with Youth at Risk, an organisation that works with the most difficult and damaged young people. He then spent four years working and training with Noël Janis-Norton, becoming a parent trainer, family coach and specialist in boys' behaviour. He also worked with children with a wide range of learning difficulties.

In 2000, in response to cultural changes that Luke believes have left us without the traditions and role models to produce healthy and balanced young men, he set up Boys to Men, a consultancy and training organisation that works with youth professionals and teachers, as well as families. Among the courses offered by Boys to Men are:

For parents
- Parenting classes in different parts of the country
- One-day workshops
- Father and son summer camps in Suffolk
- Private consultations and a range of skills booklets

For professionals
- Workshops on working with men and boys
- How to set up parenting courses and train facilitators
- Creating policies and procedures for managing behaviour and supporting the development of boys

Boys to Men
E-mail: info@boystomen.co.uk
Website: www.boystomen.co.uk

Despite the organisation's name, many of the courses and materials on offer are equally relevant to women and girls.

For more information about Boys to Men, and useful resources on parenting, fathers and sons, men's work and related subjects, please visit the website.

OTHER USEFUL ORGANISATIONS

Barrington Stoke, 10 Belford Terrace, Edinburgh EH4 3DQ Tel: 0131 315 4933 Website: www.barringtonstoke.co.uk. Books for dyslexic, reluctant, disenchanted and under-confident readers.

British Dyslexia Association 98 London Road, Reading, Berkshire RG1 5AU Tel: 0118 966 2677 Website: www.bda-dyslexia.org.uk. Information on dyslexia and local associations for parents.

Contact-a-Family 209–211 City Road, London EC1V 1JN Tel: 020 7608 8700 Helpline: 0808 808 3555 E-mail: info@cafamily. org.uk Website: www.cafamily.org.uk Support and advice for families with disabled children.

Family Caring Trust 8 Ashtree Enterprise Park, Newry, Co Down BT34 1BY Tel: 028 3026 4174 Website: www.familycaring.co.uk Courses, books, videos and games to support families.

Families Need Fathers 134 Curtain Road, London EC2A 3AR Tel: 0207 613 5060 Website: www.fnf.org.uk Support for parents concerned about keeping in touch with children after the break-down of a relationship.

Gingerbread Helpline: 0800 018 4318 Website: www.gingerbread. org.uk Support organisation for one-parent families.

Hale Clinic 7 Park Crescent, London W1B 1PF Tel: 0870 167 6667 Website: www.haleclinic.com Leading clinic offering alternative and complementary treatments, and advice on allergies and asthma.

Hyperactive Children's Support Group 71 Whyke Lane, Chichester, West Sussex PO19 7PD Tel: 01243 551313 Website: www.hacsg. org.uk Information on dietary help for hyperactivity.

Landmark Education Third Floor, 163 Eversholt Street, London

NW1 1BU Tel: 020 7969 2020 Personal development courses, including some to help parents be in charge and move away from a culture of blame.

National Family and Parenting Institute 430 Highgate Studios, 53–79 Highgate Road, London NW5 1TL Tel: 020 7424 3460 Website: www.nfpi.org.uk Campaigning and advice-giving charity.

Parenting Education and Support Forum 431 Highgate Studios, 53–79 Highgate Road, London NW5 1TL Website: www. parenting-forum.org.uk Information on parenting courses all over the country.

Parentline Plus Helpline (24 hours) 0808 800 2222 Website: www.parentlineplus.org.uk Offers support, provides information and runs parenting courses.

INDEX

Buy Vermilion Books

Order further Vermilion titles from your local bookshop, or have
them delivered direct to your door by Bookpost.

That's My Boy! by Jenni Murray	£9.99
How to Behave So Your Children Will Too! by Dr Sal Severe	£9.99
Positive Parenting by Elizabeth Hartley-Brewer	£6.99
Helping Your Anxious Child by Dr David Lewis	£7.99
Teach Your Child to Read by Annis Garfield	£10.99

FREE POST AND PACKING
Overseas customers allow £2.00 per paperback

BY PHONE: 01624 677237

BY POST: Random House Books
C/o Bookpost, PO Box 29, Douglas
Isle of Man, IM99 1BQ

BY FAX: 01624 670923

BY EMAIL: bookshop@enterprise.net

Cheques (payable to Bookpost) and credit cards accepted

Prices and availability subject to change without notice.
Allow 28 days for delivery.
When placing your order, please mention if you do not wish
to receive any additional information.

www.randomhouse.co.uk